CHACO CANYON

ARCHAEOLOGY

CHACO

Robert H. Lister

and

Florence C. Lister

AND ARCHAEOLOGISTS

CANYON

University of New Mexico Press
Albuquerque

Library of Congress Cataloging in Publication Data

Lister, Robert H.
    Chaco Canyon.

    Includes bibliographical references and index.
    1. Indians of North America—New Mexico—
Chaco Canyon—Antiquities. 2. Chaco Canyon (N.M.)—
Antiquities. 3. Archaeology—New Mexico—Chaco
Canyon—History. 4. Excavations (Archaeology)—New
Mexico—Chaco Canyon. 5. New Mexico—Antiquities.
I. Lister, Florence Cline. II. Title.
E78.N65L57   978.9′82   80-54566
ISBN 0-8263-0574-1   AACR2

First edition

Designed by Editype Data Services

For
FLORENCE HAWLEY ELLIS
Scientist, Mentor, Friend

CONTENTS

Figures

PREFACE

Chaco Canyon, New Mexico, contained a sizable Prehispanic population for several thousand years. Although it is only a small area of the American Southwest, it has fascinated adventurers and scientists alike for over one hundred years. The history of the canyon's exploration and excavation makes a good adventure story, both physical and intellectual. In the first place, the present bleak environment would seem to weigh heavily against the success of sedentary settlements. Yet a phalanx of communal dwellings, roofless now and beaten back to earth, testifies not only to the tenacity of the human spirit but also to humanity's unique adaptability. In the second place, the unraveling of the mystery of these early dwellers attracted a colorful parade of figures drawn from Western Americana—army men, Indian scouts, cowpokes, traders, drifters, government officials, Navajos, and, eventually, scientists—who in themselves contributed to the allure of the canyon.

It is the latter group, students of human culture, whose diligence, inquisitiveness, and sheer perseverance gradually have pried from the tough matrix of the past the pageant of life that once played on this stage. In the best empirical tradition over the course of this century, each successive team of investigators carefully has built upon the work of its predecessors, with the result that now, aided by the invaluable resources of archaeological maturity and complex technology, a prehistoric civilization is more intimately understood than any of the pioneers of these studies would have dreamed possible. Moreover, the information gained about what may have happened to the Chacoans also sheds light upon their neighbors, now similarly absent from the scene. To demonstrate this dramatic, painstaking reclamation of the past, the ensuing pages are presented within a historical framework. A summary of what is now known of the human habitation of the canyon appears in chapter 7, following the history of Chaco archaeology. An appendix summarizes all the archaeological investigations of the canyon, including site maps, for those who wish more detailed, specialized knowledge.

Our personal involvement with Chaco antiquities stretches back some forty-five years to the mid-1930s, when as students, camp hands, neophyte instructor and ranger, we were so captivated by the challenges of the region's prehistory and history that it became a lifetime pursuit. In the 1970s, this interest culminated in the direction of a long-term, multidisciplinary research project, some of whose results are summarized here for the first time.

As this book went to press, we learned that the federal government had changed the name and adjusted the boundaries of Chaco Canyon National Monument. Legislation enacted by Congress on December 19, 1980 created a new, larger entity to be known as Chaco Culture National

Historical Park. Outlying areas that were not part of the old national monument are now protected by the extension of its boundaries. News of the new name reached us too late to be reflected in the text of this book.

In compiling this review of Chaco Canyon archaeology, we owe much to many. The information upon which we have drawn starts with the descriptive accounts of Lieutenant Simpson and William H. Jackson and continues with the pioneering archaeological work of Richard Wetherill and George Pepper. It progresses through the extensive endeavors of Neil M. Judd and his associates to the activities of Edgar L. Hewett and his colleagues and students, and into the era of National Park Service excavation and stabilization led by Gordon Vivian. Finally, the history of exploration concludes with the diverse efforts of the Chaco Center. It is the writings and reports of this host of Chaco investigators, and conversations with many of them, that have provided most of the material for this presentation. To all those individuals, past and present, we extend our sincere appreciation and genuine thanks.

We particularly are grateful to Jim Judge, the entire Chaco Center staff, and the National Park Service for allowing us to include descriptions of many unreported activities and results of their in-depth examination of Chaco Canyon culture. Illustrative materials, which are as meaningful as words in a work of this sort, have been kindly provided by the Arizona State Museum, the University of Arizona Press, the American Museum of Natural History, the Museum of New Mexico, the National Geographic Society, the National Park Service, and the Smithsonian Institution. We are happy to acknowledge the assistance of staff members from those institutions.

CHACO CANYON

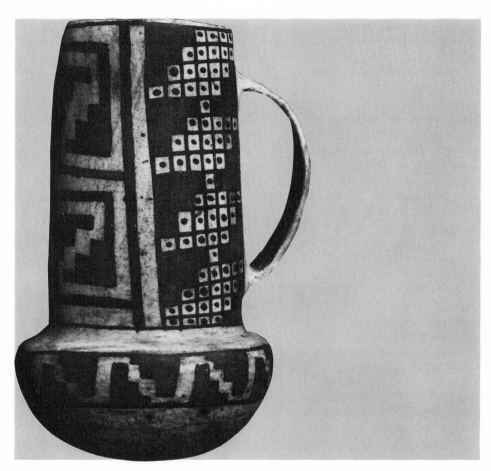

1 MILITARY AND SURVEY PARTIES

Tucked away in bleached out, craggy northwestern New Mexico is one of America's richest archaeological zones, now known as Chaco Canyon. Subject to dramatic temperature extremes and devoid of trees and year-round running water, the canyon's sandy bottomlands are cut deep by an arroyo; the terraces above are now given over to saltbush, snakeweed, prickly pear cactus, and stunted grasses. Imprisoned by walls of treacherously spalling tawny sandstone, this is a forlorn region seemingly uninviting to sedentary farmers. Today the canyon contains no settlement. Rather, Navajo herdsmen eke out a marginal existence about its perimeters. Yet dozens of tumbled multiroomed and multistoried communal houses are strewn like fallen soldiers along the canyon floor and surrounding mesa tops, mute evidence of the complex Neolithic agricultural society that endured there for so long. More impressive than the massive ruins themselves is the evident force of the human spirit that was responsible for their erection. That generating current of incalculable strength, a coalescence of drive, adaptability, and muscle power, supercharged a cultural efflorescence in Chaco Canyon and adjacent areas of the Four Corners unique in Prehispanic North America. Rather than being a record of the rise and fall of a civilization, the Chaco remains are essentially those of a slowly accelerating progress. Upon reaching a crescendo, Chaco terminated in a comparatively short time when the ancient people walked away from it, leaving homes and associated features intact. At a later date they regrouped in several distant localities, but by then whatever motives originally led them to build had, for unknown reasons, largely evaporated.

Knowledge of the lonely ruins in Chaco Canyon seems to date from the mid-seventeenth century. At that time, a number of military forays from the Spanish outposts straggled along the Río Grande Valley were mounted against the warlike Navajo, who had claimed the territory as their own long after the original occupants had deserted the canyon lands. Unfortunately, most of the early Spanish records that might shed light upon the actual first encounter with Chaco antiquities are presumed to have been destroyed during the Pueblo Revolt of 1680, which drove the Spaniards from their northernmost holdings.[1]

Not until the middle of the eighteenth century did sufficiently peaceful conditions prevail to permit the reinstated Spaniards to drift westward into the outlying uplands and valleys leading toward the Chaco. Land grants issued to Ignacio Chávez and Joaquín Maesta in 1768 were described as having as one boundary a white mesa called Mesa de Chaca. The place noted is probably the eastern edge of what is now known as Chacra Mesa, immediately south of Chaco Canyon. The grantees were admonished not to impinge on the prior rights of the Navajos who occu-

3

pied the region, not to dispossess or expel them, and to treat them with love and Christian sincerity, thereby attracting them to the Holy Faith and vassalage to the Sovereign. The lower Chaco drainage attracted no Spaniards because of the lack of water and sufficient browse for stock. Hence it served as a buffer between the seminomadic Navajos to the west and the tillers of the soil, both Indian and Spanish, to the east in central New Mexico. The vestiges of the earlier inhabitants of the Chaco were not mentioned.

In 1774, renewed warfare with the Navajo forced the Spaniards to concern themselves again with the western frontier. One of several maps drawn at that time by Bernardo de Miera y Pacheco bears the name *Chaca* in the correct location for Chaco Canyon. There is no depiction of ruins on the drawing, but there are a number of little hoganlike symbols around the name *Chaca* which may imply Navajo occupation. It is not known whether Don Bernardo visited Chaco, but a later descendant claimed that the mapmaker had seen the Chaco ruins and had produced drawings and ground plans of them. No such documents have ever been located.

By the nineteenth century, some very specific references to localities that can be identified with modern names began to appear in the documents. The earliest, in 1804, was a report by a Spanish civil official at Jémez Pueblo who, in trailing stock stolen by Indians, overtook the Navajo culprits at a place called Agua del Ratón, probably present-day Ratón Springs, near the Chaco ruin of Pueblo Pintado. In fact, one of the first names applied to Pueblo Pintado was Pueblo del Ratón. Also early in the 1800s, Lt. Vicente López led a party of armed settlers to the Chaca Mesa, where he defeated the Navajos. Spanish forces are believed to have penetrated the Chaco area proper during a series of skirmishes in 1818–19. After that a group of Navajos from the Chaca Mesa are said to have traveled to Jémez to buy corn.

An 1823 description by José Antonio Vizcarra of a trip down Chaco Canyon contains the first definite reference to the local ruins. In June of that year, Vizcarra led a force of men westward from Jémez, across the Río Puerco and on to Torreón, then over the eastern Chacra Mesa. Apparently on the fourth night they camped at La Agua de San Carlos, on the headwaters of the Chaco drainage. From there it was six leagues (fifteen miles) to Pueblo Pintado, identified as the first Pueblo del Ratón. He wrote that the Chaco Wash, which he called the Arroyo de San Carlos, did not have permanent water but was flowing during his march. He also observed that some lands along the arroyo were good for pasturing stock and others were superior for dryfarming. He correctly surmised that the Chaco, although making many turns, finally joined the San Juan River to the north.

Figure 1. Chaco Plateau and vicinity

Vizcarra seems to have continued down the canyon the next day to a place called El Peñasco seven leagues (seventeen and one-half miles) to the west. This may have been Peñasco Blanco, the westernmost of the large ruins in Chaco Canyon (see fig. 2). On the way, he noted remains of several pueblos so old that their inhabitants were unknown to Europeans. During the return trek, his troops made one of their camps at Cerrito Fajada, obviously present-day Fajada Butte, a prominent Chaco Canyon landmark. The trail established by the Vizcarra party, passing through Chaco Canyon west into Navajo lands and the San Juan Basin, became a much-traveled route until an easier road was developed in the 1860s from Albuquerque to the west and north. Scattered names and dates scratched on vertical canyon walls and an occasional ring of stones around a dead campfire form a desert registry of the passage of soldiers, missionaries, and saddle tramps.

Throughout the Mexican period, awareness of the Chaco remains was evidenced by a trickle of casual references to them, such as that by Josiah Gregg, author of the classic *Commerce of the Prairies*,[2] but the information, often garbled, probably did not come firsthand. The first substantive report on the Chaco antiquities came at the opening of the American era. In 1849, in pursuit of marauding Navajos who continued to harass isolated farms and haciendas, a young officer of the Army Topographical Engineers, First Lt. James H. Simpson, found himself in a fascinating world of jumbled, jagged walls projecting above mounds of fallen debris and windblown earth the likes of which he had never seen. Nothing in his past experience had prepared him for the hundreds of contiguous rooms of beautifully shaped and coursed stonework piled one on top of another into three or four stories to form great sweeping arcs, some with beamed ceilings, plank floors, and mud plaster still in place. All this in an empty, sun-baked landscape whose silence was broken only by the occasional screech of a stray hawk or the crash of a dislodged rock tumbling down a cliff. As he rode from east to west through Chaco Canyon, Simpson set to work with great excitement and care, measuring, describing, and examining each abandoned house complex that he saw. Eventually he had documented seven of the major ruins and several smaller ones and had assigned them names supplied by the Indian and Mexican guides accompanying the party. These included Pueblo Pintado, Una Vida, Hungo Pavi, Chetro Ketl, Pueblo Bonito, Pueblo del Arroyo, and Peñasco Blanco (see figs. 3 and 4). Drawings and maps executed by two artist brothers in the detachment, Richard and Edward Kern, enhanced this initial report.[3]

To appreciate Simpson's sharp eye for detail, one need only turn to his account of Pueblo Pintado:

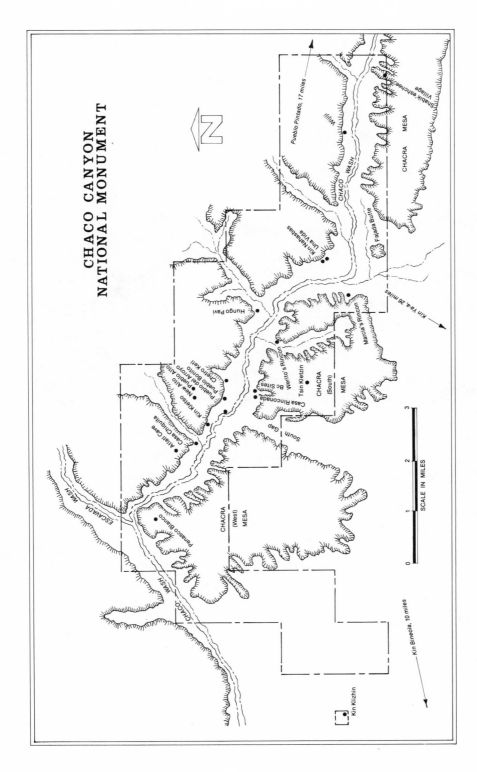

Figure 2. Chaco Canyon National Monument

Figure 3. Pueblo Pintado, the easternmost Chaco ruin and the first to be described. Photo by Victor Mindeleff, 1888. *Courtesy of the Smithsonian Institution*

Figure 4. First photograph of Pueblo Bonito, taken by
Victor Mindeleff in 1888. View looking north across the
west end of the ruin; Threatening Rock stands behind
the pueblo against the north cliff of Chaco Canyon.
Courtesy of the Smithsonian Institution

It discovers in the masonry a combination of science and art which can only be referred to a higher stage of civilization and refinement than is discoverable in the works of Mexicans or Pueblos of the present day. Indeed, so beautifully diminutive and true are the details of the structures as to cause it, at a little distance, to have all the appearance of a magnificent piece of mosaic work.

In the outer face of the buildings there are no signs of mortar, the intervals between the beds being chinked with stones of the minutest thinness. The filling and backing are done in rubble masonry, the mortar presenting no indications of lime. The thickness of the main wall at base is within an inch or two of three feet; higher up, it is less—diminishing every story by retreating jogs on the inside, from bottom to top. Its elevation, at its present highest point, is between twenty-five and thirty feet, the series of floor beams indicating that there must have been originally at least three stories. The ground plan including the court, in exterior development, is about 403 feet. On the ground floor, exclusive of the outbuildings, are fifty-four apartments, some of them as small as five feet square, and the largest about twelve by six feet. These rooms communicate with each other by very small doors, some of them as contracted as two and a half by two and a half feet; and in the case of the inner suite, the doors communicating with the interior court are as small as three and a half by two feet. The principal rooms, or those most in use, were, on account of their having larger doors and windows, most probably those of the second story. The system of flooring seems to have been large transverse unhewn beams, six inches in diameter, laid transversely from wall to wall, and then a number of smaller ones, about three inches in diameter, laid longitudinally upon them. What was placed on these does not appear, but most probably it was brush, bark, or slabs, covered with a layer of mud mortar. The beams show no signs of the saw or axe; on the contrary, they appear to have been hacked off by means of some very imperfect instrument. On the west face of the structure, the windows, which are only in the second story, are three feet two inches by two feet two inches. On the north side, they are only in the second and third stories, and are as small as fourteen by fourteen inches. At different points about the premises were three circular apartments sunk into the ground, the walls being of masonry. These apartments the Pueblo Indians call *estufas,* or places where the people held their political and religious meetings.

Inevitably questions arose. Who were the gifted masons who obviously had labored long and hard upon these homes in the wastelands and then left them to crumble? And how could so many men have maintained themselves in this arid, unyielding environment? Simpson, like most of his contemporaries, favored a Mexican derivation of the Chacoans; such a point of view reflected the prevailing ignorance at that time of the prehistory of the Southwest. No one seems to have placed much importance upon the fact that rather than being the remains of temples, shrines, or palaces, the Chacoan structures were the homes of ordinary citizens. However, rather than accepting the customarily proposed Aztec connection, Simpson hypothesized an earlier Toltec source. More than a century later archaeologists would again look to Mexico and the Toltecs as an important factor in the latter chapters of Chaco's story. As to survival, Simpson could only suggest that the arroyo, which contained a shower-swollen flow in August of 1849, once had been a sizable river whose waters supported garden plots on either bank. Evidence of farming activities had weathered to oblivion soon after they had ceased. Although he did not conceptualize it, this first serious student of Chaco civilization intuitively recognized the level of technical knowledge and extraordinary effort that enabled prehistoric people to convert a desert into an oasis without the aid of metal tools or animal power.

Simpson's obscure report caused no immediate stampede of either the curious or the treasure seekers. Chaco continued, as it had for centuries, to doze along quietly, its monumental Indian apartment houses slowly slumping back to earth. Then, a quarter of a century after Simpson's visit, activity picked up.

First came Professor Oscar Loew, who, after a brief survey of a few days, once more proclaimed Chaco to be an outpost of the Aztecs.[4] In 1877, he was followed by William Henry Jackson, a photographer attached to the Geological and Geographical Survey of the Territories directed by F. V. Hayden.

Engaging the same Jémez Indian who had guided Lt. Col. John Macrae Washington's entourage, of which Simpson had been a member, Jackson entered the canyon by the usual eastern gateway, which brought him first to Pueblo Pintado—a brown ledge looming on the horizon. During the four or five ensuing days, Jackson reexamined, mapped, and amplified descriptions of all the sites previously explored by Simpson twenty-eight years earlier. In addition, he visited Kin Kletso (fig. 5) and Casa Chiquita in the canyon bottom and a newly discovered major site on the mesa north of Pueblo Bonito. He named it *Pueblo Alto* because of its elevation and panoramic view of the surrounding country, although the guide thought his people knew it as the Jugador, or gambler. Jackson is credited with discovering and describing for the first time several of the

Figure 5. Victor Mindeleff's 1888 photograph of Kin Kletso. *Courtesy of the Smithsonian Institution*

Figure 6. One of the Chaco stairways discovered by Jackson in 1877. This example is on the north wall of the canyon near Chetro Ketl. *Courtesy of the Museum of New Mexico*

stairways the ancient Chacoans had hewn from or erected against the slick cliffs behind Pueblo Bonito and Chetro Ketl (see fig. 6). At Pueblo Bonito, Jackson saw the names of Lieutenant Simpson, Richard Kern, and several others, with the date August 27, 1849, scratched into the soft plaster of one of the northern roofed rooms. Jackson also noted the several holes that unknown vandals had poked through the exterior walls in their search for relics. This man was also the first to comment upon the great amount of natural deposition that had taken place since the prehistoric population had abandoned the area, sedimentation that was particularly visible from his camp in the bottom of the arroyo. From his account[5] it is apparent that in the interval between his visit and that of Simpson the gash in the built-up alluvium had deepened and widened considerably.

It was still eleven years before the chance discovery of the major ruins in the Mesa Verde area of southwestern Colorado some 150 miles north of Chaco Canyon, but Jackson already had spotted several lesser habitations in the cliffs of Mancos Canyon during his work there with the Hayden Survey. Furthermore, he recently had personally visited the living Hopi villages to the west and was aware of a growing corpus of anthropological data about them. Taking these clues of past and present into account, Jackson was quick to recognize that the Chaco remains were essentially yet another facet of the same cultural manifestation; the Aztec affiliation conjured up by earlier observers was laid to rest.

With all these plusses in the realm of observation, the Jackson expedition was not a complete success. Being a photographer by trade and aware that he was documenting an emerging frontier in which there was great interest in the East, Jackson saw a pictorial bonanza in the impressive artifactual record of Chaco and the stark beauty of the locale. As he explored the dusty length of the canyon, he took over four hundred shots with his cumbersome eight-by-ten camera. But to his great dismay, the new untested film he had used was a total failure, and none of his exposures would develop. Not until sixty years later did he have the opportunity to return to Chaco. By then, he had been repeatedly scooped.

Some calculations made by this astute observer while visiting Chetro Ketl (shown in fig. 7) are of special interest:

> In this ruin there was at one time a line of wall running around three sides of the building, 935 feet in length and about 40 feet in height, giving 37,400 square feet of surface, and as an average of 50 pieces of stone appeared within the space of every square foot, this would give nearly 2,000,000 pieces for the outer surface, for the exterior wall alone; multiply this by the opposite surface, and also by the interior and transverse lines of masonry, and, supposing a symmetrical terracing as we will find it will swell the total up into more than 30,000,000, embraced within about 315,000 cubic feet of masonry. These millions of pieces had to be quarried, dressed roughly to fit their places, and carefully adapted to it; the massive timbers had to be brought from a considerable distance, cut and fitted to their places in the wall and then covered with other courses; and then the other details of window and roof making, plastering, and construction of ladders, must have employed a large body of intelligent, well organized, patient, and industrious people, under thorough discipline for a very long time.

The cultural impact of aboriginal energies certainly was not lost upon Jackson.

As a consequence of Simpson's impressions of the principal Chaco ruins and Jackson's expanded observations of them, nine of the major ruins in the immediate Chaco Canyon area and other archaeological, geological, and geographical features of the region were documented by the 1880s (see figs. 8 and 9). Both of these early investigators concentrated

Figure 7. Chetro Ketl in 1920. View is east across the ruin, which is unexcavated except for a small section cleared by the School of American Research at the southeast corner. *Courtesy of the National Geographic Society*

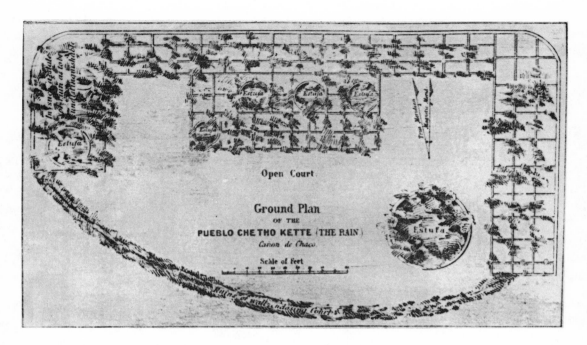

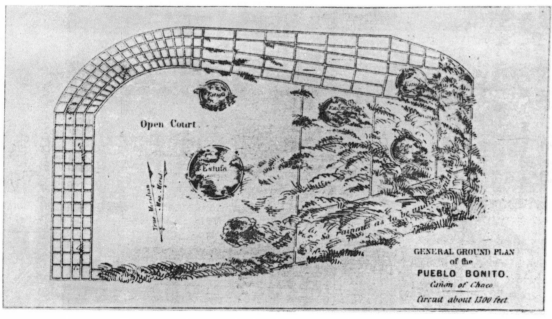

Figure 8. Plans of Chetro Ketl and Pueblo Bonito prepared in 1849 by Richard and Edward Kern to accompany the journal of Lt. James H. Simpson, the initial description and drawings of some of the Chaco Canyon ruins. From Simpson's *Navajo Expedition, Journal of a Military Reconnaissance from Santa Fe, New Mexico to the Navajo Country Made in 1849*

their attention on the north side of the canyon, where the largest structures are situated, now isolated from each other by expanses of drifted soil and detritus. They did not find the great ceremonial structure of Casa Rinconada and the concentration of small sites that carpet the south floor of the canyon. The large outlying ruins to the south and west of the main stem of the canyon proper were yet to be reported.

Simpson and Jackson inspired further works on Chaco Canyon. In 1881, Lewis Henry Morgan, famous for his studies of the Iroquois and of ancient societies, published an article on American Indian house types which contained a section on the Chaco edifices.[6] His account was a compilation from the reports of Simpson and Jackson. Morgan never was in Chaco Canyon, although he had visited the Aztec Ruin north of the canyon.

Toward the end of that same decade, Victor Mindeleff of the Bureau of American Ethnology spent six winter weeks photographing and surveying the central Chaco sites as part of his monumental study of Pueblo architecture.[7] When this comprehensive volume appeared, it contained little information on Chaco, but it did describe the living pueblos of the 1880s. It was intended as a forerunner for other architectural studies, including one on the valley ruins of Chaco Canyon. That monograph never was completed, but it might well have reinforced the proposition that Chaco had been one segment of a long Pueblo Indian continuum. Mindeleff had more success with his photographic film than had Jackson and, eleven years later, in 1888, produced the first pictorial record of the Chaco sites. His views of Pueblo Bonito furnish evidence that the pothunters already had arrived and had breached its walls in many places.

One person who is known to have been drawn to Chaco by stories of its splendid, and possibly lucrative, ruins, was Scott N. Morris, father of the pioneer Southwestern archaeologist, Earl H. Morris. Scott drove a trench through the large refuse mound to the south of Pueblo Bonito in 1893 but failed to find any artifacts of value.[8]

Meantime, sheepherders from ranches near the hamlets of San Mateo, Cabezón, Torreón, and Cuba to the east continued to use the Chaco region for winter grazing, bedding down their flocks in the protection of Pueblo Bonito's high rear wall and adjacent cliff and using available wood from the ruins for their campfires. The first large-scale cattle operations moved into the area in the 1870s. One outfit, the LC, built several stone buildings for a ranch headquarters under the cliff near Peñasco Blanco in 1879. They soon abandoned their Chaco holdings and had moved into southeastern Utah by 1896.

In the wake of the publicity resulting from the interest of the scientific community, the general public, represented by adventurers, casual travelers, and writers, soon began to visit and popularize the decaying ruins, even though it meant a trying horseback or wagon ride of several days across an expansive stretch of desolate terrain. One of the writers was Charles Lummis, who explored Pueblo Bonito in 1888. He then concentrated on writing books and articles to bring the grandeur of the Southwest to the attention of the American people. Another author was F. T. Bickford, who for eight days in 1890 wandered through Chaco houses. Bickford's article on Southwestern archaeology appeared in *Century Magazine* during that same year.[9]

Despite its new-found fame, at the end of the nineteenth century Chaco Canyon still was only superficially known. True, most of the principal ruins had been described, photographed, and mapped as well as their unexcavated condition would allow. Nevertheless, information as to their age, architectural details, contents, builders, and general place in the scheme of prehistoric Southwestern development remained shrouded in mystery. Then a series of events—settlement by whites near Chaco Canyon and the first scientific excavations and related studies—ushered in a new era.

Figure 9. Wiliam H. Jackson's drawing reconstructing Pueblo Bonito and his map of the site, both prepared during his visit to Chaco Canyon in 1877. From the *Tenth Annual Report of the United States Geological and Geographical Survey of the Territories*

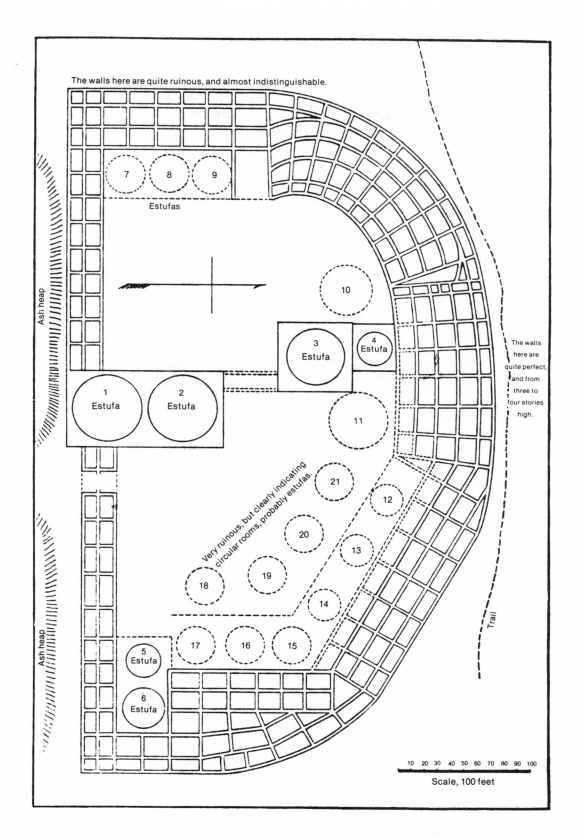

The walls here are quite ruinous, and almost indistinguishable.

7   8   9

Estufas

Ash heap

10

3
Estufa

4
Estufa

1
Estufa

2
Estufa

11

The walls here are quite perfect, and from three to four stories high.

21

12

Very ruinous, but clearly indicating circular rooms, probably estufas.

20

13

18

19

14

Ash heap

5
Estufa

17   16   15

6
Estufa

Trail

10 20 30 40 50 60 70 80 90 100

Scale, 100 feet

2 COLLECTORS, DILETTANTES, AND SCIENTISTS

A pioneer of Chaco Canyon archaeology, Richard Wetherill is also associated with the world famous cliff dwellings of Mesa Verde, where he began his archaeological career.[1] One of the discoverers and first exploiters, he claimed to have located 182 ruins in the precipitous canyons of Mesa Verde and to have helped unearth four large assortments of "relics" each numbering in the hundreds of specimens. In the process of reporting these discoveries, he acquired a certain degree of fame.

At least three interrelated factors were involved in such success. First, at a time when there was widespread curiosity about the new western frontier, Wetherill, his brothers, and their colleagues found themselves on the threshold of one of the continent's fascinating mysteries, the sort with universal appeal: a lost world once peopled by a now unknown, vanished race. Second, like a seasoned angler, Wetherill developed an intuitive sense of where to seek out exotic cultural traces and how best to get at the tangible goods they contained. And finally, the logistics of building houses in great arched cavities set several hundred feet above canyon floors on sheer cliff faces, often with all access to them now sluffed away, stimulated public interest. Surrounded by a verdant stand of cedar and juniper, with exhilarating vistas over a distant horizon of receding green mesas and wildly eroded pinnacles, and augmented by a dry condition that preserved both fragile and substantial wares just as they had been discarded by their owners, these remains excited the imagination of the active and armchair explorer alike.

Richard Wetherill soon turned to adjacent regions of the rugged Four Corners, where he found comparable habitations and loot. Under the pompous name of the Hyde Exploring Expedition, one such excursion to the Grand Gulch of southeastern Utah was undertaken in a formal business partnership with New Yorkers Talbot and Frederick Hyde. Heirs to a small fortune from their grandfather's Babbit Soap Company, the brothers used their wealth to underwrite their interest in the West and its antiquities. The Hydes subsequently donated over twelve hundred articles recovered in this venture to the American Museum of Natural History in New York, and the excavators and sponsors received a burst of publicity.

Wetherill himself got caught up in the intellectual challenge of his new-found vocation. He began to describe the cultural milieu of the area and devised two terms that have been retained in the scientific vocabulary of the Southwest. One was *Anasazi,* a Navajo word meaning the Ancient Ones, which has been refined specifically to denote the ancestors of the modern Pueblo Indians, the former inhabitants of much of the Colorado Plateau. The other term was *Basket Maker,* by which Wetherill meant those he considered predecessors of the Anasazi. This group, first found in the moisture-free overhangs of Grand Gulch, appeared not to have produced pottery but instead relied for containers on skillfully woven baskets. Modern research has shown these two groups to be facets of one unbroken physical and cultural continuum rather than distinct societies as Wetherill believed.

With these archaeological experiences behind him, Wetherill then became more identified with the modern history of Chaco Canyon than he had been with that of Mesa Verde. He spent a large part of his adult life there. At various times he was an excavator applying the full gamut of his newly learned skills to Pueblo Bonito, the area's greatest monument; a trader to the local Indians; and a homesteader struggling against long odds to make a living off the uncooperative land. Ultimately, too, he was shot to death in Chaco Canyon. He is buried in a bleak little grave in the shadow of Pueblo Bonito, to which he had devoted so much of his energy.

Wetherill first came to Chaco in the autumn of 1895 while serving as a guide for a peripatetic Kansas family named Palmer. These people had a penchant for traveling about the West by wagon, entertaining small gatherings along the way with concerts and shows to meet expenses. Before leaving his ranch near Mesa Verde in Mancos, Colorado, Richard had written Talbot Hyde that he was going to New Mexico to see if he could locate some more accessible ruins where he could spend the winter and find different kinds of relics. The Chaco-bound party outfitted in Durango with supplies for two months. Barrels for extra water were secured to the two wagons making the trip. After six days of traveling south down the Animas River, fording the San Juan River just east of Farmington, and crossing the barren sandy expanse below the San Juan, they safely arrived at the Chaco Wash a few miles west of where the Escavada Wash joins it. As they approached the canyon, they encountered flocks of Navajo sheep and goats, a few hogans near meager cornfields, and some rifle-toting Indians on horseback, who gave them no trouble. The arroyos were not running; the land was dry.

The party turned the wagons to the east and, moving along the north side of the wash, entered Chaco Canyon, passing below Peñasco Blanco and by Casa Chiquita and Kin Kletso before coming in sight of Pueblo del Arroyo and Pueblo Bonito. Camp was made in the sheltered spot between the high north wall of Pueblo Bonito and the nearby towering, almost vertical, cliff of the canyon. The Palmers slept in a wagon, as was their custom, and Richard spread his bedroll out on the ground.

Wetherill and Mr. Palmer, sometimes accompanied by Palmer's eighteen-year-old daughter, Marietta, explored the Chaco for a month despite increasingly colder weather and frequent sandstorms. They poked over all the large ruins and many of the smaller ones between Peñasco

Blanco and Pueblo Bonito. A little digging was done in the mass of tumbled debris at Pueblo Bonito and in the mounds of lesser sites across the canyon near the break in its walls known as South Gap. Most of the Chaco ruins surpassed anything Wetherill had seen, being much larger and more complex than the cliff dwellings with which he was familiar. In the effort to understand the ruins better, Wetherill asked near-by Navajos in their own tongue what they knew about the abandoned villages and how the country might have looked when the tribe first filtered into the area.

About the middle of November, with winter closing in, the group broke camp and rode out of Chaco over that long-established trail to Jémez Pueblo, then on to Santa Fe and Albuquerque, stopping at several other Indian villages along the way. From Albuquerque, Richard again wrote Talbot Hyde,

> Not having anything important on hand this winter I have taken the opportunity to visit the ruins of New Mexico. Those of Chaco Canyon being the greatest in New Mexico and almost unknown—every one so far having tried to get Relics there making a total failure of it—for that reason more than any other I wished to examine them—I was successful after a few days search in finding relics in quantity—the ruins there are enormous—there are 11 of the large Pueblos or houses containing from one hundred to 500 rooms each and numerous small ones—how many I do not know but there must be more than 100. I stayed there until I had gotten 40 pieces of pottery. . . . Grass and water is plenty—wood is scarce. A wagon can be driven to the Ruins in 5 or six days from our Ranch.[2]

This letter and others that followed were instrumental in directing the attention and funds of the Hyde Exploring Expedition to Chaco Canyon for the next four years.

Under the nominal scientific direction of Professor F. W. Putnam of the American Museum of Natural History and Harvard University, the field supervision of George H. Pepper, a twenty-three-year-old former Putnam student who had never been to the Southwest, and with Richard Wetherill as foreman, the Hyde Exploring Expedition commenced work at Pueblo Bonito in May of 1896. Pepper had met Wetherill at the Alamo Ranch in Mancos and, together with one of Wetherill's brothers and two local cowhands, hauled a load of supplies to Chaco Canyon. A tent camp was set up behind Pueblo Bonito on the spot where Wetherill and the Palmers had camped earlier. An iron wood stove, propped up on rocks against the wall of the ruin, was the kitchen. A few Navajos were engaged as laborers. Pepper presumably left most of the camp chores, the obtaining of supplies and hired hands, and the directing of the digging to Wetherill. He did not take to manual labor and so confined his own activities to planning and inspecting the excavations, meticulously cataloging and describing the artifacts recovered, preparing detailed measurements and plans of the excavated units, and carrying out necessary office work. Much of his time was spent in his tent where he had fashioned a desk from old crates. Wetherill and Pepper kept a photographic record of the digs together, but Wetherill seems to have taken most of the pictures (see figs. 10 and 11).

Drawing upon past experiences, Wetherill assumed that, despite the lack of success of other excavations, the two large refuse mounds in front of Pueblo Bonito would yield burials and rich mortuary offerings of pottery and other items. Revolting as it may seem today to have placed one's dear departed into a hillock of garbage accumulated at the front door, Wetherill had found this practice widespread in the ruins he had probed previously. Therefore, for a month, the Pueblo Bonito trash heaps were extensively trenched, sometimes up to a depth of eight to ten feet (see fig. 12). Not a single burial was encountered, and very few specimens worth keeping were recovered. Instead, they learned, as had Scott Morris three years earlier, that the mounds consisted of tons of debris from construction activities and a mass of rubbish from the pueblo's homes. The latter included broken pottery, worn-out apparel and implements, scraps of animal bones, floor sweepings of ash and charcoal, and a lot of wind-blown sand. Thus, the question of where the inhabitants of Pueblo Bonito had disposed of their dead was raised after only the first month of digging.

Disappointed, Pepper shifted the laborers to the refuse mounds resulting from occupation of the smaller house units on the south side of the canyon where Wetherill and Palmer previously had found the first ancient burials (including some forty earthenware pots) exhumed in Chaco Canyon. Pepper and Wetherill both knew that the Hydes expected a return in the form of specimens for their investment and that the first month's work had produced nothing. The trash mounds of the lesser villages obligingly yielded additional burials, thirty in all, and another array of pottery. It was difficult to explain what appeared to be a puzzling difference in burial practices between the people of Pueblo Bonito and those of the pueblos across the canyon.

Fearful of the dead, two of the Navajo diggers quit when the first human skeletons were uncovered. But there were other problems that summer in keeping the small crew of laborers. Some of them had never worked for wages before, and they could not adjust to the white man's

Figure 10. Portion of the Hyde Exploring Expedition
camp set up north of Pueblo Bonito for the 1896 season
of digging. *Courtesy of the American Museum of
Natural History*

Figure 11. Part of the Navajo excavation crew and their families at dinner at the Hyde Exploring Expedition kitchen set up against the rear wall of Pueblo Bonito, 1896. *Courtesy of the American Museum of Natural History*

Figure 12. A trench through the Pueblo Bonito
refuse mound, the first excavations of the Hyde
Exploring Expedition. George Pepper is seated
between his Navajo workmen. *Courtesy of the
American Museum of Natural History*

hours and work habits. A few were content to leave after their first payday, the fifty cents a day they had earned jingling happily in their pockets. Others had to leave to participate in ceremonial functions. Those who stayed lived in nearby hogans or camped in or near Chaco Canyon. While their husbands worked for the expedition, the wives set up their looms and wove items to sell to members of the staff. Pepper was a good customer and is said to have encouraged the women to weave new-style items after he tired of the ordinary rugs. He claimed to have had the first runners and pillow tops woven that initial season in Chaco. It is also possible that he promoted the weaving of the first sand-painting design tapestry.

In July, excavations were resumed back at Pueblo Bonito, this time in the north central part of the ruin itself (see fig. 13). Thirty-seven rooms and one kiva were cleared before the season ended in September. Work was accomplished one room at a time. First, the fallen rocks on the surface were loosened with picks and thrown aside; then, the dirt and rock fill in the room was shoveled out and away from the tops of the walls. Picks and shovels routinely were used to free the consolidated debris as the digging progressed down to the floor. Smaller tools, knives, spoons, and hands were employed to locate and remove specimens from the surrounding dirt. Artifacts and architectural features found in the fill and on the floor were measured and mapped with respect to their location in the room and were described in the field notes. All specimens were identified with the number of the room from which they came. Photographs were taken during and after the excavation of a room or of special finds. When a series of rooms had been excavated and recorded, they were backfilled with dirt and rocks dug from adjacent rooms. This was the most efficient and least expensive way of handling the tons of rubble that covered Pueblo Bonito; however, it left few sections of the site open for future observation.

Many of the Pueblo Bonito rooms contained the sorts of things Wetherill and the Hydes had anticipated finding in the ruin. Moreover, several rooms had objects verging on the spectacular. The season's haul filled a freight car when shipped to the museum in New York. Included were a cache of 114 cylinder-shaped pottery vessels from a single room, a quiver containing 81 arrows, over 375 carved wooden staffs that probably served as prayer sticks in ritual observances, a cylindrical basket encrusted with a mosaic of turquoise and shell, six wooden flutes, a number of stone effigies of birds, frogs, and tadpoles—some with inlays of turquoise—and a quantity of turquoise beads and pendants.

The expedition had been successful in producing a valuable museum collection. It had cost the Hyde brothers about $3,000, of which $600

Figure 13. Digging the first rooms and kivas in the
northwest section of Pueblo Bonito. Hyde Exploring
Expedition, 1896. *Courtesy of the American Museum of
Natural History*

went to Wetherill for his half-year's work. Nonetheless, as might be expected, friction had developed between Wetherill and Pepper before the field season ended. Wetherill wrote to Talbot Hyde suggesting that in the future he would prefer to be "put on a different footing" with Pepper, implying that he felt himself better qualified to direct the field operation. Hyde did not take the suggestion; Pepper remained field director for the duration of the project.

Wetherill married Marietta Palmer that fall. Thereafter she was a member of the Chaco team, serving as cook for the staff, clerking in the trading post after it was established, and raising a family. For the next three summers, the Hydes continued their support of the Pueblo Bonito excavations. Relationships between Wetherill and Pepper remained strained throughout their association, leading to periods of avoidance and hostility.

The following three field seasons saw the excavations confined to Pueblo Bonito. A total of 190 rooms and other features were cleared, using much the same technique as had been employed the first year. Some of the excavations and findings are shown in figures 14–19. At the close of each excavation season, the materials recovered were shipped to the museum in New York.

In spite of his assiduous record keeping, Pepper never wrote a final report on Pueblo Bonito. He did publish four short articles describing his more spectacular finds,[3] but the continual pressure of museum duties delayed the work that would have climaxed the main effort of his archaeological career. In 1920, twenty years after the field work was finished and ten years after Pepper had left the American Museum, he published his slightly embellished field notes, which are of limited value and then only to those familiar with Pueblo Bonito.[4] They are primarily a descriptive record, room by room, of observations and measurements of architectural features and a listing of artifacts found. They do reflect Pepper's attention to detail, but interpretations and significance of the archaeological evidence generally are lacking.

In the five pages of conclusions in Pepper's report, he clearly associated the Chaco ruins with the ancestors of the modern Pueblo Indians. He did not address himself to the antiquity of the sites, but he believed that Pueblo Bonito had been occupied for many years, perhaps centuries. Stratigraphy, he thought, would be a good technique for unraveling the history of the settlement, and his records indicate that such investigations, never before applied to a Southwestern site, had been planned for Pueblo Bonito. He further stated that variations in construction techniques exhibited in the masonry walls of various sections of Pueblo Bonito had temporal significance, as did different styles of doorways and ceilings.

Figure 14. Kiva 16, Pueblo Bonito, after excavation by
the Hyde Exploring Expedition in 1896. Shadow of the
photographer, probably Richard Wetherill, and the
large view camera whose glass plates produced the expedition photographs reproduced in this volume. *Courtesy of the American Museum of Natural History*

Figure 15. Looking for turquoise beads in dirt taken from one of Pueblo Bonito's excavated rooms. View is part of the Hyde expedition camp at the rear of the ruin. Left to right: Navajo Indian; Orian Buck, freighter; George Pepper; Richard Wetherill. *Courtesy of the American Museum of Natural History*

Figure 16. Room 62, Pueblo Bonito, as excavated by the Hyde expedition. Note the plastered walls, wall niches, and floor cists containing baskets and pottery vessels. *Courtesy of the American Museum of Natural History*

17.

18.

Figure 17. The original ceiling of pine beams and willow twigs in Room 14B, Pueblo Bonito. This room was cleaned out and used as the Hyde expedition kitchen and storeroom in 1896. The following year the room was incorporated in the first Wetherill trading post when that structure was attached to the north wall of the ruin. *Courtesy of the American Museum of Natural History*

Figure 18. Room 28, Pueblo Bonito, showing part of the pottery cache uncovered by the Hyde expedition. In all, four layers of vessels were found, totalling 114 cylindrical jars, 18 pitchers, and 8 bowls. This is the third layer. *Courtesy of the American Museum of Natural History*

Figure 19. Close up of the third layer of pottery in the cache in Room 28, Pueblo Bonito. Thirty vessels, including 17 cylindrical jars, 6 bowls, and 7 pitchers were found in this layer. *Courtesy of the American Museum of Natural History*

19.

Certain of the habitation rooms, in addition to the subterranean chambers known as kivas, were thought to have been used for rituals. Relating the archaeological evidence to practices of the modern Pueblos, Pepper identified one particular ceremonial room as having belonged to the Macaw clan because it contained the remains of several macaws.

The artifacts from the pueblo were said to have been those expected among a sedentary people who had reached a high level of development. Perishable items, such as ceremonial sticks, wooden arrows, fragments of cloth, pieces of buckskin, and sandals and cordage of fiber were remarkably preserved in the dry debris of deeply filled rooms. The aesthetic attainment of the pueblo's occupants was reflected in the color designs found on wooden tablets and the encrusted and mosaic work on exceptional pieces such as inlaid scrapers, a mosaic-covered basket, and animal effigies. The use of turquoise in beads, pendants, and inlays, Pepper believed, exceeded that of any other Southwestern site. He conjectured that the source for the turquoise was Los Cerrillos near Santa Fe. Regarding pottery, Pepper concluded that the majority of the vessels found were of the rough-surfaced corrugated type of cooking jars and the grayware with geometric designs in black. The tall straight-sided cylinder jars, all found in a cache in one room, represented a form not yet seen in other regional sites. Perhaps they had been used in special observances for holding ceremonial sticks as part of altar paraphernalia. Verification was implied by the discovery of a large number of these sticks in an adjacent room. Bone and stone artifacts, exhibiting a wide range of form and probable usage, were similar to those from other Pueblo centers, but a few items fashioned from both of these materials were identified as ritualistic because of special decorative techniques found on them. A number of mortars and metates had been used for pulverizing various minerals for pigments. There was no evidence of human bones having been made into implements, but Pepper added that the occurrence of cracked and calcined human bones raised the question that perhaps the people of Pueblo Bonito ate human flesh. Shells appeared commonly in the refuse, worked into such forms as mosaics, bracelets, pendants, and beads or left in their entirety. Several trumpets made of conch shells also were retrieved. Although suffering more from decay than any other class of artifacts, basketry was represented by many examples, mostly in the shapes of large and small containers resembling bowls.

After four seasons, Pepper ended his association with Pueblo Bonito as puzzled over the paucity of human burials within the town or its trash heap as he had been at the conclusion of the first sterile month. A few skeletons had been found in several so-called burial rooms. These units appeared to have seen secondary usage for the deposition of bodies of particularly important personages inasmuch as they were accompanied by consequential offerings. But the grave sites of the bulk of the populace must, in Pepper's opinion, lie concealed beneath thick deposits of sand and mud to the west or east of the structure.

Each year's campaign at Pueblo Bonito had its up and downs. The ruin continued to give up quantities of specimens, but this success was tempered by financial problems, absenteeism among the Navajos, and, most alarming of all, the realization that some of the Indians were pilfering artifacts from the digs. How many specimens were taken by Navajo workmen who sold them to nearby traders is, of course, not known. When such incidents came to Wetherill's attention, he handled them in a manner that did not disrupt his crew, as most surely would have happened had he accused one of them of being a thief. He quietly arranged to have the missing articles purchased from the Indian or from the person to whom they had been sold. One unusual well-known Chaco specimen, a small jet frog with eyes and collar of turquoise, disappeared the day it was discovered only to turn up months later at a trading post near Farmington.

During the first and second summers' work in Chaco, Wetherill came to realize that a trading post in Chaco might be a good business undertaking. He had noted that the local Navajos, and those who came from elsewhere to work for the Hyde Exploring Expedition, had to ride many miles to obtain provisions and to market their stock, wool, and rugs. Therefore, during the winter he sent two of his brothers, Al and Clate, and a helper, Orian Buck, to Chaco to build a modest structure to be used for a trading post (fig. 20). It was planned as a small one-room building joining the north wall of Pueblo Bonito and connected with one of the roofed rooms of the ruin. Stone and timbers from the Anasazi buildings were convenient materials. In 1898 when the post was completed and stocked, Al and Clate departed, leaving Buck to run it.

The Chaco Canyon Trading Post was such a profitable endeavor from the start that in another year the expedition, using the same readily available materials, built a more spacious and substantial structure. This was a rectangular three-room affair (fig. 21). One room served as the Wetherill residence, the second was a bedroom and office for Pepper, and the third was the trading post, which became a joint endeavor between Wetherill and the Hydes. Although burdened with her first child, Marietta tended the store most of the time. As manager, Wetherill was entitled to 10 percent of the profits. Thus the Wetherill family became permanent residents of Chaco and in due time moved their possessions from the Alamo Ranch in Mancos to their new home. Marietta learned to trade with the Navajos and soon established good relations with them. Some of them taught her to weave.

The new Pueblo Bonito trading post flourished. Navajos from an ever

Figure 20. East end of Pueblo Bonito in 1897. First Wetherill trading post is under construction against the north wall of the ruin. Note the succession of holes broken through the base of the wall to gain access to the first floor rooms. *Courtesy of the American Museum of Natural History*

Figure 21. West end of Pueblo Bonito in 1898. The first Hyde Exploring Expedition building, whose three rooms were used as Wetherill's home, a trading post, and George Pepper's quarters and office are shown. Two seasons of excavations had opened up numerous rooms and kivas. *Courtesy of the American Museum of Natural History*

widening area brought their business to Wetherill, who paid premium prices for good rugs and saddle blankets, provided them with Mexican pesos for their silversmithing, and helped improve their flocks of sheep.

Even though there was little attention paid to the expedition activities and findings, word of its accomplishments spread to other archaeologists working in the Southwest, and scientific journals carried notices of the program. Among the scientists who visited Chaco during the Pueblo Bonito excavations was Warren K. Moorehead, curator of the Department of Archaeology of Ohio State University. He brought a small party to Chaco and, apparently with the approval of the Hyde expedition, did some digging in Pueblo Bonito and other ruins.[5]

Another frequent visitor was Dr. T. Mitchell Prudden, a long-time friend of the Wetherill family, who on many occasions had been guided by various of the brothers on his extensive trips throughout the Indian country. Trained in medicine and a professor at Columbia University, Prudden became a dedicated and knowledgeable scholar of Southwestern archaeology and ethnology. His writings, both technical and popular, described his trips and discoveries and were important contributions to Southwestern anthropology. Much of his field work focused upon the earlier, smaller Anasazi ruins rather than on the later, more spectacular ones.[6]

During the first season of field work for his study of the physical anthropology of the Indians of the Southwest and northern Mexico, Aleš Hrdlička, of the United States National Museum, also made the pilgrimage to the Pueblo Bonito camp and returned several other times. He compiled anthropometric measurements of the Chaco Navajo, as well as of all available prehistoric skeletal remains. Furthermore, he wrote detailed observations of Navajo life that constitute a brief ethnography of the Navajo at the turn of the century.[7]

Professor Richard E. Dodge, a New York geologist, conducted research in the canyon for two summers. During that time, he assisted in the preparation of the map of Pueblo Bonito. Dodge was interested in the geological circumstances at the time of the occupation of the canyon in comparison with present conditions, any evidence of climatic or geographical change, and determination of the time lapse between the abandonment of the sites and the present day. He studied the banks of the Chaco Wash, particularly where buried cultural deposits were exposed, the comparative weathering of the rocks used in different building periods in Pueblo Bonito, and the depths of soil deposits that had accumulated about the major Chaco ruins. He became convinced that the Chaco communities had been occupied for a great length of time because of the depth of clay and of sand deposited by water and wind around them and the fact that evidences of human activities could be seen at a depth of almost twenty feet below the present canyon floor.[8]

Professor Putnam, scientific director of the Hydes' excavation program in Chaco from its inception in 1896, did not visit the ruins until the fall of 1899, at the end of the fourth and final full-scale field season (fig. 22). Despite his sixty years, Putnam was eager to see everything he could of Chaco, and Wetherill tried to accommodate him. On horseback, they explored the canyon from one end to the other and rode out to some of the larger sites adjacent to the Chaco, including Kin Bineola fifteen miles southwest of Pueblo Bonito. Accomplishments and expenditures up to that time were reviewed. Putnam stated that the cost to Talbot and Frederick Hyde had been in the neighborhood of $25,000, but that the materials recovered probably exceeded those from any previous similar effort in this country.

The American Museum of Natural History never has displayed the entire Pueblo Bonito collection and probably never will because there are countless duplications among the vast number of objects. It has, however, from time to time included the more significant artifacts in its exhibits. A rough, incomplete itemization made in 1901 listed 50,000 pieces of turquoise, 10,000 pieces of pottery, 5,000 stone implements, 1,000 bone and wooden objects, a few fabrics, fourteen human skeletons, a small number of copper bells, and the jeweled frog mentioned above. Some items from the collection are shown in figures 24–27.

Putnam made a second visit to Chaco in the fall of 1901. At this time government investigations of the Hyde Exploring Expedition took place that shortly thereafter made further archaeological work impossible in Chaco. During this sojourn in the canyon, Putnam was joined by Alfred M. Tozzer of Harvard's Peabody Museum. At that time, Tozzer, who was soon to embark upon a highly successful career among the Maya of Mexico and Central America, was primarily concerned with Navajo linguistics and ethnography. However, he assisted Putnam and others in digging in some small sites near Chaco where seventeen burials were uncovered.[9]

A matter that bothered Wetherill and the Hyde brothers from the beginning of their explorations and excavations in Chaco Canyon was their right to dig in the ruins to the exclusion of others. At that time, there were no restrictions against excavating Indian ruins on public lands such as Chaco Canyon. However, there was no legal way for an individual to keep others from working in the same site except by agreement, keeping secret the location of productive areas, or forcefully prohibiting others from "jumping claim." As news of the Hyde Exploring Expedition's success slowly became known, a few others, such as the Moorehead party

Figure 22. Professor Frederick W. Putnam, American Museum of Natural History, scientific director of the Hyde Exploring Expedition at the time of his visit to Chaco Canyon in 1899 during the last season of work at Pueblo Bonito. *Courtesy of the American Museum of Natural History*

Figure 23. The Hyde Exploring Expedition warehouse, blacksmith shop, and stable west of Pueblo Bonito during the peak of the trading post enterprise, 1901. *Courtesy of the American Museum of Natural History*

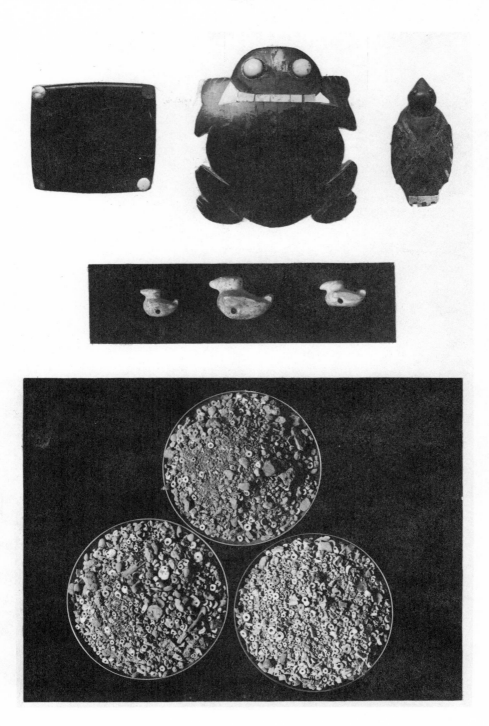

Figure 24. Examples of turquoise objects recovered
from Pueblo Bonito by the Hyde Exploring Expedition.
Above: items inlaid with turquoise, jet plaque, jet frog,
hematite bird; center: bird-shaped beads; below: part of
the assortment of over 2,300 beads and small pendants
found in a single room. *Courtesy of the American
Museum of Natural History*

Figure 25. Painted stone mortar as found by the Hyde
expedition in Room 80, Pueblo Bonito. Inset shows
details of design painted in red, orange, blue, and green.
Height of mortar, 8½ ". *Courtesy of the American
Museum of Natural History*

Figure 26. Miscellaneous artifacts from Pueblo Bonito. Upper left: human head of an effigy pottery vessel; upper right: sandal woven of yucca fiber; center: fragment of a sandstone disc covered with cloisonné design in black, red, yellow, and white; lower: trumpet made from seashell from the Gulf of California. *Courtesy of the American Museum of Natural History*

Figure 27. Examples of two forms of pottery vessels recovered from Pueblo Bonito. Upper: Black-on-white pitchers, about 7″ high; lower: Black-on-white cylindrical jars, about 10″ tall. *Courtesy of the American Museum of Natural History*

and some individual relic seekers, came to dig in Chaco. Sensing that there would be proliferation of such activity by additional groups, Wetherill undertook to secure his privilege, and that of the Hydes, to work in certain Chaco sites by starting procedures to file a homestead claim to lands that included the major ruins of Pueblo Bonito, Chetro Ketl, and Pueblo del Arroyo, as well as the several buildings constructed by the expedition. One complication after another delayed the granting of the patent for years. Two sections of railroad land near the ruins were purchased in Marietta's name, and Frederick Hyde filed a homestead claim on land south of the ancient rubble in South Gap. The latter move was never finalized.

Shortly before 1900, certain concerned persons from lay and professional ranks began to speak out against the rapidly growing practice of uncontrolled searching for and sale of relics in Southwestern Indian ruins. In their view, sites were being vandalized and scientific information destroyed. Recovered specimens were ending up in private hands or on the shelves of curio stores rather than in institutions of learning. They appealed to the government to put an end to such activities.

One of the leaders of this mounting protest was Dr. Edgar L. Hewett, then president of New Mexico Normal University in Las Vegas and later director of the Museum of New Mexico and School of American Research in Santa Fe. A humanistic scholar, Hewett had traveled extensively throughout the northern Southwest. He recognized the urgent necessity of permanently protecting and preserving its archaeological remains, most of which were situated on lands of the public domain. He pointed out their scientific potential, arguing that only qualified individuals should be allowed to excavate in them. If set aside, they would be examples of outstanding prehistoric cultural achievements available for the enjoyment and edification of future generations. The codification of regulations that would guard all objects of antiquity on federal lands and the creation of preserves or parks around areas where concentrations of significant ruins existed were proposals which Hewett and other archaeological allies took to Washington. After several years of working with various governmental officials, in 1906, during the administration of President Theodore Roosevelt, they were successful in having Congress pass what is referred to as the Antiquities Act.

The bill legally prohibited appropriating, excavating, or damaging any historic or prehistoric ruins or objects of antiquity on the public lands of the United States. It also empowered the president to proclaim as national monuments any lands owned or acquired by the federal government that contained historic landmarks, historic or prehistoric structures, and other objects of historic or scientific interest. Before his term had expired, President Theodore Roosevelt had named the first eighteen national monuments. These included Chaco Canyon, which was so designated in 1907. Until the National Park Service was created in 1916, administration of the monuments was handled by whichever federal department had jurisdiction over the land.

Protection of the great ancient structures of Chaco Canyon was one of Hewett's main objectives. As early as the spring of 1900, he protested to the surveyor general of the General Land Office against the activities of the Hyde Exploring Expedition, describing their work at Pueblo Bonito as nothing but vandalism. This turned government attention to the Chaco for the first time, and a special agent, Max Pracht, was sent from Santa Fe to investigate Hewett's charges. However, the agent did not go to Chaco but instead talked with seemingly informed citizens in and about Durango, Colorado. The result was that he reported favorably upon the operations sponsored by the Hydes and recommended no action against them.

Hewett was a determined individual and, whether his actions were directed solely toward criticism of the methods employed by Pepper and Wetherill or reflected his desire to conduct his own excavations in Chaco, he renewed his complaints in the fall, this time aided by political support of a former territorial governor of New Mexico and his fellow members of the Santa Fe Archaeological Society.[10] Complaints also were levelled by others against the Hydes' expanding livestock and trading dealings and the drilling of oil wells. Navajo Agency officials investigated the latter rumor to learn that the drilling was only for water at the expedition store, which was not on Navajo land. Nevertheless, their report added that the expedition was hauling off many thousands of dollars' worth of pottery and relics. The officers promised to keep watch on them. Meanwhile, protests, charges, and counter-charges developed to the point that the commissioner of the General Land Office issued an order prohibiting further digging by the Hyde expedition at Pueblo Bonito until a thorough investigation could be made.

The person assigned to examine the condition of the Chaco ruins and to review the activities of the Hyde Exploring Expedition was S. J. Holsinger, special agent of the General Land Office, stationed in Phoenix, Arizona. The order to undertake the investigation was issued in December 1900, but, due to Chaco's rigorous winter weather, he did not travel there until the following April. Holsinger spent four weeks in the canyon, living in the expedition's boardinghouse at Pueblo del Arroyo. Saddle horses were procured from Richard Wetherill, who also served as Holsinger's guide on most trips to every important Chaco ruin. It is known that Frederick Hyde was in Chaco during at least part of the investigation because Holsinger took statements from him and from Wetherill for use in the final report.[11]

The special agent's main objective was to investigate the charges made by Hewett and his associates that the Hyde Exploring Expedition had contributed to the "spoilation and destruction" of the Chaco sites. Those in charge of the project, furthermore, had claimed that all the relics excavated were donated to a public museum in New York while in fact it was believed that they were sold wherever they would bring the greatest return. This accusation Hyde, of course, denied.

Holsinger put a great deal of effort into his investigation and report, which for the first time detailed many aspects of the aboriginal Chaco development not previously made available to the public. But implicit in his writings was the same respect felt by earlier observers for the sheer will of a simple people which caused them to work together to survive in a demanding environment. Besides personally visiting all the large sites and some of the smaller ones, he wrote three detailed volumes about the canyon's physical setting and archaeological remains, took a number of photographs, and interviewed those who directed the work as well as some of the Navajo employees. In many cases, he compared the condition of the sites with Jackson's descriptions made twenty-four years earlier, verifying Jackson's observations about many of the ruins, supplementing them in some instances, and noting changes that had occurred in the structures in the time between the two visits. In addition, he suggested interpretations of certain prehistoric practices by referring to customs of the modern Pueblos, customs he learned either from Pueblo ethnography or from listening well to what Hyde and Wetherill had to tell him. The account is the only contemporary general description of the work of the Hyde Exploring Expedition. It also contains brief descriptions of six previously unrecorded notable Chaco ruins—Casa Rinconada, Sin-Kle-Zin (Tsin Kletzin), Kin-Kla-Tzin (Kin Klizhin), Kin-Mi-Ni-Oli (Kin Bineola), Kin-Yai (Kin Ya-a), and a structure southeast of the canyon that he did not visit.

Considerable attention was given to the physical characteristics and climate of Chaco Canyon. Holsinger wrote that the canyon proper is a wide wash on the west side of the Continental Divide, coursing in a northwesterly direction, which, after being joined by several tributaries, empties into the San Juan River. It had been cut by thousands of years of erosion into Tertiary sandstones and more recently had filled to within fifty to one hundred feet of the top with sand and sediments. This deposit forms the floor of the canyon and averages in width from a quarter- to a half-mile. Through the valley floods have cut a channel from ten to thirty feet deep and from twenty-five to several hundred feet wide. The arroyo exposes strata of fine sediments or adobe and a coarse white sand. It contains evidence of human utilization in the form of potsherds, charcoal, and ashes, to a depth of ten to fifteen feet. The latter situation, which had been alluded to in Jackson's earlier account, points out the extent to which deposition of water- and wind-borne sand and soil has taken place in Chaco Canyon during and since Anasazi occupation. Holsinger adds that Jackson, in 1877, noted soil reaching up to the bottoms of the windows of Chetro Ketl's first-floor rooms; however, in 1901, soil had entirely covered the windows and almost banked to the roof line of the first-floor rooms.

The land was characterized as desert and unfit for modern agricultural practices. Winters were described as cold, summers as hot. Summer sandstorms, some of several days' duration were lucidly pictured:

> . . . for many days the horizon line is entirely closed and objects cannot be distinguished 100 feet from the observer. At such times it is difficult to follow trails or well travelled roads and the wayfarer takes his life in his hands unless he depends upon the keen instinct and sharp eyes of a Navajo, to whom every trail and sand drift is well known, to guide him.
>
> The only tolerable season is from June to October. During this period the rains occur and nature exerts herself to redeem the desert. However, at best the scattering vegetation only lends a blending of green to the somber brown and yellow of the landscape.

The matter of water supply in Chaco, both at the time of Holsinger's stay and during prehistoric times, was considered. The Hyde Exploring Expedition relied upon a 20-foot-deep well in the bottom of the arroyo (an attempt to obtain a better supply by drilling a 350-foot well at the southwest corner of Pueblo Bonito had produced only brackish water unfit for use). Neither living springs nor running water were noted, but Holsinger stated that poor quality water could be found in the vicinity of every ruin by sinking shallow wells in the sand. He felt that the sources of water available to the aboriginal inhabitants were similar to those of modern times, but that the Chaco Wash then had not been so deep. Even when it was not flowing, water could have been secured by scooping out depressions in the bed of the arroyo.

The special agent either observed, or had called to his attention, many ancient attempts to obtain and control the meager supply of water. He wrote:

On every side one may find evidence of a continuous struggle against arid conditions and laborious effort on the part of the inhabitants, not only to secure water for irrigation but for domestic purposes.

The natural tanks on the cliff above Pueblo Bonito were believed to have provided some of the domestic water for that community. A seep in the canyon west of Pueblo Alto probably furnished water for those who resided there. Holsinger went to some length to describe, for the first time, features discernible near several ruins that were associated with irrigation practices. He correctly identified remains of dams, reservoirs, or ditches in the vicinity of Una Vida, Peñasco Blanco, Kin Klizhin, and Kin Bineola, but mistook a segment of a prehistoric road at Kin Ya-a to be a canal. Near Kin Bineola he wrote:

> . . . there is now a dry lake where water was impounded by means of a wall and earthworks. From this lake a canal carried the water some distance to available agricultural lands. The line of embankment forming the canal may be observed for a mile or more curving around the base of the low rolling hills. For a considerable distance, at one point, the canal is walled up on the lower side with solid masonry, still in good state of preservation.

At Kin Klizhin, six and one-half miles southwest of Pueblo Bonito, he examined

> . . . well preserved remnants of a stone dam with a wasteway on the east side cut in solid rock. From this dam an ancient ditch, now a mere depression, conveyed the diverted and impounded water to a tract of about 200 acres of agricultural land.

Pueblo Bonito, which he called the "ruin of ruins, the equal of which in point of magnitude and general interest, is not to be found among the world's collection of discovered prehistoric structures," and the excavations that had been conducted therein, obviously occupied most of Holsinger's attention. He learned that the Navajos called the place Sa-bah-ohn-nee, "the house where the rocks are propped up," because of the presence behind the ruin of the huge monolith whose base had been reinforced by heavy timbers and a masonry wall by the old inhabitants. This great isolated wedge of rock, known recently as Threatening Rock, was termed the Elephant in Holsinger's time. It towered above Pueblo Bonito and had been considered a threat to the community when it was occupied. Holsinger was in agreement as to its instability.

Holsinger was able to record greater detail about Pueblo Bonito than had earlier writers because he spent a longer time at the site than had the others. Also, he profited from the fact that a portion of the structure had been excavated and some of its contents revealed. Probably of greater importance, the excavators were present to explain things to him. Like prior visitors, he considered the excellence of architecture to be one of the greatest features of the Chaco ruins. The use of perfect right angles, circles, and ellipses impressed him:

52

> The long, graceful sweep of the stupendous, curving outline of the buildings, the perfectly formed doors and windows of uniform size in each tier or story of rooms, and the mosaic and laminated effect in the masonry, are all convincing proofs that the builders were adept in the use of the trowel and stone hammer.

The several kinds of masonry used in constructing habitations and kivas were outlined, as were techniques of building doors and windows and fashioning floors and ceilings. Rubble-cored walls were said to be reinforced in places by placing long timbers in their centers. Quarries from which the sandstone building material was obtained were thought to have been located on the mesas one to three miles back from the canyon rim.

Even with the overall high quality of construction, Holsinger did observe several defects in the methods employed, such as the occasional failure to break joints in laying stone, the building of walls or partitions flush with old walls without properly uniting them, and the use of rubble cores for walls which did not always bind the veneers together properly and hence allowed moisture to penetrate and split the walls. He assumed that certain sections of Pueblo Bonito had been consumed by fire because the exposed masonry and wall plaster had been turned to a brick red color; he wondered if the conflagration had happened during or after occupation. The practice of placing new clay floors over litter that had accumulated on old floors was mentioned and was said to have disadvantages because, as years rolled by, the living surfaces gradually approached the ceiling. He also observed, or was informed by the archaeologists, that the ruins of an earlier structure existed beneath the old city. This was indeed new information which brought with it a flood of new questions. What kind of structure, how old, and built by whom?

Ever observant, Holsinger commented at length on the great quantity of cedar and pine timbers employed in the erection of Pueblo Bonito, explaining that the cedar may have grown from 25 to 30 miles distant.[12]

Pueblo Indian traditions, he remarked, noted that large timbers had been dragged and carried for distances up to 100 miles by their ancestors. He also believed it likely that some of the big pine logs had been cut in the more mountainous terrain along the upper reaches of the Chaco drainage, hauled to the wash, and floated down to the canyon during floods. This theory was reinforced while Holsinger was there by a flash flood that raged through Chaco Wash, running six feet deep and appearing powerful enough to have carried heavy timbers.

In discussing the excavations at Bonito, Holsinger noted that Pepper and Wetherill started at the southwestern corner in the outside series of rooms. When that row was excavated around to the northern section of the ruin, the second and then the third tiers of rooms were cleared. Excavation was accomplished by opening a series of pits that might encompass one or several rooms. Each pit was numbered and was dug to a depth of two or three stories to reach the ground floor. Pits were successively back-filled as new pits were opened. In some instances, roofs were removed to facilitate the work. Supposedly, the diggers did not take off roofs that were "in a perfect or tolerable state of preservation," but Holsinger remarked that while this might have been the case, many sound roof timbers had been cut off flush with the walls and taken away. He also said that the expedition dismantled and shipped to the museum several rooms found in a perfect state. All stones and timbers were marked so that the units could be reconstructed at the museum, but this does not seem ever to have been done. The northwestern portion of Pueblo Bonito had contained about fifty rooms, open or partially so. When discovered, these rooms had intact roofs and were free of detritus of the building. Some of them had been broken into by early explorers, and others had been dismantled by the Hyde Exploring Expedition. Only twenty such rooms remained according to Holsinger, who described them as being in "virgin condition."

Like Jackson, Holsinger was intrigued by the stone-cut Chaco stairways. He stated that every Chaco communal house was provided with one, the finest example he thought being that at Chetro Ketl. He also recorded the existence of an ancient roadway connecting Chetro Ketl and Pueblo Alto. It is described as being twenty feet wide, walled up to grade with loose rock, and filled with soil. He traced the feature from the top of the Chetro Ketl stairway, thence westward along a narrow terrace paralleling the canyon for about one-half mile to a sandstone ledge where there were indistinct remains of a broad flight of twenty steps cut in the rock. The road then followed a groove cut for several hundred feet in a flat rock outcropping, crossed a wash, and continued north to Pueblo Alto.

It is apparent from several of Holsinger's statements that the Hydes, like other diggers of their time, considered the amassing of large collections of artifacts their primary goal. Concurrent with excavations at Pueblo Bonito, said Holsinger, crews sought out small ruins for a distance of twenty miles up and down the canyon and dug in their cemeteries (refuse mounds) for the pottery and other relics associated with burials. Such remains in the canyon had been practically exhausted, but many undisturbed sites were found in the side canyons and on the nearby mesas. Holsinger himself was not immune to the excitement of archaeological discovery and, with a crew of Navajo shovel hands, tested several small ruins from which he recovered a few pots. Many burials in the smaller Chaco villages are characteristically covered with sandstone slabs that were placed over the corpse and its funerary furnishings at the time of interment in the refuse heap. Diggers learned to dig or probe the trash for these slabs, knowing that they were apt to find skeletons and artifacts beneath them. Today, these old diggings are easily identifiable by the partially filled holes and the presence of slabs thrown aside from the graves.

After exploring Pueblo Bonito and viewing the assortment of articles recovered by the diggers, Holsinger wrote a brief reconstruction of the domestic life of the occupants. He stated that they had lived as farmers, like the cliff dwellers and modern Pueblo Indians, depending on corn supplemented by beans, squash, wild nuts, and native plants. The dog and turkey were domesticated, the latter being raised in pens in some of the pueblo's rooms. Meat was provided by deer, small game, and birds. Meals were prepared in the manner of the present-day Pueblos. Corn and other vegetal foods were ground on metates with manos. Food was cooked in firepits over open fires. A well-developed ceramic art produced gray, corrugated cooking and storage jars and decorated black-on-white bowls, pitchers, jars, and effigy vessels for table use and ceremonial purposes. The Pueblo Bonito people were described as hewers of wood, builders of stone, tillers of the soil, and not given to warfare. Weapons were said to be rare, and those manufactured probably were for hunting. Stone tools such as hoes, trowels, hammers, axes, knives, and wedges occurred in profusion, but very few arrow points were found. Clothing was said to consist of loin cloths of yucca fiber or cotton, sandals of yucca, stockings or leggings of fibers, and robes of feathers, skins, or textiles. Religious practices were compared to those of the Pueblos, involving ceremonial kivas with kachina recesses and sipapus—the small floor opening symbolic of the mythical entrance to the spirit world—and the use of ritual wands and sacred fires. Holsinger concluded this section of his report by wondering where the people of Pueblo Bonito went and whether their departure was due to enemy pressure, disease, or famine.

Holsinger's work devoted considerable thought to the matter of ownership of the lands upon which the principal Chaco ruins are situated. In summary, he stated that when excavations were begun by the Hyde Exploring Expedition, Pueblo Bonito stood upon part of the unappropriated public domain unclaimed by settlers and so remained, notwithstanding the fact that the expedition had erected several buildings upon it, until November 26, 1900. In May of that year, Richard Wetherill filed a homestead entry on a quarter section near Chaco that contained one valuable ruin, Kin Klizhin. In November, application was made to change the entry to a piece of land that embraced Pueblo Bonito, Chetro Ketl, and Pueblo del Arroyo but, according to Holsinger, had no potential for farming. Wetherill averred that he originally had intended to file on the lands upon which the three major ruins were located to keep off interlopers, that he did occupy the land, and that the error had been made by a surveyor. When the mistake was discovered, Wetherill took steps to have it corrected.

Holsinger implied that there was something irregular about the homestead claim, describing the land Wetherill sought to claim as strictly desert and asserting that he used it for trade and not as a homestead. He listed the buildings on the property, all erected by the expedition, as a company store where Wetherill also lived, a boardinghouse, employees' quarters, warehouse, stables, and blacksmith shop, all valued at a total of approximately $10,000. It was noted that all archaeological materials recovered from Pueblo Bonito had been obtained prior to the amended filing and most before the date of the original entry.

On frequent occasions during the investigation both Frederick Hyde and Richard Wetherill avowed good faith and disclaimed any intention to defraud the government either in filing the homestead entry or in removing relics from public lands. The Hyde brothers claimed to have acted purely upon philanthropic impulses in an endeavor to further scientific research in archaeology and ethnology, stressing that the work at Bonito had been conducted according to professional standards and that the entire yield of artifacts had been deposited at the American Museum of Natural History. They entertained no promise or hope of financial remuneration. In fact, their desire to continue work at Pueblo Bonito led Wetherill to submit a written proposal to Holsinger offering to relinquish all claim upon the ancient houses and to retain for himself only the part of the land not occupied by the ruins in return for a permit to allow the expedition to complete its excavations.

Holsinger's findings were not overly critical of the manner in which the Hyde Exploring Expedition had conducted its explorations and disposal of the specimens gathered, but it was clear that he felt that certain activities, such as removal of timbers from the old structures, were not proper. He did not write an opinion covering the matter of the Wetherill homestead claim. Rather, he reviewed details about it and gave his evaluation as to the condition of the lands embodied in both the original and amended entries and the use to which those lands were being put. He strongly recommended, however, that a national park be created to protect and preserve the ruins, a move which effectively delayed for many years any action upon Wetherill's homestead claim and blocked further Chaco explorations by the Hydes. Boundaries of two possible areas for the proposed park were outlined, one of such size as to include the so-called Escavada Badlands north of Chaco Canyon, which are of geological significance, and the other of lesser dimensions, to encompass only the large Chaco sites. Recognizing the possible ill effect the establishment of a park might have upon the Navajo residents of the area, he suggested that they be allowed to remain on the land.

The investigative report also pointed out that after the Hydes had been ordered to suspend their excavations in Pueblo Bonito, they had turned to Indian trading as a major venture. This certainly was the case, for when Holsinger was in Chaco, the company had developed a chain of twelve trading posts, with an inventory of $100,000, scattered over the Navajo country. Headquarters were maintained at Chaco, where a post office named Putnam, for the scientific director of the expedition, was established. Company wagons operated between the posts and rail heads at Thoreau and Farmington, hauling freight, mail, and passengers. There was even talk of building a railroad into Chaco. Wetherill had charge of the operation locally. Frederick Hyde, who had not participated actively in the archaeological program except as a financier, became heavily involved in the business as he assumed general supervision. He not only oversaw the business but also promoted the sale of Navajo blankets and Indian curios in the East by giving public lectures about the Indians and arranging for demonstrations and sales of their arts and crafts in stores in Chicago, Philadelphia, Boston, and New York. The expedition even opened several retail outlets of its own in New York.

When Special Agent Holsinger finished his brief stay in Chaco, the first chapter in the history of Chaco Canyon archaeology came to an end. Although his report was not completed and forwarded to the General Land Office of the Department of the Interior until seven months later, the temporary suspension of excavation of Pueblo Bonito remained in effect. The Hyde Exploring Expedition never resumed its program in archaeology because, in 1902, the order became permanent. And in the same year, Wetherill was notified that his homestead entry had been denied.

The efforts of Hewett and his associates to have the scientific significance of the Chaco Canyon ruins recognized by government officials was given a decided thrust forward by Holsinger's report, and steps to set the area aside as a federal preserve were intensified. In 1902, the commissioner of the General Land Office recommended in two letters to the secretary of the interior that 746 square miles of the Chaco region be designated as "Chaco Canyon National Park." Five years later, part of the area became a national monument.

The termination of the Hyde excavations at Pueblo Bonito also marked the conclusion of Wetherill's active participation in archaeological explorations. For a short time, he continued to engage in the mercantile operations of the Hyde expedition. However, friction between Wetherill and his employers, aggravated by their New York business manager, who wished to eliminate his influence with the Hydes, finally caused him to be relieved of all connections with the company in January 1903. One charge brought against him, apparently circulated to the Hydes and federal officers by the business manager, was that Wetherill was illegally digging in the Chaco ruins and selling the relics. Whether this was a false charge or not remains unknown. When Wetherill's association with the Hyde brothers came to an abrupt end, he bought the Pueblo Bonito trading post. His remaining years were devoted to that enterprise and to developing his Chaco homestead claim by ranching and farming so that it would qualify under the Homestead Act.

The Hydes' participation in Indian trading reached a peak during the winter of 1901, when they operated seventeen trading posts, several large warehouses, and a fruit-drying facility. The costs of the overly rapid expansion apparently exceeded the limits to which the wealthy Hyde family was willing to invest. Furthermore, Frederick Hyde's handling of the business appears to have been subject to his whims and impulses rather than to sound business principles. Several trading posts were sold by the end of 1901; during the following year all of the others were disposed of. It was then that the store at Chaco became the property of Wetherill.[13]

Many people were relieved when the Hydes withdrew from the trading post business. Established traders naturally did not welcome the competition from the large-scale, far-flung operation. The Bureau of Catholic Missions formally had complained about the company's methods of acquiring and operating their posts, their prices, methods of collecting debts, and their general disregard for Navajo rights. Nevertheless, the enterprise did help revive the fine art of Navajo weaving at a time when it was rapidly degenerating, and it promoted the sale of Navajo rugs in the East at a time when the market was still in its infancy.

Surely, the rapid turn of events that led to the conclusion of the

57

archaeological work in Chaco Canyon and the Indian trading post business must have brought great disappointment to Wetherill. Still, he had coped with adversities all his life and did not easily accept defeat. He appealed the suspension of his homestead entry and applied himself diligently to developing the Chaco lands and to running his own Pueblo Bonito trading post. Another agent of the General Land Office, Frank Grygla, was dispatched to reexamine Richard's homestead claim in 1905 and, following his stay, submitted a report strongly in Richard's favor.[14] Since Holsinger's visit, Wetherill had constructed an earthen reservoir to impound irrigation water, following an old Anasazi custom, and had built five more buildings at his Triangle Bar Triangle Ranch headquarters. He reportedly had sixty acres planted in corn, five in wheat, and two in a family garden. Livestock owned included 200 horses, 50 head of cattle, 5,000 sheep, 4,000 chickens, and about 100 rabbits. The ranch, in addition to the homestead, included three sections of railroad land purchased in Marietta's name and other railroad property that was leased. His stock also grazed on the public domain and on Navajo allotments, usually on a share arrangement. At one time thirty Navajo families herded sheep for him on shares. Grygla's report also stated that Wetherill had cleared six rooms and a kiva in "a ruin," which lends credence to the charge made earlier that he was illegally probing the Indian sites.

In 1907, action to suspend Wetherill's homestead entry was dropped, at which time he proceeded to file final proof of his claim. However, this action was promptly protested because it had been found that there were deposits of coal on the land. Furthermore, several months after the Antiquities Act of 1906 was passed, representatives of the Department of the Interior asked Wetherill if he would sign title to the three ruins, as he had offered to do years before. This he promptly did, thereby reducing his homestead entry in size from 160 to 113 acres. The coal matter delayed action on his claim for another five years. Finally, in November 1912, the government granted him a patent to the land. By then, Wetherill had been dead for more than two years.

As a rancher and Indian trader, Wetherill's relationships with people and his business dealings were looked upon much as were his undertakings in archaeology, damned by some observers and commended by others. When operating his ranch and store at Chaco Canyon, he soon was at odds with the Indian Service and those in charge of the Navajo agencies at Shiprock and Crownpoint, who did everything in their power to get him out of Chaco. One bitter bone of contention was that rather than turning to agency officials, the Navajos went to Wetherill, a man who had lived among them for years and who understood their culture and language. This did not sit well with the government representatives who, even though the Wetherill ranch was not on the reservation, maintained an informal surveillance of all of Wetherill's affairs. He was accused of mistreating the Navajos, of stealing their stock, of using strong-arm tactics in collecting debts, of illegally fencing off Navajo or public lands for his private use, and of counseling the Navajos to ignore Indian Service regulations and notices.

Wetherill was able to counter many of these accusations; others he ignored. Some of them may have been true, for he was characterized as a strong man, fearless and a bit ruthless but no more so than others of his kind at that time and place. He must have held the respect of many of the Chaco Navajos who sought his advice, went to him when they needed credit or medical attention, traded with him when they could have gone elsewhere, and ran sheep on shares with him.

Ranching the Chaco mesas and plains was difficult, for range conditions and stock water there are subject to the vagaries of summer rains, heat, and winds as well as winter cold and snows. It was equally difficult to farm the alkali-laden canyon bottom, which usually suffers from lack of moisture, occasionally from too much rain, and frequently from excessive temperatures and blowing sand. The Triangle Bar Triangle had its good years and its bad ones. When the elements were favorable, Wetherill's herds of cattle and horses and flocks of sheep increased and were fat. Adverse conditions reduced the number of his stock and left them in poor shape. The local Navajo, primarily sheepherders, were equally affected. When times were hard, they had little cash to spend at the trading post and only small amounts of wool to sell. Under such circumstances, Wetherill, like other traders, extended credit to his customers to tide them over until better days came around.

Unpaid bills of his creditors mounted until the store had outstanding extended credit of around $8,000 owed by Navajos and $3,000 by Anglos and Mexicans. Marietta also had notes from Indians totalling over $1,500. Wetherill tried to collect his debts but failed in most cases, sometimes because of interference from the Indian Service. Reluctantly, he sold the trading post to a Spanish American early in 1910. The buyer probably was of the Miera family of Cuba, New Mexico, members of which were active in the mercantile and sheep businesses.

After the trading post changed hands, Wetherill continued to operate the Chaco Canyon ranch and to press for collection of his debts. The latter action and disputes over grazing rights on particular parcels of land led to troubles with some Navajos. However, an incident that culminated in his death was provoked by one of his cowboys, Bill Finn, who had severely beaten a Navajo after an argument over a horse. When friends and relatives of the injured Navajo came to Chaco Canyon to avenge the abuse, a lot of bad talk, including threats to kill one another, were exchanged between the Indians and Wetherill. Shortly afterward, in the late afternoon of June 22, 1910, as Wetherill and Finn were driving a herd of cattle from the vicinity of Pueblo Bonito down the canyon toward the Escavada, they were confronted by Chiishch'ilin Biyé, one of the Indians with whom Wetherill had had words.

The several versions of the murder present such conflicting detail that it is now impossible to reconstruct an unbiased account. Some say that the Navajo ambushed the two cattlemen as they rode toward the setting sun, unable to see their assailant, and that they did not return his fire. Wetherill was shot dead. Finn escaped and fled back to the ranch house. Another version, the one presented by the Indian Service in defense of the Navajo, states that after the argument with Wetherill, the Indian obtained a rifle and rode down the road toward Wetherill and Finn, who were driving the herd of cattle. When Chiishch'ilin Biyé was within 150 yards of them, the white men saw him and started toward him. As they galloped to within 25 yards of him, the Indian jumped off his horse and gunfire erupted. Wetherill was shot off his horse; Finn reined up and sped back to the ranch house. Wetherill was killed by a slug from a .33 caliber Winchester that pierced his right hand and entered his chest. The Navajo walked to the prone body and, at point blank range, fired another shot, tearing away half of Wetherill's head.

Chiishch'ilin Biyé gave himself up at a nearby trading post, where he was arrested. When he was finally brought to trial two years later, he was judged guilty of voluntary manslaughter and sentenced to five to ten years in the State Penitentiary at Santa Fe.

After Richard's death, Marietta Wetherill tried to hold the ranch together and collect the moneys due the estate. The assets of the ranch and the uncollected debts were appraised at over $17,000, but on the day of his murder, Wetherill's Albuquerque bank balance was only $74.23. Aided by friends and court appointees, but frustrated by Indian Service interference, Mrs. Wetherill managed to salvage enough to pay her lawyers' fees and settle a loan that Richard had obtained before his death in order to buy some sheep. She had a small sum left with which to attempt a fresh start.

Less than a year after the event that left her widowed with five small children, Marietta leased the homestead to a sheep rancher, closed the ranch house at Pueblo Bonito, and with her young family and few possessions drove her wagon east up the canyon. She passed the great silent ruins that had been so much her life since that day in the fall of 1895 when she, Wetherill, and her parents first had driven into Chaco Canyon to see if the ruins lived up to the stories they had heard. Wetherill remained behind, cold in a grave in sight of the Anasazi. In a few years, Marietta had to let the Chaco property go for taxes.

On her own, Marietta tried ranching near Cuba, New Mexico and then ran a ranch and trading post at Sanders, Arizona. She wandered from one Southwestern town to another, finally settling down near Albuquerque, where she passed away in 1954. As she had wished, after cremation her ashes were placed in the grave with her husband at Pueblo Bonito.

Until the Hyde Exploring Expedition began intensively to excavate Pueblo Bonito, there had only been guesses as to what sort of archaeological remains a large Chaco site would yield. Previous descriptions of the leading Chaco ruins had emphasized their magnitude, the architectural skills with which they had been built, or the broken pottery and other artifacts scattered about them, such observations being possible without digging. Sketch maps had been drawn of most of the ruins, based upon the patterns of standing walls and interpolation of units that lay buried beneath the huge mounds of rubble. The myth that the sites had been built by the Aztecs had been rejected as they were correctly attributed to the ancestors of the modern Pueblo Indians. Similarities between the domestic and ceremonial architecture of the Chaco ruins and that of Pueblo villages had been noted. The arid landscape of Chaco had caught the interest of all the earlier writers, as had the severity of the elements, followed by opinions about the probable climate at the time the Indians populated Chaco.

The work of George Pepper and Richard Wetherill at Pueblo Bonito and other Chacoan sites answered some of the questions posed previously, but it also created many puzzling problems that remained unsolved at the conclusion of their investigations. The Pueblo Bonito excavations provided the Hyde brothers and the American Museum of Natural History with a massive collection of artifacts, thereby fulfilling the primary goal of the expedition. The objects recovered proved to be generally similar to those found in other ruins throughout the San Juan country, including the cliff dwellings such as those at Mesa Verde. However, Pueblo Bonito yielded greater quantities of tools and implements of all types than had been found in any previously excavated ruin, in addition to some unique specimens and great quantities of objects fashioned from turquoise.

Techniques for dating archaeological materials had not yet been developed, so Pepper could only conclude that the Chaco sites were prehistoric. But the presence of ruined house structures beneath sections of Pueblo Bonito made it apparent that an entire village had existed and fallen into ruins before Pueblo Bonito had been built, thus arguing for a lengthy occupation. Distinctions between the small ruins in and about Chaco and the great community structures in the canyon could be discerned in architecture, artifacts, and burial practices, but their temporal relationships were unclear. Objects that could be related to ceremonial activities received emphasis, reflective of the orientation of most American archaeology at the time. This is exemplified by the fact that all four of the articles Pepper wrote on Pueblo Bonito were descriptions of specimens presumed to have been of ritual nature.

From an archaeological point of view, it is fortunate that the Hyde Exploring Expedition was not allowed to complete the excavation of Pueblo Bonito. They might have found more artifacts, but they would not have gained additional knowledge about the ancient Chacoans. Archaeological methods, dating techniques, and the formulation of theoretical problems to be solved by systematic excavation had not evolved to a state where they could provide insight into the behavior of past peoples. However, the Hyde brothers, George Pepper, and Richard Wetherill should be looked upon as pioneers in the new field of Southwestern archaeology. The Hydes' money had been spent prudently. Their collection from Pueblo Bonito is one of the finest ever assembled from the Anasazi domain, and, under the custodianship of the American Museum of Natural History, is still of great value to students of the Southwest.

The crates of Chaco specimens shipped to New York at the end of each field season; the sketches, photographs, and notes concerning architectural details, and a number of popular articles and several notes in scientific journals all contributed to the recognition of the archaeological wealth of Pueblo Bonito and Chaco Canyon. Unfortunately, attention was focused upon material accomplishments of the Pueblo Bonito occupants with particular emphasis on the unusual, the bizarre, the outstanding. Little was written about the vast number of objects that had been employed routinely in everyday activities. The skillful utilization of available resources to make implements needed to obtain and prepare foods, to quarry and shape building materials, to process fibers and fashion them into clothing, and to manufacture an array of ornaments received minimal notice. In final analysis, the most significant results of the Hyde Exploring Expedition came about from objections to its activities. These were, first, the passage of the Antiquities Act of 1906, and, second, the creation of Chaco Canyon National Monument.

3 ARCHAEOLOGISTS, GEOLOGISTS, AND CHRONOLOGISTS

C haco Canyon slumped back into its characteristic solitude following the years of intense activity of the Hyde Exploring Expedition. Some intrepid ranchers moved in on the old Wetherill lease or appropriated the range for their cattle and sheep, and the trading post and post office continued to function on a limited scale in the old Hyde boardinghouse. The only unusual stirring of the prevailing calm was an oil strike at Seven Lakes, eighteen miles south. A small rush ensued, with 3,000 claims filed on lands already allotted to the Navajos. However, because the field was not a big producer, this activity was short-lived, though some of its abandoned equipment still litters the Chaco Canyon roadside today.

As a national monument, Chaco Canyon was little more than a location on a map. The Indian trader at the Chaco post was appointed non-salaried caretaker of the ruins. He did not attempt supervision of the monument but provided some protection to the ruins by observing and knowing the business of all persons wandering about Pueblo Bonito and vicinity. Periodic examinations of the Anasazi houses were performed by officials of the General Land Office. They reported in 1915 that only a dozen parties had visited the area. A year later, this was up to one hundred persons. In 1917, a National Park Service informational pamphlet tersely described the trip to Chaco Canyon:

> The reservation can only be reached by team, mountain hack, and camping outfit from Farmington, New Mexico, and from Gallup or Thoreau. This service may be procured at from $6 to $8 per day, with driver, exclusive of the cost of feed and subsistence. The trip . . . will consume from two to three days on the road each way.

Although the two decades after the termination of digging at Pueblo Bonito saw little research in Chaco Canyon, the study of Southwestern prehistory was forging ahead elsewhere. Extensive explorations and intensive excavations extended from the brick red cliffs of the Kayenta region in northeastern Arizona to the cool evergreen mesas east of Santa Fe, where in past times the Pueblos had to retreat from the bellicose, hard-riding Comanche of the southern plains. Involved were no more than a dozen men whose names were to become the cornerstone of regional archaeology as they worked under the auspices of such distinguished institutions as the American Museum of Natural History; Peabody Museum of Harvard University; Phillips Academy, Andover, Massachusetts; the School of American Research of the Archaeological Institute of America, Santa Fe; and the Bureau of American Ethnology, Washington, D.C. Because everything they found was new and interesting, an aura of excitement compensated for the inevitable sore muscles, sunburns, and sometimes sterile trenches that are part and parcel of field archaeology. But from their unstinting efforts on the Colorado Plateau came a broader understanding of the Pueblo continuum, that is, the period of the early Basket Makers, the climax of the Anasazi civilization, and then its subsequent decline before and just after the arrival of the Spaniards in 1540. The slowly accelerating cultural dynamics were largely unknown. How the Pueblo people evolved from sedentary hunter-gatherers, who lived in mud and stick cubicles in the shelter of a natural recess in cliff faces, to horticulturalists with appropriate accoutrements such as pottery and substantial communal fixed abodes erected in the open, could not be determined at this time. The regional differences recognized in such cultural attributes as architecture and ceramics were assumed to indicate that progress had not been uniformly achieved throughout the entire Anasazi domain. How much time such advancement might have required likewise had not been determined, but a general consensus that as much as several millennia were at stake later would be shown to be a gross exaggeration. Several new techniques for developing relative and absolute chronologies were devised so that archaeologists could order the mounting volume of data resulting from rigorous field work.

One was the principle of stratigraphy wherein, barring evidence for disturbance, materials found at the lower levels of deposition were considered older than the ones above. A developmental sequence derived from the careful excavation at one site could then be related to those at others, depending upon similarity or disparity of certain categories of remains. The result was the development of a relative chronology of sites. Pottery, particularly in fragmentary form (sherds), assumed a special importance as a stratigraphic indicator because of its imperishability, its abundance in late- and post-Basket Maker contexts, and its frequent stylistic modifications reflective of various kinds of human behavior and periods of culture change.

The second dating device was a new science known as dendrochronology just then being perfected by an astronomer, A. E. Douglass. Based upon the annual growth rings visible in cross sections of coniferous trees, such as had been customarily used in Anasazi construction, a remarkable master chart of growth patterns slowly was formulated. If either preserved or charred wood of suitable kind were available, a scientist could accurately place his particular site within a thousand-year time span from the present back to the era of Christ. It should be remembered, however, that this precision had not yet been achieved when archaeological attention again turned to the Chaco antiquities. All that could be said at that time was that some beams recovered at Pueblo Bonito had been cut forty to forty-five years before others from Aztec Ruin, a large settlement to the north of Chaco Canyon that appeared to have shared a Chacoan cultural orientation.

Even though still in a formative stage, these diverse excavation and analytical activities led to a hypothesized sequential scheme applicable to prehistoric Southwestern cultural evolution.[1] In it, the grandest houses of Chaco Canyon were seen as representative of a stage known as Pueblo III, or the apogee of the Anasazi continuum, with those below them obviously belonging to an earlier but still undefined horizon. It was at this state of the regional archaeology that Neil M. Judd emerged to lead the next comprehensive program in Chaco Canyon.

A Southwesterner with exploration and archaeological experience in the mesa lands of southeastern Utah and northeastern Arizona (he was a member of teams that discovered the natural wonders of Rainbow Bridge and the Indian cliff dwellings of Betatakin and Inscription House), Judd had secured the backing of the National Geographic Society for a five-year project of further explorations of Pueblo Bonito and the neighboring ruin of Pueblo del Arroyo as well as corrollary studies of the past and present physiography of the canyon, the relationships between the large and small settlements, the development and distribution of Chaco ceramics, and the agricultural practices of the old Chacoans (see fig. 28). Pueblo Bonito was selected because the work already done there by the Hyde Exploring Expedition demonstrated the wealth of material objects concealed in the site but left unanswered many questions about the structure at the peak of Pueblo civilization. Furthermore, over half the site had not been disturbed by Pepper's work. Pueblo del Arroyo was chosen for simultaneous investigation because its proximity made work feasible and because it was believed that earlier materials underlay the surface structures. Judd was to organize and direct the program, and for that purpose the United States National Museum, for whom he worked, granted leave of absence for four months annually. Each summer's investigations were authorized by the Department of the Interior; all archaeological material collected was donated to the U.S. National Museum for the benefit of the American public.

In 1921 when the National Geographic Society Expedition set up field operations, Edward Sargent, who leased the old Wetherill homestead and used the Chaco buildings as headquarters for some of his sheepherders, permitted Judd and his staff to occupy the facilities. However, Sargent's lease was cancelled, and Judd was forced to establish a tent camp on the adobe flat just south of the crumbled heap of Pueblo Bonito on the edge of a long, cellarlike pothole that had been the Hyde Exploring Expedition's storeroom for wool and Navajo blankets. Water was provided by a

Figure 28. Neil Judd visits Pueblo Pintado in 1920 while reconnoitering Chaco Canyon sites prior to selecting locales to be excavated by the National Geographic Society. *Courtesy of the Smithsonian Institution*

well dug in the nearby arroyo and was pumped into a tank elevated above the tents; gravity carried it down into the kitchen and to a location near the ruin where mud mortar was mixed for wall repairs. The kitchen was walled in and had an earth-covered roof to protect it from spring sand storms. A box wrapped with burlap sacking and dampened by a dripping pan on top functioned as a refrigerator. Gasoline lanterns provided light.

Local Navajo workmen were employed, augmented by a contingent from Zuñi Pueblo which at times brought the total number of hired hands to almost thirty. Judd was criticized by some for mixing Navajos and Pueblos on his work force because it was thought that cultural differences and traditional animosities would cause conflicts between the Indians and problems for the field supervisors. However, the two groups proved to be compatible and provided Judd with an efficient group of diggers, the Zuñi being described as somewhat more steady and less temperamental than the Navajos. The Navajo employees lived in their nearby homes, but the Zuñis, being a long way from their village, had to make camp in the canyon. Each Sunday night a bonfire blazed in front of the expedition's tents while the Zuñi entertained themselves, the staff, and visitors with impromptu songs and dances. Usually numbered among the spectators were Navajo neighbors who sat on their horses at the edge of the firelight while enjoying the proceedings.

The summer field seasons from 1921 through 1927 lasted from four to six months, depending upon length of winter, number of spring sand storms, and timing of summer downpours and flash floods. The staff varied in number from season to season, but when the project was running at full capacity, it included the director, two or three field assistants who usually were graduate students in archaeology, a stenographer-bookkeeper, a geologist, a surveyor, a truck driver, a photographer, an architectural draftsman, and a cook. At times, according to necessity, staff members doubled in various duties. One such individual, O. C. "Pete" Havens, hired from a nearby trading post as stenographer-bookkeeper, turned into one of those rare individuals in an archaeological camp, a man of all trades. Pete kept the automobile engines in repair, nursed the gasoline pump that provided water for the camp and for repairs to the ruins, drove a truck out to Thoreau on the railroad seventy miles to the south for supplies and mail, and somehow found time to take most of the photographs that illustrated Judd's several reports.

Unexpectedly, Pepper's published field notes became available the same summer the National Geographic campaign opened. This permitted Judd to avoid duplication of effort; now he knew what rooms had been excavated and later backfilled by the Hyde team and what they had contained. Also, in order to estimate the rate of erosion in the canyon and to gauge changes within the site itself, Judd was fortunate to obtain the physiographic studies made by Professor Dodge in 1900 and 1901 for comparison with those Kirk Bryan of Harvard was to undertake during the present program. Judd also gained access to the 1887–88 Mindeleff photographs of Chaco ruins and Pepper's unpublished negatives. However, Judd's excavation techniques differed from those used at Pueblo Bonito in the past. Instead of going through the ruin like a gopher, recovering the archaeological materials from the excavated features and then filling them again with the spoil dirt, Judd planned to carefully clear each designated unit, gather the specimens and data from it, and remove the dirt fill and rock debris so that the architectural elements would be left open and visible. As had the earlier excavators, Judd's crew relied upon the pick and shovel and smaller hand tools for general digging, but peeling away the enormous amounts of rubble that covered the site was a time-consuming effort that demanded additional measures. Some dirt and rock were carried short distances by wheelbarrows or horse-drawn wagons. However, most of it was transported on horse- or mule-drawn slips or scrapers to places where it could be loaded into small ore cars set on narrow gauge railroad tracks, as in a mine, and then pulled by mules to a dump (see fig. 29). Dirt and unworked or broken stones were deposited in the Chaco Wash, where they periodically were flushed away by summer floods that raced down the canyon. Many of the fallen wall stones were carefully stockpiled for future use in repair work.

The combined forces of time, nature, and unsound construction methods had taken their toll upon the great empty masonry shell that was Pueblo Bonito. But considerable damage also had been wrought by thoughtless men who had dislodged or chopped off wooden supporting beams and lintels, punched out sections of wall, or, as with the Hyde expedition, had removed entire roofs in order to get at a room's fill. Moreover, Judd's proposed procedure of leaving cleared portions of the structure exposed placed it in further jeopardy. Therefore, with admirable foresight, the National Geographic Society authorized all necessary measures to forestall deterioration. Standing walls were strengthened in order that they might be preserved, broken masonry was patched, missing door lintels were replaced, and other reasonable precautions were taken to check further decay. Floors of some rooms and areas around them were sloped to carry water away from the bases of standing walls, and in some deep interior rooms, drainage holes were sunk in the middle of the floor, filled with rocks, and covered with sand.

The two hills of consolidated trash at the entrance to Pueblo Bonito were as tantalizing to Judd as they had been to previous diggers in Chaco, most recently Nels Nelson and Earl Morris of the American Museum of

Figure 29. The National Geographic Society expedition
used mine cars pulled over narrow-gauge track by mules
to remove dirt and rocks from the excavations in Pueblo
Bonito, 1924. *Courtesy of the National Geographic
Society*

Natural History. For three seasons, Judd's crews dug into them with the same negative results. By 1921 pottery was becoming recognized as a handy gauge for measuring the age and cultural affiliation of Southwestern ruins, and Judd postulated that the sequence of local development in the art of pottery making would be revealed in the stratified trash layers. An undisturbed section was found in the west mound and a twenty-foot-deep trench was sliced through it. But the excavators observed that pottery types considered as early in the evolutionary scale were deposited above fragments known to be late. Something was obviously awry.

The explanation for this seemingly topsy-turvy stratigraphy did not come until 1924, when the trench was extended into and through the pueblo itself, making it possible to reconstruct the way in which the village had grown. It then became clear that the earliest occupants of Pueblo Bonito had lived in a relatively small crescent-shaped complex of rooms in the northwest section of the site. They had deposited their trash south of the village. Later, as the community went through almost continual expansion, it engulfed the area of the first dump, at which point the spot for dumping trash was moved farther to the south in front of the much larger town. Somewhat later, a very large kiva, or circular ceremonial room, was sunk into Pueblo Bonito's west court. Subsequently, this was razed to be replaced by other structures. But preparations for the subterranean chamber had cut into the drifts of rubbish from the early village. Builders of the kiva had carried the unearthed trash outside the newly enlarged building and thrown it on the refuse mound already rising there, thus placing sherds of early pottery types on top of, or mixed with, later types. In so doing, they created a dilemma that archaeologists came to call "reverse stratigraphy."

The study of the staggering amount of pottery recovered in the trash mound and pueblos was turned over to Frank H. H. Roberts, Jr., and Monroe Amsden, both of whom went on to become stalwarts of the discipline. The results surpassed Judd's fondest hopes; a stylistic progression of some twenty-one distinct types was demonstrated. The availability along much of the Colorado Plateau of potting clays low in iron content permitted the production of a light gray material that carried black geometric decoration for nonculinary vessels, making these Anasazi wares almost unique in the New World. In the western region of Anasazi culture, for example in Monument Valley, red pottery was common, but the Chaco Canyon ware was gray. Without the use of any mechanical aid such as the potter's wheel or formal firing kilns, the good Chaco pottery was exceptionally well made, being hard, thin walled, with carefully controlled contours and fine-lined designs executed with surehanded draftsmanship. The pottery also offered proof that at some time later in the canyon's prehistory people bearing either Mesa Verde pots or their stylistic tradition dwelt there.

The Hyde Exploring Expedition had excavated a total of 190 rooms and kivas in Pueblo Bonito. Unknown persons cleared 5 other units and 2 kivas some time between 1900 and 1920. To these figures, the National Geographic Society project added 138 ground floor rooms and 24 kivas, 2 of which were a style known as Great Kivas. At the conclusion of all this effort, and taking into consideration the excavation's analytical studies of ceramics and other artifacts as well as the steady refinements being made in dendrochronology to supply absolute dates, it was possible for Judd to delineate the original settlement and to trace the subsequent additions to the structure until it reached its final form. He also confirmed the presence of earlier ruins beneath Pueblo Bonito and discovered the foundations of a planned addition to the community that was never completed.

The results of each of the field sessions at Pueblo Bonito were summarily reported in the Smithsonian Institution's annual reports on explorations and field work. The National Geographic Society also publicized the work they were sponsoring in five popular articles in the *National Geographic Magazine* between 1921 and 1929.[2] A. E. Douglass wrote the first volume recording the more technical aspects of the Society's researches in Chaco Canyon.[3] It appeared in 1935; however, other reports in the technical series were long delayed. It was not until 1954, twenty-seven years after the field work was completed, that Kirk Bryan's geological report[4] and Neil Judd's first volume on Pueblo Bonito[5] were issued. In 1959, the Pueblo del Arroyo monograph[6] appeared, and in 1964, a second volume on Pueblo Bonito[7] was published, both authored by Judd. Obviously Judd had fallen victim to the same set of circumstances at the National Museum that had plagued Pepper at the American Museum, namely that other pressing museum responsibilities left little time for the analysis of the huge collection from the field, the digesting of excavation notes, and the writing of reports. But Judd stuck to it, completing some of his accounts after he had retired.

According to Judd's interpretation, one which was not shared by all contemporary or later colleagues, Pueblo Bonito was built upon a slight elevation that was first occupied during Pueblo I times by a pithouse village that belonged to a group who were not ancestral to the Pueblo Bonito occupants. After the abandonment of the pithouse settlement, the "Old Bonitians," a Pueblo II cultural manifestation, moved in from some part of the San Juan Basin to the north, bringing with them a new set of cultural attributes. They built the nucleus of Pueblo Bonito, a widespreading, rudely constructed crescent of one-story houses with storerooms in the rear (figs. 30, 31). Exterior walls were of wall-width spalled

Figure 30. The northeast foundation complex as outlined by the National Geographic Society expedition in
1925. This planned addition to Pueblo Bonito was abandoned in favor of a substitute addition to the southeast
portion of the pueblo. Judd's tent camp is seen along
the arroyo in the upper left. *Courtesy of the National
Geographic Society*

Figure 31. Pueblo Bonito after completion of excavations and the fall of Threatening Rock in 1941. View is to the southeast. Building at the southwest corner of Pueblo Bonito was built by the National Park Service as a residence for the custodian of the area. The University of New Mexico field school facility can be seen at the foot of the far canyon wall. *Courtesy of the National Park Service*

slabs of sandstone embedded in the surplus of adobe mortar, Judd's Pueblo Bonito Type I. Some interior walls were made of upright posts and mud. Several subterranean kivas were built in front of the village, and the communal trash pile was beyond the kivas. This original settlement was occupied from about A.D. 828 to 935, when a second group of migrants from the north arrived to join the original occupants.

The newcomers were the "Late Bonitians,"a Pueblo III people who introduced pottery and architectural practices of their own. They greatly enlarged the pueblo, expanding it and remodeling it from its arc-shaped beginnings to a D-shaped multistoried urban community. The pueblo then passed through a series of construction periods, each marked by a distinct style of precisely laid wall masonry. All stone construction of the Late Bonitians featured veneer and core walls; however, the veneer progressed through a series of styles differentiated by size and arrangements of blocks and chinks of friable and laminate sandstone elements (see fig. 32). Three principal types can be distinguished between A.D. 1011 and 1130. The first Late Bonitian variety, Judd's Pueblo Bonito Type II, has a veneer combining blocks of soft, friable sandstone dressed on the exposed surface and chinked all around with thin slabs of harder laminate sandstone; the second style of the Late Bonitians, Judd's Pueblo Bonito Type III, employs bands of thin tablets of laminate sandstone neatly arranged between smoothed uniform-size blocks of friable sandstone; the last style, or Judd's Pueblo Bonito Type IV, features a veneer of laminate sandstone blocks of fairly regular thickness laid with a minimum of mud plaster between.

Kivas were built into the room blocks and dug into the courtyards. Late Bonitian trash was dumped in abandoned rooms and in the two mounds directly in front of the town. Masonry retaining walls were constructed around the piles of refuse in order to curtail refuse drift. Threatening Rock (see chapter 2) was propped up with pine poles and a wide stone terrace. It is the houses, pottery, and other artifacts these Pueblo III people made that are now accepted as a distinct social development, the Chaco Culture.

The two groups, each with its own cultural heritage, lived side by side in Pueblo Bonito, maintaining distinct ways of life for about a century. However, it appears that the Late Bonitians usurped leadership of the village immediately upon arrival. Then the Late Bonitians departed, leaving the community in the sole hands of the Old Bonitians for a while until they, too, drifted away from Chaco. Judd characterized the Old Bonitians as old-fashioned and unchanging and the Late Bonitians as alert and progressive; he believed that the two were culturally several generations apart.

Figure 32. Judd's four principal types of masonry at Pueblo Bonito. I: spalled sandstone slabs of wall width laid in abundant quantities of mud. II: rubble veneered with casual blocks of friable sandstone dressed on the face only and chinked all around with chips of laminate sandstone. III: rubble veneered with matching blocks, either of laminate or dressed friable sandstone or both, alternating with bands of inch-thick tablets of laminated sandstone. IV: rubble veneered with laminate sandstone of fairly uniform thickness with a minimum of mud mortar between. *Courtesy of the National Geographic Society*

In its later stages, immigrants from north of the San Juan River, bearing a Mesa Verde–type culture, joined the inhabitants of Pueblo Bonito and remained there until final exodus from the community. Presence of these northern Anasazi is identified particularly from the sudden appearance in late trash deposits of pottery typical of Mesa Verde. It may be distinguished from Chaco wares by differences in shapes and decorative elements and by the use of a vegetal pigment for painting black designs on white vessels rather than the characteristic mineral paint used by the Chacoans.

Judd estimated that Pueblo Bonito at the height of its fame, A.D. 1000–1100, included 651 rooms (not all of which were occupied simultaneously). They stood a maximum of four stories and housed possibly 1,000 persons (figs. 33–35). He suggested that the likely causes for abandonment of the great town were reduction in available arable land, deficiency of rainfall, and increased erosion. Perhaps these factors forced groups of the populace to move south toward the Zuñi Mountains.

Pepper's rich finds had caused many people to think of Pueblo Bonito as a treasure house. Realistically viewed, Judd's recovery of specimens in no way approached the quantity and quality of remains unearthed by the first investigators. Rather, Pepper's crew was lucky; they stumbled upon a series of undisturbed burial chambers that produced most of their more dramatic finds of pottery and turquoise ornaments. Not that Judd's discoveries were second-rate (fig. 36). He did encounter some very rich specimens, for example a 2,500-bead turquoise necklace and pendants. Nevertheless, for the most part, his collection is more characteristic of the utilitarian cultural residue found in typical Anasazi sites. Judd also was careful to remove all specimens from his diggings, including great quantities of potsherds, which made his collection less impressive than Pepper's selected assortment of artifacts.

In attempting to reconstruct the Chaco environment during the three centuries of Pueblo Bonito's existence, Judd made use of specialized studies in biology and geology which he correlated with archaeological evidence. With regard to the ancient forest that supplied the tremendous number of timbers required for construction of the town, he pointed out that he had located a relict stand of pine trees within fifteen miles of the ruin and that a few old conifers still grew in side canyons and on terraces above Chaco Canyon. Elder Navajos recalled a time when a few more were in the area but stated they had cut them down for firewood. Portions of the fallen trunk and buried root system of a large pine that had stood in the west court of Pueblo Bonito when it was an active community were uncovered by the excavators. Its last readable ring yielded a date of A.D. 1017, but an unknown number of rings were missing from its eroded

Figure 33. Portion of the well-preserved cribbed log roof of Kiva L as excavated by the National Geographic Society in 1923. Fourteen layers of pine logs or sections of logs, totalling 350 timbers, rose domelike from six basal pilasters to cover the circular ceremonial chamber. *Courtesy of the National Geographic Society*

Figure 34. Based upon Judd's excavation data, Dr. Kenneth J. Conant of Harvard's School of Architecture prepared this drawing depicting Pueblo Bonito as it probably appeared in its heyday. View is north across Chaco Canyon and the Chaco Wash. *Courtesy of the National Geographic Society*

Figure 35. Dr. Conant's drawing of a portion of the east court of Pueblo Bonito as it may have appeared about A.D. 1050. *Courtesy of the National Geographic Society*

Figure 36. This carefully coiled turquoise necklace, accompanied by two pairs of eardrops, was found by Neil Judd in a shallow depression between two flagstones on the floor of Room 320, Pueblo Bonito. The necklace of well-matched minute beads had been strung in four loops each 14″ long. *Courtesy of the National Geographic Society*

outer surface. Adding up the evidence, Judd concluded that a pine forest once had existed in close proximity to Pueblo Bonito. He further believed that through reckless felling of those trees, man himself had brought about a devastating cycle of erosion that he was incapable of halting. Each year the denudation of the soil and lowering of the water table continued to the point where people could no longer farm.

The studies of the Harvard geologist Kirk Bryan indicated that the existing arroyo is at least the third arroyo to have evolved at Chaco. Over the centuries, floodwaters in the canyon have alternately deposited beds of alluvium and later breached those deposits with gullies similar to the present erosion channel. These cyclical periods of sedimentation and erosion were triggered by slight climatic changes affecting vegetation, which in turn largely regulated floodwaters. Noting the great numbers of rushes used for mats and roofing (fig. 37), Judd postulated that the climate at the time of Pueblo Bonito occupation must have been slightly wetter than at present.

In an effort to document the history of the present Chaco arroyo, Judd drew upon Simpson's 1849 account and the memory of an old Navajo whose knowledge of Chaco supposedly went back to 1842. Judd inferred that, in those times, the arroyo had been inconspicuous and intermittent and that a ribbon of willows and cottonwoods marked its course. Grass grew tall and thick on either side of the drainage. Water could be had by digging potholes along the arroyo bottom. By 1877, Jackson found Chaco Wash gutted from end to end by the arroyo that was then ten feet deep opposite Pueblo Pintado and entrenched to a depth of sixteen feet at Pueblo del Arroyo. The arroyo therefore was deeply cut into the floor of the canyon before livestock were introduced into the area on a large scale about 1878.

Bryan compared the present-day arroyo (figs. 38 and 39) with one that evolved in Pueblo Bonito times. His research supported the assumption that a prehistoric arroyo reached its climax, and a depth of twelve to thirteen feet, about the middle of the twelfth century, basing the time upon datable potsherds found in the bottom of the gully. That arroyo, like the modern one, could have changed Chaco Canyon from a suitable place of residence into an uninhabitable wasteland. Refill of the wash and sedimentation of the canyon took place between A.D. 1250 and 1400, according to Bryan. Then an equilibrium was reached, and Chaco Canyon again became a fit place in which to live, until erosion set in again in the mid-nineteenth century.

Domestic water available to the Chacoans and their predecessors in Chaco Canyon was trapped in the deep natural potholes in the rock on the mesa above Pueblo Bonito or, more often, was drawn from a series of

83

willow- bordered water holes in the canyon bottom that were freshened by runoff from rains and melting snows. At times when there was no surface water in the canyon, the high water table made it possible to obtain limited quantities by scraping out shallow depressions along the course of the drainage. Seeps that exist today in several *rincones,* or side canyons, may have been flowing springs if past conditions were a bit more moist. Irrigation, although recognized to have been undertaken in the past, was thought not to have been too successful because of the presence of a large amount of sodium in the soil. In solution, sodium makes it difficult for water to penetrate the soil, leading to deposition of alkalies that impoverish agricultural lands.

Even though Judd referred to the decrease of arable land through erosion as the principal reason for the abandonment of Pueblo Bonito, he did note several other factors that created problems of varying magnitude and duration for the Chacoans. Some are closely tied to the reduction of farming resources, such as dwindling food supplies that could have promoted internal dissent and family fission. On the other hand, architectural evidence, especially the presence of sealed exterior doorways and ventilators and the eventual complete enclosure of the town, suggests successive measures to strengthen their defenses against marauders. The Late Bonitians left only a single town gate in the southeast corner of the west court when they accomplished their second expansion program. Shortly thereafter, the passage was reduced to ordinary door width. Subsequently, it was completely blocked with a masonry wall. From that time on, the town had no gates and no open doorways on outside walls. Access must have been by ladders that led up and across the roofs of the one-story rooms that enclosed the structure on the south side.

National Geographic expeditions dug Pueblo del Arroyo intermittently during four seasons as workers could be spared from the large undertaking at Pueblo Bonito. The report on Pueblo del Arroyo is based upon the excavation notes of Karl Ruppert, who was in charge of the digging, supplemented by Judd's memoranda and data resulting from study of the collections at the U.S. National Museum. This major site is situated just 400 feet southwest of Pueblo Bonito on the edge of the Chaco arroyo, as its name implies. Judd wrote that it is not beyond reason that it was built by a group migrant from the larger town. Tree-ring dates for the site range from A.D. 1052 to 1103, falling within the last half of Pueblo Bonito's life span. Both the architecture and the ceramic complex further demonstrate a contemporaneity with Pueblo Bonito, particularly with Judd's Late Bonitians. But Judd also noted that the Chaco-tradition builders of Pueblo del Arroyo did not long maintain sole possession of

Figure 37. Mat of willow twigs as revealed by the National Geographic Society expedition on the floor of Room 320. The willow shoots were fastened together by string threaded through holes punched through them at intervals. Mats served as beds, and the dead frequently were placed to rest upon them. *Courtesy of the National Geographic Society*

Figure 38. The eroded bank of Chaco Wash about four miles east of Pueblo Bonito. The floor of a Basket Maker pithouse, and a metate associated with the structure, are 13½ feet below the present canyon surface. *Courtesy of the National Geographic Society*

Figure 39. The Chaco Wash running bank to bank after
a summer downpour. *Courtesy of the National Park
Service*

the village. As a body or as stragglers they moved on, and the bearers of a Mesa Verde type of culture came in to take their place. As in Pueblo Bonito, this arrival of an alien people is indicated by changes in pottery and construction techniques.

Pueblo del Arroyo had been visited and named by Lieutenant Simpson in 1849. Jackson camped in the arroyo near the ruin in the spring of 1877 and remarked that he could discern in its banks the outline of a buried prehistoric arroyo. When Bryan studied the geological history of Chaco Canyon, he identified the refilled arroyo cut recorded by Jackson as part of the ancient arroyo that probably influenced the abandonment of Pueblo Bonito, as well as Pueblo del Arroyo and other Chaco communities, in the eleventh and twelfth centuries. Victor Mindeleff took a number of photographs of the ruin in 1888 that show previous digging in the site by unknown persons, including holes broken through walls.

The National Geographic Society excavated 44 ground-floor rooms and 7 kivas in Pueblo del Arroyo, but Judd estimated that the structure had 284 rooms and 14 kivas and may have had a maximum population of 475. In ground plan, the village resembles the D shape of Pueblo Bonito (see fig. 40). It consisted of a rectangular block of rooms with extensions at each end that connected by a series of one-story structures enclosing a courtyard. The main room blocks stood three and four stories high and were terraced down to a single story adjacent to the court. Masonry corresponded to two of the later styles in Pueblo Bonito, Types III and IV, but was not as well executed nor its relationship as clear. Ruppert described it "as being the product of many individuals each of whom built according to his personal preferences but with left-over materials, the choice building stones having been utilized elsewhere."

Although a planned community, Pueblo del Arroyo typically was subject to constructional changes throughout its existence. Ground-floor rooms appear to have been used mainly for storage, with living quarters being confined to upper stories. Bins equipped with slabs of stone for grinding corn and other commodities were present on the floors of some dwellings. The pattern of doorways between rooms on the same level suggests a grouping of certain rooms into suitelike arrangements. This could indicate the occupation of adjacent units by members of a family or clan. Some such complexes had no outside doorways, requiring at least one room in each unit to have a hatchway in its ceiling for access to the suite. Ventilators, or small windowlike openings, were present in both interior and exterior walls. As in Pueblo Bonito, most doorways and ventilators had been sealed. Also reflecting Pueblo Bonito, there had been only a single gateway into the courtyard of Pueblo del Arroyo, and it had been blocked at some time during the life of the settlement.

Figure 40. Aerial photograph of Pueblo del Arroyo after excavation. This is one of a series of pictures of Chaco Canyon ruins and other Southwestern sites taken by Charles and Anne Lindbergh in 1929. *Courtesy of the Museum of New Mexico*

Northern San Juan influence on Chaco, or occupation by groups from that area, is suggested at Pueblo del Arroyo by the remains of a tri-walled tower near the back of the building. It is a type of structure well known in southwestern Colorado. Judd believed that the tower at Pueblo del Arroyo was never completed. In testing the feature, he found that its walls had been begun but then torn down. The stones apparently were used elsewhere; only the lower foundation stones were left in place.

No external trash deposits were located. If Pueblo del Arroyo had only a short occupation, as is supposed, the amount of refuse deposited outside the town may have been a modest accumulation that easily could have been covered by silt during a time of alluviation. There was a considerable amount of household rubbish in some of the rooms and kivas that had fallen into disuse, and in a few of these over a dozen burials were made. Unfortunately, all but three burials had been disturbed and widely scattered. These three were complete when found, but many of the others were restored from fragments found amidst household sweepings and in debris resulting from the collapse of upper-story rooms. None of the burials had rich furnishings. Restorable pottery vessels make up the bulk of the collection from Pueblo del Arroyo.

The last season of Judd's work in Chaco Canyon, which saw him wind up the excavations at Pueblo Bonito and probe a number of puzzling features on the mesa above Chetro Ketl and Pueblo Bonito, also witnessed the first excavation of one of the lesser Chaco sites. Over the years, many small-house pueblos had been plundered by pothunters, and some had been tested by archaeologists. But no one had bothered to dig in a pithouse village, although there were a few unimpressive surface indications of such settlements distributed about Chaco. These were simply complexes of shallow depressions, possibly an occasional outline of stone slabs set on edge, and a skimpy scattering of household discards. Frank Roberts had located one such site in 1926 while sampling a small pueblo ruin in the upper Chaco Canyon for the National Geographic Society. From his knowledge of the Chaco cultural sequence and the ceramics of the area, he concluded that the potsherds lying on the surface, added to other evidence, indicated that the zone had been home to a cruder, less highly developed people than those of the Pueblo culture. Therefore, in 1927, after he had joined the Smithsonian Institution's Bureau of American Ethnology, Roberts returned to Chaco to dig the site, hoping to obtain information about an imperfectly known phase of Southwestern archaeology. Working from Judd's camp at Pueblo Bonito, he cleared eighteen dwellings, a kiva, and forty-five storage cists at the locale which he named Shabik'eshchee Village, a Navajo name for a sun symbol that someone had pecked on a large rock near the ruin.[8]

The village sits on top of the mesa that forms the south wall of Chaco Canyon, about nine miles east of Pueblo Bonito. Excavations revealed that the crude but quite substantial houses were formed by a shallow pit about ten to fifteen feet in greatest dimensions and two and one-half feet deep, circular to rectangular in contour. Sometimes they were lined with vertical slabs, and roofed over with a pole, brush, and mud superstructure that was supported by four posts set in the floor. The posts probably carried a rectangular framework of beams upon which were placed the upper ends of small slanting poles, the lower terminals of which were embedded in the earth around the perimeter of the pit. The rectangular space at the top of the framework was covered by a flat roof of poles around a central opening for the exit of smoke. Both the sloping sides and the horizontal area of the wooden structure had been covered with twigs, bark, dirt, and plaster. Most of the units appeared to have had an entryway on the south side. From the main room, a passage gave access to a small, conical, semi-subterranean chamber covered in the same manner as the living room. A little opening in the side of the antechamber allowed a person to stoop through it into the antechamber and then crawl through the low passageway into the house. Figure 41 shows the plan of such a pithouse.

Little remained of the interior furnishings of the abodes. Near the center of the room was a shallow mud- or stone-lined firepit. Between it and the doorway was an upright stone slab normally set into the earth which probably served as a deflector to prevent cold air, drawn through the opening, from blowing directly onto the fire. Frequently, rows of upright slabs of stone were embedded in the floor to form a binlike compartment on the south side of the chamber. Between the firepit and the north wall, there usually was a small circular hole in the floor, analogous to the *sipapu* of later kivas considered by many present Pueblo Indians to be the mythical place of emergence through which their ancestors passed on their journey from the underworld to the surface of the earth.

One circular pit structure much larger than the rest, forty feet in diameter and three feet deep, was placed among the smaller dwellings. It had a low bench around its interior wall, both it and the wall above being faced with sandstone slabs. Floor features included firepit, deflector, and four post holes. There had been no antechamber, entry to the pit building probably having been through an opening in the roof. Roberts interpreted this large pit structure to have been a forerunner of the circular ceremonial room associated with later Anasazi ruins which became known as the Great Kiva. He went on to theorize about the origins of the two styles of kivas found in Anasazi sites. The small, more numerous type perhaps was dedicated to the performance of the clan's seasonal cycle of ceremonies. Probably these observances once had been held in the family

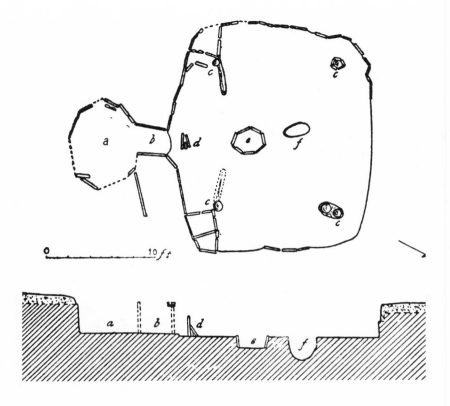

Figure 41. Plan of a Shabik'eshchee Village pithouse and postulated method of construction. a, antechamber; b, passage; c, post holes and support posts; d, deflector; e, firepit; f, sipapu; g, compartment wall; h, slabs lining periphery of pit; i, plastered walls; j, pole and brush framework; k, earth and plaster covering on superstructure; l, smoke hole. From Roberts's *Shabik'-eshchee Village, A Late Basket Maker Site in the Chaco Canyon, New Mexico*

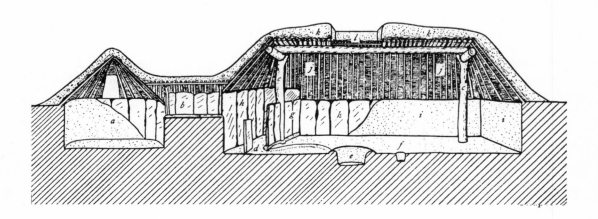

dwellings such as those at Shabik'eshchee Village, and for that reason the small kiva retained many of the features of the early type of habitation. On the other hand, more important ceremonies, those involving participants from an entire community or from several towns, were conducted in the large Great Kiva structures. The Great Kiva thus was used before the clan kiva evolved from the pithouse dwelling. It continued in vogue along with the smaller religious chambers after those modifications were made.

Randomly scattered throughout the village in close proximity to the houses were bins, or cists, for the storage of corn and other foodstuffs. Simple in form, they were constructed in the same fashion as the dwellings but on a smaller scale.

Two concentrations of village trash were located and trenched and fourteen burials were uncovered in various scattered locations around Shabik'eshchee Village. No definite cemetery could be found. Burial furnishings, specimens from the refuse deposits, and items recovered from the fill of pit structures constituted the collection from the site. It was limited to articles of earthenware, stone, and bone because the open setting of the village and its shallow deposits allowed destruction by moisture of all perishables.

The ceramic specimens were most significant because they represented the first true pottery of the Anasazi and hence a major technological advancement. Simple and crude, they also reflect the conservative nature of the people in that their black designs for the most part were direct carry-overs from previous motif vocabularies expressed on earlier basketry.

Roberts relegated Shabik'eshchee Village to a cultural stage that bridged the gap between the less complex Basket Makers, who made no pottery, and the early Anasazi who had been residents of the arc-shaped town beneath Pueblo Bonito. By the taxonomy then in vogue, it was termed Basket Maker III, later to be revamped by Roberts into Modified Basketmaker. He was unable to assign the site to an absolute temporal slot because the tree-ring dating system had not been perfected at the time of his studies. Years later, a group of charcoal specimens obtained from the village yielded construction dates of A.D. 753 and 757, or more than a century earlier than the first occupation at Pueblo Bonito. Subsequently, the dating was pushed still farther back into the sixth century.[9] Shabik'eshchee Village assumed the role of a type site for Basket Maker III in Chaco Canyon. For many years it was the only carefully excavated and reported example of this formative period in Anasazi history.

93

4 STUDENT ARCHAEOLOGISTS

C haco Canyon offered an ideal laboratory for training students because of the dense concentration of Anasazi civilization within its walls. Isolated from campus distractions, a select few were free to focus upon proper methods of excavation and sharpen their reasoning powers by mentally re-creating a past milieu from the surviving random scraps of archaeological information. Being an educator with experience in directing field schools, Edgar L. Hewett appreciated the possibilities presented by Chaco not only for teaching but also for making an important contribution to the growing body of knowledge of the Anasazi. Hence, for the first time, New Mexico institutions took the lead in Chaco Canyon archaeology. Also for the first time, women joined the ranks as part of the School of American Research–University of New Mexico expedition. Two years after the National Geographic Society work closed down, Hewett directed new excavations back in the canyon. Some of the old Wetherill facilities served as field headquarters, and Judd's dump cars and track were moved to Chetro Ketl to help in hauling dirt.

Prior to Judd's work at Pueblo Bonito, Hewett had conducted limited excavations in Chetro Ketl (in 1921). He cleared rooms and kivas in the southeast room block, tested the Great Kiva in the east plaza, and trenched the extensive refuse mound east of the town. When work was resumed in 1929, excavations picked up where they had left off and continued for the next eight seasons. Hewett was assisted in the field by staff members of both sponsoring institutions and by students from various universities who spent one or more summers obtaining on-the-job training in archaeology. Paul Reiter, later to join the staff of the University of New Mexico, served as field supervisor during most of the operation. He was helped in various chores from time to time by Stanley Stubbs, subsequently a staff member of the Laboratory of Anthropology in Santa Fe; by Gordon Vivian, who was to cast his lot with the National Park Service and spend much of his life excavating and preserving Chaco ruins; by Florence M. Hawley, who also joined the University of New Mexico faculty as a specialist in Southwestern archaeology, ethnology, and dendrochronology; by Anna O. Shepard, on the way to a career in the technical aspects of ceramics for the Carnegie Institution; and by others from the Museum of New Mexico and similar bodies.

Chetro Ketl, Pueblo del Arroyo, and Pueblo Bonito form a trio of massive, generally contemporaneous, canyon-bottom sites almost within shouting distance of one another. The inhabitants of these and numerous other smaller settlements in the vicinity undoubtedly made up the densest population center in all of Chaco during the eleventh century. Rising next to the north wall of the canyon, Chetro Ketl, like neighboring Pueblo Bonito, had been visited and described by every chronicler of Chaco Canyon from the time of Simpson; it suffered the same sort of vandalism from travelers, sheepherders, and pothunters as had the other great houses. Although comparable in size to Pueblo Bonito, direct comparisons are impossible since it is still only partially cleared. Estimates place its room count at no less than 500, the majority of the units being arranged in contiguous rows parallel to the straight north wall. East and west wings of rooms extend south from the main complex, and a curved alignment of one or two rows of rooms was built to connect the lateral wings, resulting in a D-shaped configuration. Kivas are situated throughout the structure, in the court, and among the rooms, and two Great Kivas are sunk into the courtyard. The north-central portion is believed to have stood four stories high at its rear and to have stepped down to one or two stories on the interior exposure. Toward the outside of town, sections stood to heights of three and four stories, dropping down in number of tiers toward the central court. The enclosing curve of rooms on the south probably was only a single story. Determining that it required about fifteen trees to provide the beams, poles, and lintels for a single room in Chetro Ketl, it is conservatively estimated that over 5,000 trees went into the town's construction. Behind Chetro Ketl on the talus slope next to the vertical wall of the canyon there are at least seven small villages, some of which were contemporaneous with the large town.

Although few final reports were published,[1] it would appear that somewhat less than half of Chetro Ketl was excavated by Hewett's expedition, including about 130 rooms in the northern and eastern room blocks, the curved front enclosure, nine kivas, two tower kivas, and two Great Kivas. The extensive refuse heap, some twenty feet deep in places, was trenched along both axes and stratigraphically analyzed. Wherever excavations were pushed to any depth, it is apparent that the ruins of an earlier structure existed beneath the town that is now visible. However, it is not clear whether those remains simply represent the first stages of the present village or whether there was a prior community that was abandoned, fell into disrepair, and was built over in later times. In places there are almost *two stories* of buildings below the present surface! As in the National Geographic Society work at Pueblo Bonito, stabilization of exposed features was undertaken concurrently with the digging, using cement and soil cement as mortar. Chetro Ketl excavations are shown in figures 42 and 43.

Few artifacts were recovered from the Chetro Ketl habitations. The lower units were almost devoid of cultural debris, and only a few of the upper structures contained refuse from which some specimens were obtained. The trash mound, on the other hand, yielded quantities of potsherds and other kinds of tools and implements that had been discarded with household rubbish. As was true of the other large Chaco towns excavated, Chetro Ketl produced very few burials.

Of the two Great Kivas situated in the Chetro Ketl courtyard, one is a remodeled ordinary kiva to which Great Kiva features had been added. The other is a true Great Kiva that had gone through several alterations during its existence. These were not the first Great Kivas of the Anasazi to be studied; Earl Morris had dug one at Aztec Ruin, and Judd had cleared two more at Pueblo Bonito. Nevertheless, certain circumstances associated with Hewett's larger example at Chetro Ketl made it particularly noteworthy.

When this chamber was opened to its uppermost floor level, it revealed a typical Great Kiva with niches in the wall, encircling bench, seating bins for the roof supports, vaults, firebox or altar, and a plaza-level antechamber from which entrance to the kiva proper was gained by means of a series of steps. Next, excavations were carried deeper, exposing the original nature of the feature and the several refurbishings it had gone through. Floor elements remained virtually similar throughout its history, but several deposits of objects, undoubtedly of ceremonial significance, were recovered from the bench and wall of the earliest unit. Then, ten carefully sealed foot-square niches, or crypts, were discovered around the wall above the bench. Upon opening them, it was found that every one contained a ritual offering, or a set of religious paraphernalia. Luckily, they had remained undisturbed from the day they had been left there by the ancients. Each cache had a great number of black and white stone and shell beads that originally had been strung as long necklaces or garlands, plus numerous pieces of both unworked and shaped turquoise. The ten necklaces are remarkable samples of Anasazi craftsmanship. Each consists of from 983 to 2,265 beads which, when restrung in the manner indicated by their arrangement in the small niches in which they were found, produce strands from seven to seventeen feet in length. It is significant that the sealed niches were never molested by later occupants of the religious edifice, but in its later, or upper, manifestation all niches were found open. If they, too, had been depositories for ceremonial offerings and had been sealed, they had been rifled.

The engineering skills of the Anasazi are demonstrated by the techniques used in roofing the large Great Kiva, a span some sixty feet in diameter. Four huge pine posts, set in holes in the floor, supported a square arrangement of heavy beams (see fig. 44). From them, smaller timbers radiated outward and downward to the top of the kiva walls. The flat central part of the roof also was covered with wooden members; whether it had contained an opening is not known. This wooden framework supported a pole, brush, and dirt covering. The method used in

42.

43.

Figure 44. Remains of the lower end of one of the four roof-support timbers found in the masonry-lined post holes of the Great Kiva at Chetro Ketl. The post measured 26 inches in diameter and may have stood 12 feet high. *Courtesy of the Museum of New Mexico*

44.

Figure 42. North-central section of Chetro Ketl during the School of American Research–University of New Mexico excavations in 1931. Note the use of mine cars to transport dirt from the diggings and the A-frames about the Great Kiva. Buckets were lowered into the kiva from cables strung between the A-frames to remove the deep fill from the chamber. *Courtesy of the Museum of New Mexico*

Figure 43. Filling buckets with dirt so that they can be raised by pulleys and emptied into the mine car during the excavation of the Chetro Ketl Great Kiva. *Courtesy of the Museum of New Mexico*

roofing the Great Kiva was nothing new to the Anasazi because they had been making roofs in this way since Basket Maker III times. Notwithstanding, construction of a frame that would support the many tons of wood and dirt required to mantle such a large area was an outstanding achievement. At Chetro Ketl, a structural detail associated with the four roof-support posts was noted later in other Great Kivas. The lower end of each massive upright, one of which measured twenty-six inches in diameter, was set down into a circular, masonry-lined pit dug into the kiva floor. Before a post was seated, however, four enormous sandstone discs, weighing between 1,000 and 1,500 pounds each, had been laid one upon another to create a solid foundation for the post. The Anasazi architects and engineers must have learned their lessons well as there was no evidence of undue settling in any of the foundations (see fig. 45).

Another variety of ceremonial structure, the tower kiva, was identified at Chetro Ketl (figs. 46, 47). The distribution of this kiva form is fairly widespread in Anasazi ruins north of the San Juan River; in addition to the two uncovered in Chetro Ketl, they are also known to occur in other Chaco sites of the Pueblo III period. In Chaco, they normally consist of a round tower, two or more stories high, enclosed within a square structure of comparable height. Those at Chetro Ketl are located in the northern sector of the pueblo surrounded by habitations. In some other Chaco buildings, but more particularly in ruins about Mesa Verde, they stand as round towers, either apart from or attached to habitation units. They apparently were elevated so as to command a view of the surrounding landscape and perhaps an unobstructed outlook to the sky.

In many cases, floor features of tower kivas are missing because they were exposed to destructive elements of nature. Hewett, however, wrote that the interior of the east tower kiva of Chetro Ketl remained intact although the roof was missing. It contained typical kiva floor elements: a bench encircling the wall, eight log pilasters upon the bench, a firepit, altar, and a subfloor ventilator. It was engulfed by square-shaped masonry walls creating triangular spaces in each corner, criss-crossed with wooden posts and sticks, then filled with dirt and debris.

Chetro Ketl is the best dated ruin in Chaco Canyon. Florence M. Hawley, once a student at the University of Arizona working with the astronomer A. E. Douglass, who developed the science of dendrochronology, collected many specimens of wood from all sections of the site. These helped date the various masonry styles and hence the history of construction of the excavated portion of the pueblo. In addition, she gathered charcoal specimens from the trash deposits and fragments that were incorporated in discarded household rubbish. She utilized the dates obtained from them to help unravel the complex stratigraphy of the

Figure 45. View of Chetro Ketl's Great Kiva after excavation. Five of the 10 niches in the lower, or earlier, wall
of the kiva's occupation can be seen. Upon excavation,
the niches were sealed with masonry; when opened, each
was found to contain a string of beads and turquoise
pendants. Eleven of the 29 niches in the wall of the later,
or upper, phase of the kiva are visible. Note the steps
from the antechamber into the kiva, the firebox, deflector, two vaults, four post holes, and the seating discs
from several of the post holes. Compare the floor features with the map of Casa Rinconada, Figure 49. *Courtesy of the Museum of New Mexico*

Figure 46. Chetro Ketl after excavation and stabilization. The rooms in the foreground provided most of the
tree-ring samples used to date the site. Hewett's east and
west tower kivas are at opposite ends of the room block
near the plaza. View is to the southeast. *Courtesy of the
National Park Service*

Figure 47. Artist's reconstruction of Chetro Ketl by
Robert M. Coffin. Note the two tower kivas in the section of the building fronted by a colonnade, and the two
Great Kivas in the plaza. The colonnade is unique to
Chetro Ketl and is thought to have been an architectural
derivation from Mesoamerica. Also observe the small
communities built along the talus adjacent to the
pueblo. *Courtesy of the Museum of New Mexico*

refuse and to assign absolute dates to the various types of pottery made and utilized by the people of Chetro Ketl.

Hawley divided the growth of Chetro Ketl into three periods. The first is the least known and longest; it was based on dates obtained from beams and other wood specimens originally associated with the lower structure. These ranged from A.D. 945 to 1030. Construction featured the use of thin, irregular, edge-trimmed sandstone slabs similar to Pueblo Bonito Type I. The second building period at Chetro Ketl exhibited rapid growth, especially in the north block of rooms, and was the most flourishing and prosperous in its history. Two types of wall construction were employed. Between A.D. 1030 and 1070, walls with rubble cores and veneers of large sandstone slabs laid in close courses and chinked around with very small spalls were built similar to Pueblo Bonito Type II. Between A.D. 1070 and 1090, Chetro Ketl masons laid up walls whose veneer consisted of alternate bands of large, well-shaped blocks and thin spalls. Hawley distinguished two categories of this type, one superior and the other inferior. Judd called all of it Pueblo Bonito Type III.

Units built during Chetro Ketl's last period of expansion, a stage marked by architectural degeneration, have produced tree-ring dates between A.D. 1099 and 1117. Three masonry styles are associated with this horizon. A type not present in all Chaco sites has wall surfaces that contain bricklike blocks chinked with very narrow courses of one or two rows of small spalls that have a tendency to fall from the wall. It is not banded. Judd did not describe this type at Pueblo Bonito. Another method, similar to Pueblo Bonito Type IV, has slabs that are more or less rectangular and are laid up without spalls over a rubble core. Hawley attributed

47.

a sixth type to a migrant group that reoccupied the town after abandonment or to a decadent group that lingered behind as the structure fell into disuse. Walls of this variation feature thick, crudely shaped sandstone blocks, one or two set side by side extending from one side of the wall to the other. Obviously there was no core, and neither banding nor spalls are noticeable. Judd did not assign this style a number at Pueblo Bonito but called it non-Chacoan, regarding it as an introduction into Chaco by peoples from Mesa Verde..

The masonry of Pueblo Bonito and Chetro Ketl stands as one of the outstanding accomplishments of the Chaco Anasazi. The architectural, engineering, and artistic skills of those prehistoric artisans are further enhanced by the realization that they labored without metal tools or precision instruments. Moreover, the sort of studies of Chaco masonry undertaken by Judd, Hawley, and others illustrates one means by which archaeologists may reconstruct, with a reasonable degree of accuracy, the history of a community through a thorough analysis and mapping of variations in dated construction techniques. Because it has been determined that the general sequence of building styles was pan-Chacoan, archaeologists now are able to extend the temporal placements of masonry styles from dated sites such as Pueblo Bonito and Chetro Ketl to lesser Chaco structures that, although still undated, exhibit similar building practices.

The results of Hawley's examination of potsherds from the town dump were instrumental in creating a chronological ordering of Chetro Ketl ceramics that in large measure duplicated those recovered at the neighboring large settlements. The sections of the dump that were probed, although deep, were found to be the result of a relatively brief accumulation of household cast-offs, ash, sand, and charcoal, plus a good deal of old trash originally deposited elsewhere in the town. In places, mounds and lenses of different materials marked the full evolution of the deposit. Dated charcoal fragments from the top and bottom of one section of the mound indicated a span of only thirty-eight years. Correlation between complexes of pottery in the dumt and in the pueblo and between calculated rate of refuse accumulation and estimated density of population pointed to some positive relationships.[2]

A postscript to the exploration of Chetro Ketl came almost twenty years after Hewett's program had ended when an arroyo that normally drained the rincón northeast of the city was unable to handle a swiftly rising runoff. This water broke from its channel east of the pueblo and coursed along the building's north wall. Lower level rooms on the cliff side of the ruin were flooded. One section of wall collapsed; the bases of many others suffered extensive damage. Gordon Vivian, by that time a

National Park Service employee responsible for preservation of the Chaco remains, immediately began emergency operations to prevent further deterioration of the old hulk of a town. At one place, the walls of a partially open first-story room with intact roof had been so weakened by the flood that it was felt that the weight of the debris in the unexcavated second story unit above it would cause the first story walls to buckle and fall. It was decided that the upper room should be cleared of its fill to the floor.

In the course of this rescue work, a thick mass of juniper bark from a collapsed roof was encountered about a foot from the floor of the upper room. This layer had effectively served as a moisture barrier for the six-inch sand and silt deposit that rested on the floor beneath the shredded bark. Partially dispersed into this dry material and covered by it were over 200 fragile wooden artifacts, many of them still bearing traces of painted decoration. Most of the specimens were thin slabs of cottonwood, carved into various shapes and painted with one to five colors. Some of the more complete examples consisted of two or more carved and painted elements originally tied together with sinew or cord laced between pairs of opposing perforations. They normally were finished and decorated on both sides, suggesting that they had been intended to be viewed from all directions. It is probable that, when assembled, some parts of the complex gear were three-dimensional and may have had movable parts. Pigments to produce green, brown, yellow, white, blue, red, and purple colors had been prepared from various organic and mineral materials and then had been mixed with a resin binder or, in some instances, with water. There were several fragments that obviously depicted parts of birds, such as heads, bills, tails, wings, and perhaps bodies. Also included in the assortment were sections of wands or staffs bearing zoomorphic motifs, representations of snakes and humans, a lattice of crossed sticks, discs with scalloped edges resembling blossoms, nonfunctional arrows with wooden fletching, and what are thought to be plumes. Most of the objects consist of pieces of slats, discs, ovates, rectangles, and hornlike forms which probably were sections of compound trappings (see fig. 48).

This unique find, the largest of its kind thus far known from any Anasazi settlement, probably represents a cache of extraordinary ritual apparatus that was utilized in public dramatization based in part on sympathetic magic. A fleeting but intriguing view is thus afforded into an aspect of the mentality of the ancient ones seldom available in more prosaic goods.[3]

Under Hewett's direction, the School of American Research and the University of New Mexico excavated two other Chaco Canyon Great Kivas during the 1930s, Casa Rinconada and Kin Nahasbas.[4] The former

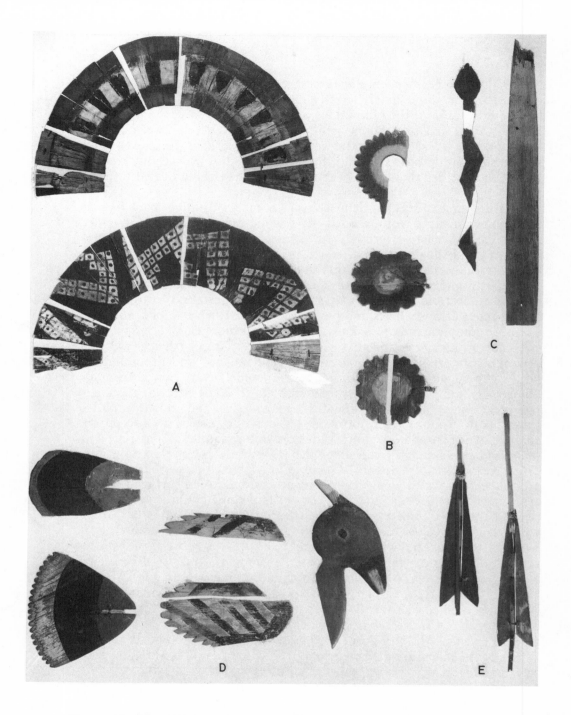

Figure 48. Examples of wooden ritual artifacts from Room 93, Chetro Ketl. A, portions of "plume circles"; B, scalloped discs; C, slat fragments; D, parts of bird tails, wings, and head; E, nonfunctional arrowshafts with wooden fletching. *Courtesy of the Arizona State Museum*

lies at the top of a low natural hill on the south side of Chaco Canyon opposite Pueblo Bonito. Gordon Vivian cleared it during the summer of 1931, and in 1933 he partially rebuilt the floor features in soil mortar, filled the eight deep breaks in the outer wall, and restored the large voids in the north and south antechambers with pine lintels. Several years later, the National Park Service stabilized the floor elements and capped the outer wall. While Casa Rinconada is an isolated structure, not part of any community, it occupies a position within one of the most densely utilized sections of the canyon. Perhaps it functioned as an intercommunity religious center for all the villages in the vicinity.

Casa Rinconada (fig. 49) is the largest excavated Great Kiva in Chaco Canyon, with an inside diameter of slightly over sixty-three feet. The major portion of it had been sunk into a layer of shale on the hilltop, but several feet of the thick exterior wall and its roof extend above the summit of the hill. There is a one-room antechamber on the south and an antechamber group of at least three and possibly six rooms on the north. Floors of both antechambers had been level with the hilltop and steps from the surface units led down into the Great Kiva. Evidence for four or more peripheral rooms, in addition to the antechambers, was disclosed. Whether these had opened directly into the kiva chamber is not clear. Floor features, which exhibit remodeling, include a bench, firebox, fire screen, two vaults, four seating pits for timbers supporting the roof, a subfloor passageway that extends under the bench and wall to emerge in the north antechamber, and several minor puzzling features. The exterior wall contains thirty-four open niches, twenty-eight forming one encircling series and six larger ones making up a second group. High on the wall are sets of small protruding poles set in horizontal sockets. The chamber had been roofed in the manner of the Chetro Ketl Great Kiva.

Very little cultural material was recovered from Casa Rinconada other than a small assemblage of potsherds, one restorable pottery jar, three crushed copper bells, and an assortment of beads. It is possible that the sanctuary originally had contained ceremonial deposits of caches similar to those in the Chetro Ketl Great Kiva because beads continually wash from the surrounding hillside as though they might have been scattered there by individuals who had rifled the kiva at some time in the past. The style of masonry used in the exterior wall and the types of pottery obtained from Casa Rinconada place its occupancy late in the Chaco sequence and into the time of migrants from southwestern Colorado.

The Kin Nahasbas Great Kiva is just west of the Chacoan town of Una Vida, near the present National Park Service Visitor Center. However, it is independent of the community, having been snuggled into the steep talus and bedrock of a point that projects out from the north wall of the

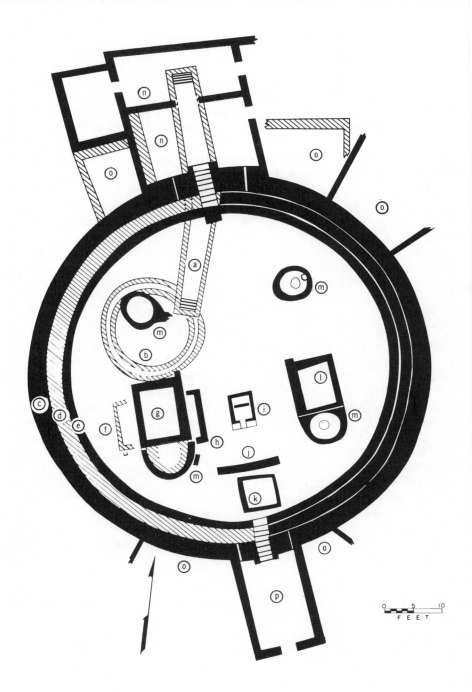

Figure 49. Plan of the Casa Rinconada Great Kiva. a, subfloor passage, lower floor level; b, circular trench, lower floor level; c, outer wall; d, original bench, later covered with veneers; e, later bench veneer; f, earlier partial vault; g, west vault; h, vault extension; i, firebox; j, deflector; k, subfloor enclosure; l, east vault; m, the roof support seating pits; n, north antechamber; o, partial peripheral rooms; p, south antechamber. *Courtesy of the National Park Service*

canyon. Like Casa Rinconada, it is only partially subterranean, but, because it was thrust into a sloping surface, its southern section stands more above ground than does the north, which was cut more deeply into the hillside.

Kin Nahasbas was studied by University of New Mexico students in 1935 as one of Hewett's ancillary undertakings at Chetro Ketl. It is smaller than Casa Rinconada and, even though indicating several construction stages, its features are of a normal, uncomplicated sort. It did lack wall niches, but so do several other Chaco Great Kivas. There is a small antechamber cut into the hillside to the north. A few artifacts, most of which had washed downslope from habitations higher up on the hill, were gathered during excavation. Pottery and masonry types imply a late date for Kin Nahasbas, possibly extending into the early 1100s. Whether the chamber was a sanctuary for nearby Una Vida, which is largely unexcavated, or was used collectively by inhabitants of the several small communities along the north side of the canyon between Una Vida and Hungo Pavi remains unknown.

Among other outlying excavations during the Hewett expeditions was that of Talus Unit No. 1 (fig. 50), a complex of lesser houses behind Chetro Ketl and occupied contemporaneously with it. It contained about thirty rooms and three kivas arranged in two- or three-story fashion on a talus mound at the base of the cliffs. Hewett noted that this ruin resembles a number of others situated in similar locations in the vicinity, and that it was a complete village with living and storage rooms, kivas, and other domestic characteristics. He postulated that it was the home of a Chetro Ketl clan. Tree-ring dates from the site show that it was built, occupied, and repaired during the eleventh century. A unique architectural device, described as a platform mound ascended by a flight of stairs, was uncovered.

Leyit Kin, on the south side of the canyon, was dug and reported upon by Bertha Dutton, who served the Museum of New Mexico and Museum of Navajo Ceremonial Art for many years.[5] The pueblo, in which Dutton cleared four kivas and seventeen of the estimated twenty-seven rooms, covers remnants of an earlier occupation as well as showing signs of late reoccupation by non-Chaco peoples. Stratigraphy, construction techniques, architectural styles, and variation in pottery types support the proposed building sequence. Unit I, the earliest, is believed to date between A.D. 800 and 950. Unit II, Leyit Kin's major building period, began about A.D. 1040, according to tree-ring dates, and is thought to have lasted into the first quarter of the twelfth century. The last stage, Unit III, represents a reutilization by Mesa Verdians, as evidenced by kiva, masonry, and ceramic modes. The habitations and kivas that constitute

Figure 50. Talus Unit No. 1 behind Chetro Ketl during stabilization activities. *Courtesy of the National Park Service*

Unit II would have been contemporaneous with active periods of construction in adjacent great communal dwellings such as Chetro Ketl and Pueblo Bonito.

The dating of both Talus Unit No. 1 and Leyit Kin, considered together with their cultural contents and size, caused some archaeologists to begin questioning the validity of classificatory schemes that treated smaller communities as the direct forerunners of larger towns. In Chaco, at least, it was becoming apparent that some of the minor villages were inhabited simultaneously with the larger towns in a sort of big-town-to-suburban-village relationship. Actually, the first inkling of this situation arose in 1929 when Anna Shepard tested one of the small houses, Site Bc114[6], across the canyon from Pueblo del Arroyo, and found that the potsherds were types common to Chetro Ketl.

The contents of a series of cavities in the north cliff of the canyon between Chetro Ketl and Kin Kletso investigated in 1932 and 1933 by

Dorothy Keur, one of Hewett's students, and Hurst Julian, then custodian of the national monument, proved puzzling. At first it was thought that the hollows in the vertical cliff wall had been utilized in the past by rodents, such as pack rats, for the storage of foodstuffs and that some man-made articles had been included with the debris that the rats had carted. Then it was realized that many of the artifacts, for example a four-and-one-half-foot-long digging stick, could not possibly have been transported by rodents. Furthermore, some of the natural cavities had been modified by people, and the openings to several originally had been sealed with mud. In addition to a haul of well-preserved natural materials such as corncobs, kernels, husks, and stalks, gourd or squash rind, seeds, stems, beans, pinyon nuts, cotton bolls and wads, yucca leaves, juniper bark, and miscellaneous seeds, artifacts in these hollows included fragments of arrow shafts, string, feather cordage, basketry, sandals, cotton cloth, potsherds, and the digging stick. It is not illogical to think that the cliff holes may have been shrines or sacred places in which offerings to particular deities were placed, a practice still observed by Pueblo Indians.

By the mid-1930s, the long-time association of Edgar L. Hewett with Chaco Canyon began to fade. Excavations at Chetro Ketl came to an end and have been resumed only on occasion by the National Park Service in conjunction with stabilization measures, as in the case of repairing the flood damage that produced the horde of wooden artifacts.

During the late years of Hewett's tenure in Chaco, land ownership became a sticky issue, as it had during Wetherill's day. Despite the fact that certain sections of land had been set aside as a national monument before his expedition, there were other parcels, surrounded by government holdings, which belonged to private individuals or had been acquired by the University of New Mexico through Hewett's efforts. A further complicating factor was that erroneous early land surveys resulted in claims and counter-claims to ownership of some ruins or even portions of ruins. Arguments among the several factions—the National Park Service, the trading post operator who had a concession from the Park Service, and the School of American Research and the University of New Mexico—grew fierce and often unreasonable. In essence, an archaeological range war was brewing. This muddled state of affairs resulted in a comic opera scenario with Hewett digging in Chetro Ketl on land leased from an individual—who supposedly owned it—and refusing to obtain an Antiquities Act permit because he assumed he was digging on private land where such an authorization was not required. Operating under the same legal cloudiness, the Park Service put up a building on land they believed to be part of the monument. Subsequent surveys demonstrated that Hewett was excavating on federal land without a permit and the govern-

Figure 51. Tseh So, or Bc 50, after excavation by a University of New Mexico field session in 1936 and stabilization by the National Park Service. *Courtesy of the National Park Service*

ment had erected a structure on property owned by the University of New Mexico. In 1949, after a long series of negotiations, the National Park Service accepted an offer originated by Hewett and supported by the University of New Mexico in which the university holdings in the monument were deeded to the Department of the Interior in exchange for other lands and perpetual, preferential rights to conduct scientific research in Chaco Canyon.

In the summers between 1939 and 1942 and for one season following World War II, the oppressive quiet of Chaco Canyon exploded as a lively throng of as many as a hundred college students descended like an invading army, digging, taking notes and measurements, washing potsherds by day, and raucously socializing from one end of the canyon to the other by night. Programs around evening campfires, dances in the dining room, lectures by visiting anthropologists, nightly gatherings at the trading post, and participation in nearby Navajo squaw dances, foot races, and softball games must have had the old Anasazi turning over in their graves.

The University of New Mexico, under whose sponsorship all this good fellowship and hard work thrived, concentrated its archaeological studies in the sector immediately east of Casa Rinconada, after erecting a headquarters complex close-by. There, on the gently sloping sandstone and

Figure 52. Bc 51, the companion site to Bc 50, principally excavated by the University of New Mexico field session of 1937. Additional sections cleared by the National Park Service during stabilization operations. *Courtesy of the National Park Service*

shale pediment that juts from the south mesa wall, rubble-strewn mounds and scatterings of trash marked the former location of a number of compact pueblos. The objective in working them was to better define the stages of the Chaco culture between Basket Maker III, as exemplified by Shabik'eshchee Village, and the classic Pueblo III times, seen at places like Chetro Ketl. For this purpose, six of the occupational sites in the Casa Rinconada area and four talus complexes along the base of the canyon wall were totally or partially cleared under the direction of Donald Brand, Florence Hawley, Frank Hibben, and Paul Reiter from the university and Clyde Kluckhohn from Harvard.[7]

The two principal sites worked in this effort, Bc50 (Tseh So) and BC51, were comparable (see figs. 51 and 52). Both were built predominantly of a masonry type described as blocks without core and were placed chronologically before the Pueblo Bonito Type I. The architectural configuration of both villages was elongated units of rooms, two or three rows deep, to which were attached the kivas. They stood only one story high but formerly may have incorporated a few two-story rooms. Beneath both ruins were substructures of slab-based, masonry-walled pithouses, suggesting a long occupation of each locale. The stratigraphy and kinds of architecture, pottery, and other artifacts reaffirm a cultural continuum from Basket Maker III (the pithouse) through Pueblo I (remains of crudely built stone walls) to Pueblo II (the surface pueblo). Additionally, some of the pottery complex from the last building phase, regarded as Pueblo II, was composed of types characteristically associated with the large Pueblo III settlements across the canyon, including some Mesa Verde earthenwares from the last days of ancient settlement. Burials, accompanied by funerary offerings, were encountered both in the refuse heaps and in some of the fill of the rooms.

Not surprisingly in view of this complex situation, tree-ring dates from the two small settlements in the canyon's south flank imply occupation coeval with that of the local metropolises standing in sentinel formation along the north. One date, A.D. 928, came from an eroded specimen of charcoal with an unknown number of missing rings which had been collected from Bc50; two wood fragments from a repaired room in the Bc51 site next door provided dates of A.D. 1043 and 1077, which coincided satisfactorily with the time of maximum Pueblo III occupation.

Another small ruin in the Casa Rinconada area (fig. 53), Bc59, excavated in 1947, manifested the same paradox as Bc51: the form and material contents were characteristic of Pueblo II times, but the tree-ring dates placed it clearly in Pueblo III times. At Bc59, the wood fragments dated the site at A.D. 1110.

As a result of the work among the small ruins such as Talus Unit No. 1 on the north side of Chaco Canyon, it had been suggested that many of those structures had been occupied concurrently with the classic towns on the same side of the canyon. This premise was not difficult to support because the towns in question were seemingly reduced versions of the more populous settlements, having similar construction and identical time of occupation. It was more difficult to explain how the Bc sites strung along the base of the southern escarpment near Casa Rinconada could have continued to adhere to a Pueblo II stage of Anasazi development while sites fitting a Pueblo III frame of reference flourished just across the canyon. How could two contemporaneous populations within a stone's throw of each other fit into two different cultural pigeonholes?

If evidence substantiated the simultaneous coexistence of two culturally diverse groups in Chaco Canyon, an explanation had to be found. In the first place, with the perfecting of the tree-ring dating method and the maturing of Southwestern archaeology, it was obvious that the Pecos Classification was too rigid. All men, even in shared environment, simply

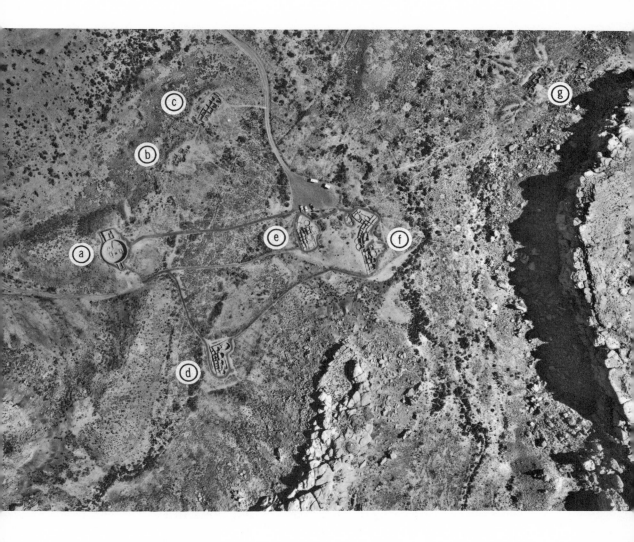

Figure 53. Aerial view of the Rinconada area on the south side of the canyon opposite Pueblo Bonito. a, the Great Kiva, Casa Rinconada; b, Bc 57; c, Bc 58; d, Bc 59; e, Tseh So (Bc 50); f, Bc 51; g, Bc 53. The Bc sites were excavated by students of University of New Mexico field sessions. *Courtesy of the National Park Service*

did not progress at the same rate. Therefore, some archaeologists, led by Harold S. Gladwin, set up a series of phases, some of which cross-cut the Pueblo II and Pueblo III stages of the Pecos Classification and others of which identified contemporary but differing ways of life: the Hosta Butte Phase to designate the small villages coeval with the great pueblos, the Bonito Phase to represent the acme of Chaco culture typified by the large towns, and the McElmo Phase to describe the Mesa Verde–like culture pattern of the migrants from the north.[8] Kluckhohn offered two other possibilities besides irregular advancement: (1) that the inhabitants of Bc50 and Bc51 and other small sites such as Leyit Kin were "either 'poor relations' or conservatives who refused to adopt the progressive architectural styles of their congeners across the canyon," or (2) that the small village inhabitants were "migrants from another region, representatives of a related but somewhat less advanced cultural heritage drawn to the Chaco by the prosperity of its inhabitants, or, conceivably, by the reputation for magnificence and power of their ceremonialism, or by the protection which these populous towns could offer." He went a step further by suggesting that the south-side villagers might even have spoken a different language.[9]

A criticism of some student training programs in archaeology is that they fail to report the results of all or parts of their field activities. Obviously, unless the findings of an archaeological project are made known to other scientists, and hopefully to the public, one of the most important responsibilities of an archaeologist is left unfilled. Hewett's School of American Research–University of New Mexico program at Chetro Ketl was guilty of this negligence. No comprehensive report upon the eight seasons' work at Chetro Ketl has ever been prepared. To a lesser degree, the University of New Mexico field school program in the Rinconada area and vicinity was guilty of the same shortcoming. Reports upon only two of the ten sites excavated by the university have been published.

A half-century had passed between the Hyde Exploring Expedition at the old city of Pueblo Bonito and the closing down in 1947 of the University of New Mexico summer programs which had concentrated on suburbia. During that time, Southwestern archaeology and the men and women who pursued it had come of age, and studies and teaching programs at Chaco Canyon had contributed substantially to the growth and maturity of both. Many Chaco trainees had met the challenge of a demanding endeavor and had gone on to merge into the mainstream of anthropology. The spectrum of Chaco Anasazi civilization now stretched from rudimentary pit dwellings of the sixth century Basket Makers to the multiroomed, exceedingly complex masonry apartment houses of twelfth century Pueblos. Although the earliest horizons from which the Basket Makers had emerged remained shrouded in mystery, the later horizons were revealed: it seemed that by the time the Anasazi left their austere homeland along the Chaco Wash, they had in some way been assimilated into a culturally compatible people dwelling eastward and southward who together survived into historic times. The major achievement of Hewett's excavation was the development of the long sequence of occupation through careful excavation. However, it could not have been accomplished without A. E. Douglass's tree-ring dating technique. This method enabled the archaeologists to assign absolute dates of occupation for each site, and unravel the sequence of utilization of sites and the time depth of Anasazi civilization in Chaco Canyon.

Student Archaeologists

5 PRESERVATION SPECIALISTS

As the University of New Mexico archaeological activity in Chaco Canyon drew to a close, the National Park Service inaugurated a preservation program for the sites already excavated. Judd had accomplished some protective measures and restoration at Pueblo Bonito, and Hewett had done the same at Chetro Ketl. However, such activity had been incidental to excavation programs, and in some instances the techniques employed, though common practice at the time, proved in the long run to be more detrimental than beneficial.

Beginning in 1933 National Park Service crews, initially under the direction of Gordon Vivian, began a stabilization program that has continued until the present. At first, attention was centered upon the two most extensively excavated great Chaco towns of Pueblo Bonito and Chetro Ketl. Aided by federal funds from various public works programs, local Navajo workmen, who had few traditional skills in masonry, were trained in ways of strengthening and preserving the existing walls of the ruins, while at the same time emulating as closely as possible the appearance of the aboriginal workmanship. Reconstruction was not attempted except in situations where missing sections of masonry or wooden building elements needed to be replaced in order to stabilize portions of walls in danger of collapse or destruction by natural forces.

The first limited Park Service conservation efforts at Pueblo Bonito included the removal of the unsightly layers of cement that earlier excavations had used to cap walls and cover areas around the kivas and over back-filled rooms. In most places, the cement had cracked badly and, instead of keeping moisture from penetrating the walls, actually was funneling water down into their cores. After the cement was taken off, several courses of stones from the tops and edges of the walls were removed and reset in their original positions in adobe-tinted cement mortar. This created a waterproof seal which visually resembled the mud used by the ancient masons and effectively kept moisture from entering the walls. The stone linings of subterranean kivas were treated in similar fashion. Comparable measures were undertaken at Chetro Ketl, but there low diversion dikes also were raised about the ruin and on top of the mesa above it to divert flash floods from the structure.

The Park Service preservation work proved so successful that in 1937 a small Civilian Conservation Corps camp, made up solely of Navajo technicians, was established near Pueblo Bonito. It functioned for the several years of that program's existence, not only at Pueblo Bonito and Chetro Ketl but also at Pueblo del Arroyo and many of the unexcavated Chaco ruins whose standing walls sorely needed attention. During winters, when inclement weather stopped work at Chaco, the crews were trucked to other Park areas in warmer climes where comparable preservation work was continued. Following World War II, the Park Service reestablished a mobile ruins stabilization unit which, like the original one, headquartered in Chaco and concentrated its efforts there. However, it also cared for ruins elsewhere in the Southwest Region of the National Park Service.

Because such preservation was a new problem and a learning experience for all involved, some of the first measures undertaken at Chaco have had to be altered. Portland cement mortar, for example, proved unsatisfactory in several ways. Pigments used to tint it sometimes varied from season to season, resulting in nonconformity of mortar color throughout a ruin. After several years, some pigments weathered to an undesirable hue. Of even greater concern was the fact that cement mortar was harder than the sandstone blocks it held in place. In some courses, where the original builders had used a relatively soft grade of rock, the sandstone eroded, leaving a weblike network of cement mortar protruding from around the masonry elements. In an attempt to avoid these drawbacks, Vivian experimented with a variety of mud-based mixtures that were at least partially waterproof, would not set up harder than the sandstone, and closely approximated the appearance of the Anasazi material. Neither he nor later soil scientists or chemists found a completely satisfactory solution. Meanwhile, the walls of the Chaco ruins are being maintained now much as they were in the Anasazi period, with mud mortar and few, if any, additives.

At one time, preservationists believed that ruins like those in Chaco could be repaired once and the job would last indefinitely. Now it is realized that the initial stabilization effort is just the beginning because the old structures must be constantly maintained, often at great expense. Such work is carried on by a local crew that labors every summer recapping sections of walls, replacing badly weathered building stones, repointing joints, and improving the drainage within the sites. The bases of walls in the Chaco ruins are particularly vulnerable to damage from surface water, an irony in a desert. The sandstone, being porous, acts like a sponge, and structural weaknesses result. Fortunately, keeping vegetation from swallowing up the ruins, which is a primary concern in preserving the Maya antiquities of Mexico and Central Mexico, is not a problem in Chaco Canyon.

In addition to the comprehensive stabilization and maintenance of the opened Chaco sites and those unexcavated ruins with exposed masonry walls, crews frequently have been diverted from scheduled projects to take care of emergencies. The repairs of flash-flood damage to Chetro Ketl is one example. Another came about as a consequence of a unique situation in Chaco Canyon. A massive 30,000-ton, 150-foot-long wedge-shaped sandstone pier rested precariously on a narrow base beside the 100-foot-high canyon wall just behind Pueblo Bonito. By the twentieth century, the slab had been treacherously undercut by scouring action of wind and water. Like many other examples along the entire north face of the canyon, it originally had been separated from the matrix of the canyon wall by a geologic process called exfoliation: a gradual widening of small vertical cracks parallel to the cliff face by the alternation of freezing and thawing eventually created a free-standing block. Typically, erosion eats at the base of such slabs, bringing eventual collapse and fragmentation into numerous large and small boulders.

That monolithic chunk of cliff figures prominently in the literature of Chaco Canyon after it was first described by Holsinger in 1901, who called it the Elephant. It was later discussed by Nels Nelson after a 1916 inspection. Judd knew it as Braced-up Cliff, the translation of its Navajo name. The Park Service referred to it as Threatening Rock (see fig. 54).

It is difficult to understand why the builders of the first unit of Pueblo Bonito chose to locate their pueblo so close to the enormous balanced rock. Though it seems unlikely, perhaps they took no notice of it when choosing a building locale, or maybe they simply refused to believe it would fall on their village. Nevertheless, midway through the life of Pueblo Bonito, after additions to the community had brought its encompassing walls even closer to this towering danger, some occupants jammed a series of supporting pine timbers beneath its undercut footing. They then built up several large platforms and buttresses of tons of earth and masonry to forestall its movement (see fig. 55). Modern engineers noted that the Anasazi supportive measures, even when first installed perhaps eight or nine centuries earlier, would have been ineffectual in stopping the shift of such a huge natural monument, but they likely had slowed erosion at its base.

Once Pueblo Bonito gained national prominence, the National Park Service grew anxious over its fate. The engineers who were called in to examine Threatening Rock confidently stated that the slab was in a stable condition and that nothing should be done to it. They predicted that it would stand erect for a thousand years. Still, measurements taken over a period of years showed that the giant stone was settling slightly. Something had to be done. It was recommended that the sand and rocks that had accumulated in the narrow space between Threatening Rock and the canyon wall be removed in order to relieve any possible outward pressure that debris might be exerting upon the rock. There were other suggestions, such as pouring a concrete foundation beneath the slab or tying its crest back to the canyon wall with steel cables. In the end, the only step taken to arrest the movement of Threatening Rock was to clean the detri-

Figure 54. Threatening Rock as it dominated Pueblo Bonito for over 1,000 years during the thriving times of the pueblo and after its abandonment. *Courtesy of the Museum of New Mexico*

Figure 55. The rock bracing built beneath and adjacent to Threatening Rock by the ancient Chacoans during the occupation of Pueblo Bonito. *Courtesy of the American Museum of Natural History*

tus from the crevice behind it, in retrospect probably increasing its instability.

Measurements to precisely determine the rate of any sway of Threatening Rock were begun in 1933 by John Keur, a School of American Research field associate. His studies revealed no appreciable settling, but nevertheless he recommended that the Park Service continue to monitor the rock for possible shifting. A Park Service ranger was detailed to measure twice daily the gap between sets of horizontal steel rods extending from the top of Threatening Rock to the cliff. The hazardous task necessitated jumping from the cliff on to the top of the monolith, and, while lying prone, reaching out with a pair of calipers to take a reading. The rock was seen to be teetering from one-quarter to one-half an inch in the midday heat.

During the night of January 21, 1941, Threatening Rock settled nine inches at its west end and twelve inches on the south, loosening several tons of sandstone that cracked away from the main mass and fell behind it. The following day, Park Custodian Lewis T. McKinney spent hours taking photographs and measurements of the damage to the rock for his report to the regional office. By midafternoon, he ran out of film and went to the trading post in the old Hyde expedition boardinghouse at Pueblo del Arroyo for a new supply. While inside the store, he felt the concussion and heard the fall. His watch indicated it was 3:24 p.m.

From their camp just east of Pueblo Bonito, several Navajos of the ruins stabilization force saw Threatening Rock buckle and fall. In that terrifying moment, one old Indian became hysterical because he feared, as did many of the tribe, that the world would come to an end when Braced-up Cliff fell. The Park Service personnel condensed their more matter-of-fact versions of the event as follows:

> The slab leaned out about 30 or 40 feet from plumb, settled sharply, and when it hit solid bottom, rocks from the top of it were broken loose and propelled into the ruin. The lower two-thirds pivoted on its outer edge and fell down the slope toward the ruin. The whole mass broke into many fragments and an avalanche of rock catapulted down the slope and into the walls of the back portion of Pueblo Bonito.[1]

A long segment of the finest part of the many-storied north wall of the town and all or portions of approximately sixty-five rooms in the northeastern section of the ruin were crushed by this disaster (fig. 56). The National Park Service briefly considered removing the jumble of rock, but the enormity and cost of the task resulted in only the smaller fragments being picked up. Those rooms and kivas that were damaged by fall-

Figure 56. Aerial view of Pueblo Bonito after the fall of
Threatening Rock in 1941 had crushed 65 of its excavated rooms. *Courtesy of the National Park Service*

ing spalls and the walls cracked by the vibration were repaired; a trail was built over and around the great disarray of rubble and boulders. Visitors to Pueblo Bonito now have a panoramic view of the site from a vantage point on top of one of the enormous remains of the rock which threatens no more. The rods anchored into the cliff for measuring Threatening Rock's movement protrude uselessly from near the top of the canyon wall.

The salvage of archaeological remains is another facet of the government's mandate in Chaco. The first project of this sort came about in 1939 when a Civilian Conservation Corps camp, not to be confused with the already mentioned Navajo ruins stabilization team, was set up in Chaco Canyon. It was a full-fledged, 200-man installation, supervised by military and civilian personnel. It built soil conservation devices, conducted rodent control programs, improved roads and trails, and cleaned up around the ruins. The C.C.C. enrollees continued a program, initiated earlier by the Soil Conservation Service, of curtailing erosion along the banks of the Chaco arroyo. The project called for the planting of nearly 100,000 tamarisk, willow, cottonwood, and wild plum trees along the bottom and edges of the wash. It has proven effective in reducing erosion, and many of the trees have grown to reach well above the arroyo banks, thus creating the only expanse of green summer vegetation to be seen in the otherwise brown Chaco landscape.

The location selected for the C.C.C. camp, near Fajada Butte on the south side of the canyon, was found to contain a small ruin that could not be avoided by the construction of the camp. Years later, when a location was chosen for the Park Service Visitor Center and headquarters near the old camp, tests revealed the presence of two other minor ruins there. These building projects and the threat of obliteration of several ancient remains by flooding arroyos led to federal excavation of a half-dozen small Anasazi sites at the C.C.C. camp location, Park headquarters, the campground, and along Chaco Wash, the results of which neatly tallied with or expanded upon work completed earlier.[2] By now there were few surprises in the architecture of the outlying complexes of cellular rooms and associated subterranean kivas or in the artifacts scattered through the dirt and fallen rubble that enveloped them. Deductions based upon the accumulated fund of information and some tree-ring dates confirmed that the National Park Service excavations represented a Pueblo II occupation in the ninth and tenth centuries followed by Pueblo III refinements in the eleventh and early twelfth centuries. Mesa Verde remains continued to share, if not dominate, the final levels in the mid-twelfth century.

Perhaps the most significant Chaco site excavated by a salvage project

Figure 57. Remains of the tri-walled structure at the
rear of Pueblo del Arroyo. View looks out the South
Gap of Chaco Canyon. Chaco Wash on the right,
Pueblo del Arroyo at the left. *Courtesy of the National
Park Service*

is the Tri-Wall unit behind Pueblo del Arroyo (fig. 57). This triple-walled
circular structure is unique in the Chaco area. Although it is usually
spoken of as an independent feature, it actually is a portion of a large
group of rooms and kivas attached in part to the outer walls of Pueblo del
Arroyo. Tests revealed that the structure, which may have contained
seventy or eighty rooms, originally extended for 115 feet along the back
of Pueblo del Arroyo and eastward parallel to its south wing for a
distance of 90 feet. Surface erosion and arroyo cutting have removed all
but traces of these latter walls, as well as part of the Tri-Wall itself.

When members of the National Geographic Society Expedition to
Pueblo Bonito were excavating in Pueblo del Arroyo, they trenched the
Tri-Wall and nearby rooms and kivas. However, when the National Park
Service under Gordon Vivian's direction began the stabilization of Pueblo
del Arroyo in 1950, no report on the Geographic's work had appeared.

Preservation Specialists

The complex had decayed into a shapeless mound, with the central depression marking the location of the Tri-Wall badly worn by the action of surface water. Since the unit was considered an integral part of Pueblo del Arroyo, it was felt that clearing it would add pertinent information about an unrecorded architectural form and would therefore benefit future scholars and visitors.

The Tri-Wall proper consists of three concentric circular walls. The center of the structure, at least when cleared, is an open circular area twenty-one feet in diameter. Surrounding it are two rings, each divided into a series of rooms, six in the inner circle and ten in the outer. The diameter of the outside ring is seventy-three feet. Interpretation of the site was made more difficult because its faced building stones had been removed in prehistoric times, a widespread Anasazi practice evident in many excavated ruins. In some instances, it was obviously more convenient for ancient builders to reuse stones and timbers from abandoned units rather than quarry a new supply of rock or fell additional trees for roofing materials. However, removal of the outer veneer of stones from the Tri-Wall, which left only the massive cores of dirt and scrap rock, caused the walls to deteriorate. Present wall heights range from mere traces to five feet. There are narrow doorways in the room wall partitions that remain but no evidence of openings in the circular walls, either between the rows of rooms or to the exterior or central interior area. Whether such openings had existed was impossible to determine because of the fragmentary condition of most of the walls. It is likely that the Tri-Wall, both the central chamber and the surrounding rooms, had been covered in typical Anasazi fashion by timber and dirt roofs. Perhaps roof hatchways served as entrances to the interiors. These would have been required had there been no openings in the circular walls.

When reports[3] on this structure appeared, they generally agreed on most details; however, Judd wrote that he doubted whether the Tri-Wall was ever completed and roofed and that he thought the walls once stood considerably higher but had been razed midway up. Both he and Vivian recognized the uniqueness of the building in Chaco. At the same time it was similar to other tri-walled units distributed northward into the Mesa Verde area. Basing his opinion upon comparative data, Vivian felt that the interior circular area of the Tri-Wall originally had contained kiva features and had been used for that purpose, as was the case in most other better preserved examples. He went on to ponder whether the surrounding rooms, some of which have domiciliary characteristics, might have been occupied by a priestly group attached to the kiva who used them as abodes, places of instruction, and storage units for ritualistic gear. In spite of attempts by others to attribute the walled buildings to an influence from Mesoamerica, he felt that they were a uniquely Anasazi statement arising from a period of intensified creativity.

The principal significance of a tri-wall in Chaco Canyon, with its tree-ring date of A.D. 1109, is that it added further support to mounting evidence that during the height of the classic Chaco communities and shortly thereafter, there were strong contacts with other Anasazi groups living to the northwest, that is, toward Mesa Verde. Mesa Verde-like architectural forms and pottery styles noted in many Chaco towns and villages postdating their abandonment by the original settlers suggest that migrants from the north actually took up residence within Chaco settlements. Some of the newcomers may have brought with them the idea of the tri-wall as a structure sympathetic to their version of Anasazi religious practices.

Archaeologists also wondered whether the simultaneous appearance of the Great Kiva in Chaco during Pueblo III times, could be related to a burgeoning religious fervor which evolved beyond and functioned above, but did not replace, the old established modes centering on societal groups and their smaller kivas. Did this mean the beginning of a specialized class of priests or an incipient theocracy?

Knowledge of Chaco prehistory improved as a consequence of excavations in other lesser towns. And as general recognition of the cultural affiliations and temporal sequence of the various construction processes, architectural vogues, and pottery variations was achieved, many of the complexities of Chaco development surfaced. The hypothesis that Chaco Canyon culture evolved in a neat, orderly pattern had to be adjusted to accommodate the simultaneous presence of diverse cultural manifestations and the coexistence of small simple villages and large complex towns. The impact of external influences on Chaco, although evident, was not understood. It was suspected that variation in plan and construction did exist between sites. Particularly straying from the great town norm were Kin Kletso, Casa Chiquita, New Alto, Tsin Kletzin, and the house block adjoining the tri-walled structure at Pueblo del Arroyo. Instead of the usual arrangement of room blocks stacked in tiers around open courts or plazas, these ruins consisted of rooms organized into compact rectilinear, multistoried complexes. In addition, the masonry of the variant sites differed from that found in the typical great communities.

When the National Park Service undertook to stabilize Kin Kletso, the opportunity was presented to examine more thoroughly one of those atypical sites. Instead of merely preserving the walls, it was decided to expose the entire structure and then reinforce it. This became a major research effort of the Park Service, with a dual mission, first, to study a type of Pueblo III Chaco ruin previously uninvestigated, and second, to prepare it thoroughly for exhibition to visitors. By that time (1951), with almost two decades of continuous experience in Chaco Canyon archaeology and preservation, Gordon Vivian initiated work at Kin Kletso, assisted by Tom W. Mathews.

Seventeen years earlier, Edwin Ferdon had studied Kin Kletso for the School of American Research. At that time, Ferdon had outlined portions of the ruin, removed some of the surface detritus, completely excavated two kivas and three rooms, and partially dug several other rooms. No report upon the work had been prepared.

After Vivian had mapped the ruin, Kin Kletso (fig. 58) was found to be a rectangular pueblo with fifty-five ground-floor rooms and five kivas. Along the north wall, the lower half of a third story is present, and there are numerous two-story walls on the front, or south.

One of the smallest of the towns, it nestles at the foot of the north canyon wall and is built over and between large boulders scattered along the base of the cliff. The masonry of Kin Kletso is probably the most homogeneous in any of the Chaco towns. The raw material employed is a soft sandstone that had been worked into rectangular blocks by pecking and rubbing. The facing or bearing stones of each side of the two-foot-thick walls make up a third of their widths, leaving only a narrow center of scrap rock and mortar. This is a decidedly different construction from the massively cored but thinly veneered building method utilizing hard laminated sandstone so prevalent at Pueblo Bonito and Chetro Ketl. In Kin Kletso, the facing pattern, which actually is the basis on which Chaco masonry types are predicated, is one of large blocks set in rather regular layers, the individual stones being separated from the courses above and below and usually from one another within the course by thin rows of spalls. The appearance in freshly cleared walls is that of substantial rectangular stones each ringed with a ribbon of small chinks. Upon exposure, the spalls tend to weather out of the joints, leaving visible only the adobe mortar. Rooms were roofed in the usual Anasazi fashion in which several pine vigas, or beams, spanned the width of the room. These were topped by smaller pine poles laid at right angles to the vigas, then by juniper splints or willow rods, and finally by earth. Rooms were entered through hatchways in the roof or through doorways. There were no exterior ground-level doorways in the pueblo, access to the habitations having been gained by climbing ladders to the upper stories and then descending through roof openings or doorways into the rooms. Some rooms had interconnecting openings; others, especially those on the lower floors, had no such apertures. These latter are thought to have been storage areas which were entered by means of hatchways in the floors of the living

Figure 58. Kin Kletso prior to excavation. Chaco Wash beyond the ruin, and the University of New Mexico archaeological field station buildings against the south cliff of the canyon. *Courtesy of the National Park Service*

rooms above them. One of the five kivas is a tower kiva. The others are the ordinary small variety. Two of them retain typical Chaco features, and the other two have some elements more characteristic of the area to the north of the San Juan.

The pottery recovered from Kin Kletso also was a comparatively pure collection consisting of a few types representative of a relatively short occupation, uncontaminated by earlier deposits and uncomplicated by discrepancies between a number of building stages. The black-on-white types, which are better time and cultural indicators than the gray, corrugated wares, formed an assemblage made up of several late Chaco modes and one that was introduced into the Chaco from the Mesa Verde region. The latter was the main kind of painted pottery at Kin Kletso. Even though arising out of a non-Chacoan tradition, some of it was probably made locally.

Six burials of children and young adults, some accompanied by pottery vessels and other burial furnishings, were found in the fill of rooms or beneath floors.

Three basic construction phases have been outlined for Kin Kletso. A square-shaped unit of twenty-eight rooms into which two kivas were incorporated came first; then, an addition of comparable size with one kiva was attached to the east wall of the original pueblo; finally, two rooms and a kiva were built against the east wall of the first addition and another kiva was added to the main room block. Whether initially each phase was built to its maximum height, or whether the upper stories were added after the ground floors of the first and second phases were completed, was not clear. Tree-ring dates from construction timbers span the period A.D. 1059 to 1124. Vivian believed that a series of dates from A.D. 1059 to 1076 resulted from the first construction effort. Another grouping at A.D. 1123 and 1124 related to the second increment. The last addition to the pueblo did not produce datable specimens. Bryant Bannister of the Laboratory of Tree-Ring Research, who studied the wood samples and based judgment solely upon their evidence and provenience, pointed out that the earlier dates came from the first-floor rooms throughout the ruin and the later ones from second-story rooms. This distribution suggested to him that portions of the ground floor were built around A.D. 1059 to 1107 and that rooms of the second floor were in place by about A.D. 1124. Regardless of whether Kin Kletso grew in horizontal or vertical increments or a combination of the two, it was a rather short-lived, late Chaco town differing in length of occupation, plan, building technique, and pottery assemblage from most of its neighbors. Its occupation can be extended another fifty years if dates of A.D. 1171 and 1178, obtained from fragments of charcoal found in firepits in the site, are accepted as representing activities of its inhabitants. Alternatively, it can be argued that the firepits from which the charcoal came were used some time about A.D. 1178 but not necessarily by the builders or permanent residents of Kin Kletso.

The excavation of Kin Kletso convincingly demonstrated that it and other similar communities within Chaco Canyon were the result of a late intrusion of peoples from the north bearing a cultural tradition which for identification purposes archaeologists have labeled the McElmo Phase, McElmo Canyon to the southwest of Mesa Verde being a region where there are many examples of this particular variation of Anasazi culture. The infusion of northern San Juan elements, slightly distinct from those that had evolved locally, had been observed in most of the Pueblo III Chaco villages and towns. Hitherto, however, it had been unclear whether some of the northerners had established residence and a peaceful coexistence in scattered ongoing Chaco communities, or whether the Chaco peoples had adopted selected ways of their neighbors. It was possible that a combination of both processes had occurred. Kin Kletso, however, seemed to verify an actual movement of outsiders into Chaco, at least some of whom built their own communities. Moreover, the material remains uncovered at Kin Kletso were predominantly non-Chacoan. Notwithstanding, occasional Chaco elements also were present, which makes it appear that the new settlers did not rule out adopting local ideas to fit their own needs.[4]

In addition to the intellectual excitement of digging and restoration, the Park Service worried that it had lost a ruin, a seemingly incomprehensible state of affairs in such a denuded area where on a clear day one can see for miles. But as usual there is a humdrum explanation. It seems that in 1901 when Special Agent Holsinger recommended that certain Chaco ruins be embraced in a proposed federal preserve, he included a site called Casa Morena, described as similar to Kin Ya-a though larger and in more ruinous condition. Holsinger gave a legal description of its location which placed it about eleven miles east of Crownpoint. Congress withdrew the land and included it with those set aside for Chaco Canyon National Monument. However, when the National Park Service found time to pay attention to the sites in the detached areas outside the main canyon and its immediate environs, they could not find Casa Morena, even though New Mexico state maps as late as the 1940s located it a short distance southeast of Pueblo Bonito.

A review of the circumstances makes it clear that Holsinger had not visited the site but, while in Thoreau awaiting the train for his return to Phoenix, had been told about a ruin whose name he interpreted as Casa Morena. Based on that conversation, he assumed it to be another of the

133

large, isolated Chaco settlements, and in so doing, caused perplexed government officials years of trouble. Since it never has been located, it appears likely that the site is one presently known as Casamero, a medium-sized Chaco-type complex named for a local nineteenth-century Navajo headman. Although not in the exact location given by Holsinger, it is in its general vicinity and fits his description. Casamero, it turns out, is on Bureau of Land Management lands, not within the national monument.

While the government archaeologists were at work trying to save and understand the Chaco monuments under their care, the administrative arm of the National Park Service prepared a history of the monument[5] and took steps to improve the facilities for the growing tide of visitors. A Visitor Center and headquarters building was constructed in 1957, and the staff swelled to include a superintendent, permanent and seasonal rangers to deal with park management, interpretation, archaeology, and protection, and a support staff. To the regret of Americana buffs, old buildings fashioned from resources pilfered from the Anasazi or imitating the unique Navajo dwellings, which were left over from the Wetherill, trading post, and university eras, were dismantled, to be replaced by characterless Park Service cinderblock administrative facilities and residences. The store, post office, and even the resident Navajos were banished from the monument. Only the unimproved access roads to the north and south, choked with sand and cut by ruts in dry spells and a slough of mud in wet ones, remained to remind travelers that this remote patch of the West was still wild.

6 ARCHAEOLOGICAL ANTHROPOLOGISTS AND ECOLOGISTS

Seventy-five years of intermittent interest in the antiquities of Chaco Canyon had exposed ruins of several ages and reinforced some of them to withstand the future. Now a veritable mountain of straggling bits and pieces of evidence about the Anasazi civilization encompassed the commonplace as well as the puzzling. The general progress of the ancient Chacoans from their first primitive one-room pithouses to their final terraced apartments was understood in broadest terms. Nevertheless, many problems posed by the successive teams of prehistorians remained unanswered. Therefore, twenty years after the work at Kin Kletso, a new cadre of shovel-and-trowel men and women attacked the province, this time armed with an updated set of theoretical concepts, analytical techniques, and space-age tools. Calling itself the Chaco Center, this research body was a joint undertaking of the National Park Service and the University of New Mexico.

In 1971, the Chaco Center's first order of business was to identify and appraise all the archaeological remains in the canyon and on adjacent uplands within the National Monument; surprisingly, this had never been thoroughly done. Such an inventory was essential not only for its inherent value but also as a basis for planning future work. A systematic sampling procedure wherein twenty 1,000-foot-wide north-south transects covering approximately twenty-five percent of the monument were arbitrarily selected and walked by survey crews led by W. James Judge. Three hundred sites were recorded. The following summer Alden C. Hayes directed a conventional, blanket-type overview of the thirty-two square miles of the preserve proper and its five detached areas. Parties traversed the entire terrain on foot and, at the conclusion of the field season, had reached the first objective of providing an inventory of the 1,751 archaeological sites the National Park Service is charged with protecting. During succeeding field operations, Hayes extended his reconnaissance outside the boundaries of the monument in order to determine the presence of sites on the mesas and in the canyons cut by the artificial geographical boundaries of the preserve. Anasazi usage of those lands could only be known if all the zones were examined. On these lands, 469 additional sites were found, resulting in an impressive total of 2,220 in the forty-three square miles within and immediately adjacent to Park Service holdings.[1] Each site's location, immediate environment, architectural or other observable characteristics, present condition, and relationship to nearby sites and natural features were fully recorded. In addition, each site was photographed, pinpointed on a map, given an identifying number, marked by a metal stake bearing its number, and scoured for a sample of potsherds and other artifacts present on its surface.

Taking into consideration all the evidence that was available from such a reconnaissance, and aware of modifications likely to come from future excavation, the painstaking survey produced significant results that expanded knowledge of Chaco occupation both backward and forward in time. First, there were a number of campsites situated beneath shallow rock shelters or on the benches outside the canyon that had been utilized long before the Anasazi came into the region. These simple remains, characterized by surface litters of stone debris, a few recognizable lithic tools, and scattered hearths and cists, were temporary stopping places of small groups of nomadic hunters and gatherers who ranged over the Southwest several millennia before Christ. Probably their presence in Chaco was never great. The foragers neither built permanent shelters nor made pottery. This early stage of culture development, widespread throughout the New World, is generally referred to as the Archaic.

Representative of the next evolutionary stage in Chaco life was a wide variety of sites which could be identified with known Anasazi cultural horizons extending from Basket Maker II through Pueblo III, or from about the time of Christ to A.D. 1250. Because the group constantly changed, few sites pertained to just one of these arbitrarily segregated levels. Many had been used for long periods of time, straddling several phases, or had been abandoned at some point to be rebuilt, enlarged, remodeled, or covered over by later people in another style. Plotting them on a master map revealed that shifting settlement patterns were responsive to such factors as changed ecological conditions or fluctuation in number of inhabitants. Expanding from a meager Basket Maker II occupation, population estimates derived from the raw survey data by Hayes place the number of Chaco Basket Maker III at about 1,000 persons, growing to around 3,500 by Pueblo II, spurting to a peak of 5,000 or 6,000 in Early Pueblo III, and finally dwindling back down to some 1,000 in Late Pueblo III. Then came the exodus.

The range of occupation groups was reflected in a variety of architectural types. Kinds of features recorded included pueblos, or permanent habitations varying in size from a few to hundreds of rooms; field houses, or single-room units that suggest seasonal or specialized use; pithouses, or subterranean habitations usually grouped into small villages; sherd areas, or activity locales devoid of habitation but marked by concentrations of broken pottery; storage units, taking the form of isolated cists or small storage chambers; religious structures, or kivas, Great Kivas, or shrines independent of settlements; stairways, including rock-cut steps and hand- and toe-holds; trails and roads; quarries; water-control devices, such as dams, terraces, and ditches; and rock art, or pictographs and petroglyphs on cliffs and boulders.

More than 600 historic Navajo remains, the largest representation of any one period in the sequence, marked the most recent human presence in Chaco. They covered the last several centuries from the early 1700s to the present. These included hogans, or houses, usually circular, of timber or rock; corrals, or stock pens frequently set along cliffs or rock outcrops; cairns, or piles of stones to mark trails and other features; and rock art that was painted or carved on bluffs and boulders near hogans.

Other than routine census taking, the survey rewarded its participants with some interesting finds and afforded them opportunity to make observations of a sort not previously possible. Such was the case when a set of Anasazi gardening tools was found cached in a crevice between two large boulders. Piled together were willow digging sticks, or dibbles, whose pointed ends were used for loosening the soil and making planting holes; wooden hoes, or sticks of oak with a knob at the top and bottom flattened and sharpened on one edge for cultivating and cutting weeds; hafted hoes with blades of stone or mountain sheep horn set into the grooved ends of cottonwood sticks and held in place by bindings of sinew and leather, which functioned like the wooden hoes; and a rectangular, concave board, notched for grasping in the hand, that was employed as a shovel or scoop. The surfaces of these wooden implements had been finely smoothed during manufacture but enjoyed a further polishing through use. Apparently, some Anasazi farmer had stashed his tools for safekeeping beneath the craggy debris at the canyon's skirts rather than cart them home. For unknown reasons, he never returned to reclaim them. The individual items of this find are not unique in themselves because samples of all of them have been recovered before, but to encounter them in a horde was a surveyor's bonus for long hours on the track. A pack rat's nest and drifting sand might have hidden them indefinitely had not his sharp eyes seen the ends of the worked sticks protruding from the deposit.[2]

Slightly more than 400 samples of rock art were noticed by the survey crews. Three categories were identified, two of which can be attributed to the past and present Indian occupants of the canyon. These are petroglyphs, or motifs cut into rock surfaces, and painted pictographs. Most Chaco Anasazi rock art is of the petroglyph variety, generally found near pueblos. It consists of geometric and curvilinear designs, especially spirals, and more rarely, naive renditions of animals and humans. Navajo rock art normally is close to Navajo habitations or corrals, is predominantly incised by steel tools, and commonly depicts human and animal figures or, on occasion, ceremonial activities and deities. Carved and painted modern graffiti left throughout the Chaco by soldiers, sheepherders, and cowpunchers consist of names, brands, and dates. When the main route between the settlements on the Río Grande west to Farm-

139

ington and Durango passed through Chaco Canyon, a favorite overnight camping spot for horseback and wagon travelers was at the foot of the cliff one-third of a mile west of Casa Chiquita. Inevitably, names, dates, and messages were scratched into the nearby rock, which hints at a passing tide of history. For instance, in 1887, an advertisement for the "H. L. Hines Store 10 miles down canyon" was inscribed, and about the same time this personal message of an unkept appointment: "Gean I cannot get no feed I cannot wait for you."

Of special interest to the Chaco surveyors was evidence of a network of what was suspected to have been signaling stations. These somewhat amorphous remains normally consist of arch or U-shaped walls of masonry, several feet high, placed on promontories within sight of one another and so situated as to link the entire Chaco populace.

Some of the survey results added little new information about Chaco prehistory. Nevertheless, they were important in the necessary corroboration of earlier finds and notions; in some respects, they substantially expanded previously gathered data. Intimately working over an area rather than concentrating upon a specific ruin complex has obvious advantages in certain aspects of the total problem. One example is the increased knowledge gained of Chaco irrigation engineering, which now is seen to have incorporated developed seeps and springs, small stone check dams across minor drainages, large earthen dams, water diversion devices, storage tanks, and agricultural terraces and garden plots. Several previously undiscovered quarries from which building stone or potter's clay had been secured were located on the barren terraces stepping back above the canyon. Other isolated Great Kivas were recorded, each surrounded by a cluster of pueblos which may have used the sanctuary as a communal ceremonial center. And additional signs of ancient roads, trails, and stairways were encountered by tramping laboriously over the ground. However, this facet of the research was more greatly expanded by one of archaeology's newest technological helpmates, remote sensing.

When the Chaco Center was established, the National Park Service encouraged the establishment of an experimental program, led by Thomas R. Lyons, to determine whether or not remote sensing, a complex analysis of various types of aerial photography, could be used to identify man-made and natural phenomena on the ground and thereby enrich the archaeological and environmental studies proposed for Chaco. For this purpose, aerial photographs of the greater Chaco Canyon region, as basic to this method of gathering data as the shovel is to the digger, were obtained from a variety of camera platforms ranging from tethered balloons to orbiting satellites. The airplane was found to provide the most useful imagery (see figs. 59–61). Depending upon the problem at hand,

Figure 59. Aerial photograph showing Pueblo Bonito, Pueblo del Arroyo, and the Tri-walled structure. The small rectangular plot in the upper left is the Chaco Canyon cemetery where Richard and Marietta Wetherill are buried. *Courtesy of the National Park Service*

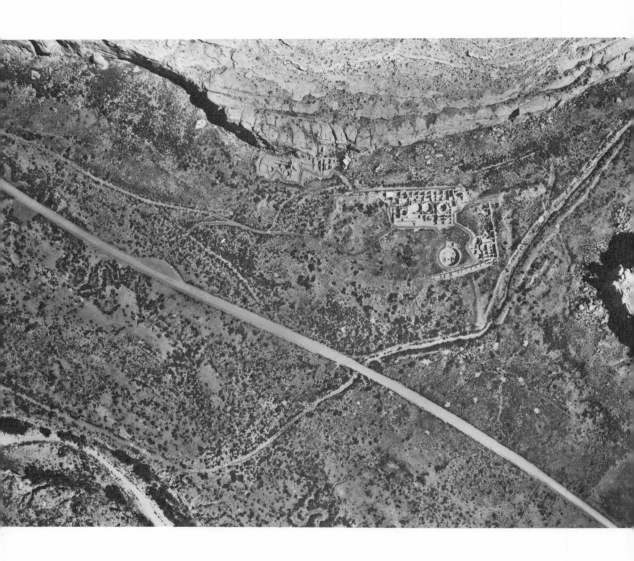

Figure 60. Aerial photograph depicting Chetro Ketl and
Talus Unit No. 1. *Courtesy of the National Park Service*

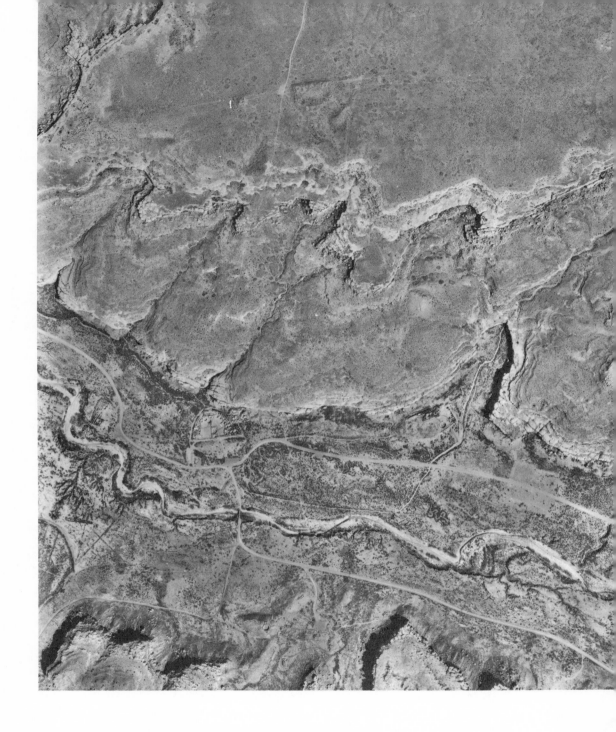

Figure 61. Aerial photograph of Pueblo del Arroyo, Pueblo Bonito, and Chetro Ketl in Chaco Canyon, and Pueblo Alto to the north of the canyon in the upper center of the picture. Faint lines extending north and south of Pueblo Alto are ancient roadways. The Chaco Wash meanders through the canyon. *Courtesy of the National Park Service*

the season of the year, and other circumstances, several types of film were employed because it was realized that the maximum amount of information could be extracted only when several kinds of imagery covering the same area were studied simultaneously.[3] Supplemental to the photographs were periodic field checks of an area being investigated to enable the technician to acquire firsthand knowledge, or ground truth, of the geological, biological, and archaeological phenomena essential to correct recognition.

Identification of objects from simple, vertical photographs were helpful for mapping sites, for initial awareness of features, and as a field aid in archaeological reconnaissance, but a drawback to such interpretation was that only the two dimensions of length and width were clearly perceived. In order to see depth, or relief, in photographs, it was necessary to obtain images from two different points in space and to view them three-dimensionally through a stereoscope. The images, a lefthand and a righthand view, or stereo-pair, were arranged beneath the corresponding lenses of the stereoscope so that the left eye looked at the lefthand photograph and the right eye the righthand view. The result was a three-dimensional image, which has much greater interpretative value than a single, vertical shot. However, both individual vertical photographs and stereo-pairs were used as the basis for up-to-date maps of the important Chaco Canyon ruins and for maps of the foremost sites excavated by the Chaco Center.

For identifying other Chaco human accomplishments and natural phenomena such as vegetation distribution, soil types, and geological forms, several electronic devices were put to use in the laboratory. They utilized complicated closed-circuit television systems to analyze black-on-white, color, and infrared imagery. One of the most useful, called an edge enhancer, accentuated all lines that appear on a photograph, making obscure or hazy lines such as walls of a ruin, edges of a prehistoric road, or a low rock outcrop stand out sharply on the television screen. Another machine was the density-slicing monitor, which transmitted to the television screen an image in which each color represented a distinctive part of the landscape, such as rock, soil, different types of flora, or water. By changing the colors, a given feature could be made to contrast with its surroundings, thus allowing more accurate definition. This device was instrumental in plotting the extent of the Chaco road system, in locating former irrigation works and cultivated fields, and in spotting concentrations of certain vegetation clusters indicative of ancient settlements. A third implement, the perspective monitor, enabled the interpreter to tilt electronically on the television screen a flat image to give it relief, making it appear three-dimensional. This helped to identify questionable sites appearing on vertical photos and to determine accurately the shape and dimensions of known unexcavated ruins.

Another remote sensing technique of the Chaco Center depended upon an infrared scanner. Operated from an airplane, it recorded differences in ground temperatures because various areas, such as rock exposures, dry expanses, moist spots, disturbed soil, undisturbed soil, and localities covered by plants, reflected different amounts of heat. It enabled field personnel to locate buried walls, silt-filled reservoirs, and ancient watercourses.

Recognition of an elaborate, far-reaching Chacoan road network came about primarily as a result of data derived from remote sensing. The Chaco Center, however, was not the first to discover the presence of prehistoric roads in Chaco Canyon. Marietta Wetherill stated in a 1948 interview that

> north of [Pueblo] Alto in certain lights you can still see what appears to be a wide roadway running down to the Escavada. In the old days this was clearly defined in the spring or early summer because the vegetation on it was different from any other and it could be traced clear to the San Juan.[4]

Her Navajo friends told her that such phenomena were "race courses." Neil Judd remarked about the "broad pathways" that connected the stairways cut in the cliffs near every principal ruin and described the "roads" extending southeast from Pueblo Alto to Chetro Ketl, as well as other examples. He stated that construction of each road had been a prodigious undertaking and, at one point, called them "ceremonial highways" but did not elaborate upon the matter. Older Navajos interviewed by Judd related that the so-called roads were more obvious in the past when they could be traced from one end of Chaco Canyon to the other and to distant sites to the north and south of the canyon. They said that most of them had been washed away or covered by sand and silt but that their locations were indicated by cuts through low knolls.[5] Gordon Vivian was aware of segments of the "roads," but he confused some of them with water control measures. His son, Gwinn, mapped several short portions of roads on the north mesa above Pueblo Bonito.

Remnants of the Anasazi roads were discerned on the aerial photos because of several of their physical characteristics. Some segments have less dense vegetation than their surroundings, while others exhibit more. These variations result from differing soil conditions and vegetative patterns. Topographically, the roadways sometimes are slightly depressed in the sandy soil. This permits a greater accumulation and retention of moisture which results in slightly increased plant density. The growth usually cannot be detected by the naked eye, but it accounts for differential reflection of sunlight that is recorded on the photographic image. In places at certain times of the day, shadows seen on the photographs mark the edges of depressed roads. Most of these identifying elements are invisible or slightly discernible from the ground. However, in a few local areas, the presence of lines of stones, mounds of dirt, or cuts in the soil indicating a road's lateral borders allows for ground recognition. Other indications of roadbeds were the broad steps cut in the edges of rock exposures or the stone and dirt fills placed in small draws over which the road passed.

The road system was not simply a set of trails, which would seem to have been appropriate for a people without beasts of burden who used it solely for pedestrian traffic. Instead, it consisted of well-engineered lines of communication that required a tremendous expenditure of time and effort to plan, construct, and maintain. The roads were laid out on preconceived routes that avoided major topographical obstacles but that cut through minor obstructions, such as low hills or shallow arroyos.

The primary roads, averaging about twenty feet in width, and the spur roads, frequently twelve feet wide, comprise a network of over 250 miles in length. It seems to relate to the period of Chaco's population expansion in Late Pueblo II and Pueblo III during the eleventh and twelfth centuries. Seven roadways of the largest complex known radiate generally northward from an opening in a stone wall attached to Pueblo Alto (see figs. 62 and 63). One of these has been traced nearly thirty miles and at one time may have connected Chaco with communities along the San Juan River. In the canyon proper, identifiable stretches of roads make it almost certain that an east-west route linked the leading communities from Pueblo Pintado on the east to Peñasco Blanco on the west. Also, the canyon centers were tied to the neighboring southern towns of Kin Bineola, Kin Klizhin, Tsin Kletzin and Kin Ya-a and to Pueblo Alto to the north of Pueblo Bonito. In addition to the north road that extended well beyond the limits of the densest Chaco settlement, there are many segments that point toward other neighboring population centers or that lead into regions possessing natural resources unavailable or of limited occurrence in the Chaco, such as timber, arable land, wild plant and animal foods, and useful minerals. At intervals along the routes, there are a number of small ruins, which are so closely associated with the roads as to suggest that they served as way stations, communication centers, or possibly as encampments for construction, repair, and protection of the system.[6]

As it is now known, the integrated Chaco road network could have had several functions, namely to provide well-defined routes for the

146

travel of groups and individuals within the Chaco sphere and between nearby community centers, to transport raw materials into Chaco Canyon and goods and materials among those affiliated towns, to facilitate communication between widely separated groups, and as a means for keeping the Chacoans together as a cohesive social force. No other aboriginal land communication system of such magnitude and purpose has been recognized north of Mexico. Certainly it was a product of group organization, controls, and a lot of human energy.

As in the case of the Chaco roads, there had been descriptions by early writers of prehistoric structures thought to direct or catch surface water. In 1901, Holsinger noted such devices at Kin Bineola, Kin Klizhin, Una Vida, Kin Ya-a, and north of Peñasco Blanco. Later, in addition to a reexamination of most of those, Judd's excavations at Pueblo Bonito exposed a series of "artificial canals or ditches" running parallel to the refuse mound in front of the site. They were described as four to ten feet wide with adobe-lined walls on the downhill side. They were thought to have carried water from the rincón northeast of Chetro Ketl. Between 1963 and 1966, Gordon Vivian mapped and photographed known hydraulic structures which later were more intensively investigated by Gwinn Vivian.[7] Finally, the Chaco Center has again devoted some attention to this phenomenon, particularly using both remote sensing and archaeological testing with special emphasis on the Kin Bineola area.

The considerable information gathered to date indicates that the Chacoans had a comprehensive plan for controlling surface water that was as well thought out and executed as their network of roads. Assuredly, advanced social and economic organization entailing planned communal endeavors, as well as practical engineering skills, are implicit in both. Elements of the water manipulation assemblage include dams, reservoirs, canals, ditches, and water diversion walls, all of which were constructed to channel runoff water to farming terraces, garden plots surrounded by grid borders, and fields. Some reservoirs also may have provided temporary domestic water to nearby towns.

There is no positive evidence that water was ever diverted from the main Chaco drainage to farm areas. Yet it is not unlikely that in the past, when the Chaco Wash or intermittent water course meandered down the canyon, its flow was turned aside to canyon-bottom fields. If the stream had periodically overflowed its banks when runoff was heavy, land alongside its banks would have been naturally watered by the floods. At times when the flow was normal, simple rock and brush diversion dams would have permitted overflow irrigation in the center of the canyon or, through the use of ditches, allowed water to be directed downstream to fields closer to the borders of the canyon. Although heavy deposits of

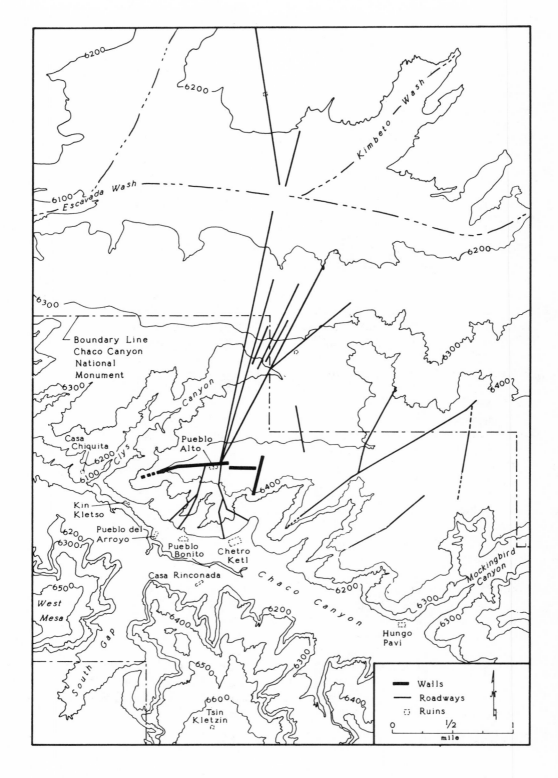

Figure 62. Map showing segments of the prehistoric Chaco road system in the vicinity of Pueblo Alto. *Courtesy of the National Park Service*

Figure 63. A cleared section of a Chaco road near Pueblo Alto. Over smooth rock the road is bordered by low, dry-laid stone walls. Where it ascends rock terraces, broad steps had been cut into the rock. *Courtesy of the National Park Service*

sediments on the canyon floor have obliterated any signs of possible irrigation means along Chaco Wash, sections of ancient canyon-bottom canals have been exposed in the arroyo banks. Whether they drew water from the river or from side canyon runoff is not clear.

On the other hand, there is abundant evidence for the capture and diversion of surface runoff water for agricultural purposes. Almost every outlying town has a system for this purpose. In fact, there is such a dense cluster of water control features in the central sector of the canyon, from Una Vida to Peñasco Blanco, that it is difficult to say whether they represent a series of individual works or one grand coordinated complex. Most such devices are on the north side of the canyon where the topography of short side canyons and a fingerlike arrangement of mesa-top drainages leading down to a broad rock bench above the heads of the canyons affords sufficient surface flow from summer downpours and rapid spring thaws for the operation of an irrigation system or systems.

Of particular importance to this water control complex, as demonstrated by Gwinn Vivian, is the expanse of bare, flat rock between the cliffs of Chaco Canyon proper and the next vertical face north of the canyon. This intercliff zone, varying in width from 1,000 to 3,000 feet, not only speeds water that drains onto it from higher elevations down into the canyon cleft but also, and more significantly, forms a vast catchment area for runoff. Because this bench of exposed bedrock is almost devoid of moisture-absorbing soil, practically all water that falls on it channels into the canyon, thereby providing maximum amounts of water from even minimal rains. It is an amazing sight in this desert to witness water rushing from the top of the canyon wall in a series of miniature waterfalls after a summer thunderstorm (fig. 64).

Commonly the Anasazi built earthen dams across the arroyos at the mouth of side canyons to impound the runoff in small reservoirs. From them, a canal extended upstream along the north brink of the canyon for a short distance. Then, by means of stone headgates and ditches, the canal water was directed downstream to fields and garden plots toward the lower, central portion of the canyon floor (fig. 65). A group of these units at the north and south sides of the canyon bottom would have placed part of Chaco Canyon under irrigation that would have functioned during or immediately after periods of runoff. Lesser networks for irrigating benches above the canyon floor also were used.

Perhaps it is significant that the water control measures seem to have been in use during the existence of the great Chaco towns and, at least within the canyon, may have been created when the Chaco arroyo became so deeply entrenched that irrigation water could no longer be taken from it. This occurred at a time estimated by some geologists to have been dur-

Figure 64. Summer rains produce rapid and violent runoff that cascades over the north canyon rim and down into Chaco Canyon. This is the resource that was captured by the Chaco water control system. *Courtesy of the National Park Service*

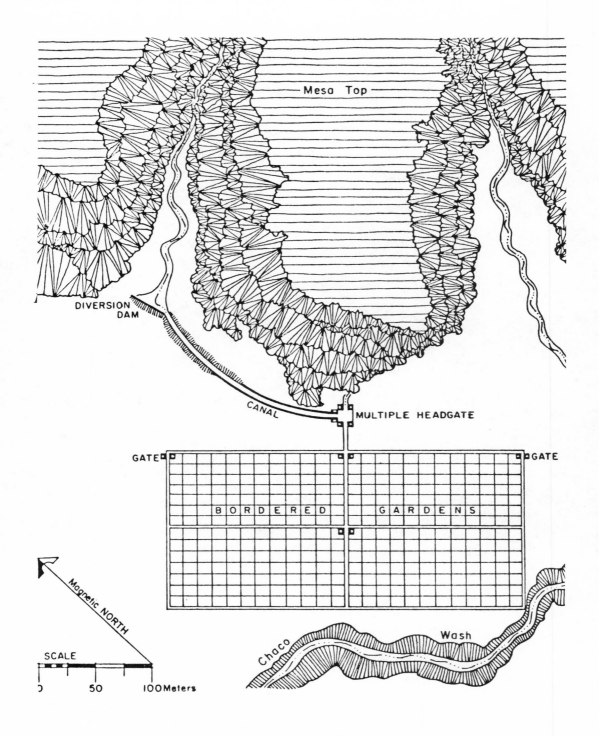

Figure 65. Schematic diagram of a typical Chaco Canyon water control system utilizing diversion dam, canal, gate complex, and bordered gardens. *Courtesy of the University of Arizona Press*

ing the Pueblo III period.[8] Thereafter, even though the Chaco arroyo and its tributaries were deeply embedded, it could have been possible for an irrigation plan to have remained adequately usable for the continuation and expansion of an agricultural community. This argues against the proposal advanced by some persons[9] that arroyo cutting would have caused lowering of the water table, which in turn forced the desertion of the area.

Other students of Chaco culture have suggested that the creation of the water control arrangement, combining Anasazi engineering abilities and the unique topographic situation that provided a mesa-top water catchment pocket next to arable canyon lands resulted in the population growth and cultural enrichment so evident in Pueblo III.[10] This explanation points out that the irrigation system was a response to a cyclical deficiency in precipitation that fostered production of agricultural products in amounts well above the subsistence level. Resulting surpluses had to be preserved for future use, hence the building surge of Early Pueblo III that added many large, well-constructed storage rooms to the existing towns and saw the establishment of new towns incorporating habitation and storage units. Once a surplus economy had been created, trade with peoples throughout the Chaco Plateau was intensified. Moreover some inhabitants of adjoining regions that continued to suffer frequent crop failures because of drought must have been attracted to Chaco Canyon because its water system afforded a more secure existence.

As data from the archaeological surveys and remote sensing investigations accrued, personnel of the Chaco Center turned to a comprehensive excavation program to rethink the entire Chaco cultural sequence, giving particular attention to horizons with limited or no previous information. Also, concurrent with this research, a series of biological, geological, and geographical problems was attacked so that human activities could be accurately related to the environmental setting.

In these latest appraisals of Chaco's past, scientists were aided by a new method of dating known as archaeomagnetic dating, which derives dates from burned clay. It is particularly applicable to Chaco sites because most of them contain some form of burned clay: mud-rimmed hearths or firepits, walls and floors of pit structures and masonry rooms baked hard by the intense heat of fire that had destroyed them.

Simply stated, the principle archaeomagnetic dating involves two factors. One, that the course of the constantly moving magnetic north pole has been charted and positions along that route have been dated; and two, that the minute linear particles of iron in clay are loosened within their matrix at certain temperatures and align themselves with the magnetic north pole. Upon cooling, the iron particles remain directed toward the pole. This means that the bits of metal in the fired clay point toward the

153

position of the pole at the time of the last fire in a firepit or when a structure was consumed by fire.

During excavation, small samples of burned clay are carefully collected and encased in blocks of plaster-of-paris. The orientation of the clay is meticulously determined before being removed from its original context. The samples then are sent to the Earth Sciences Observatory at the University of Oklahoma, where the plaster cubes containing the clay are placed in a machine in the exact position in which they were found in the field. The device measures the direction in which the iron particles in the clay are pointing. Once that azimuth is determined, it is extended mathematically from Chaco Canyon to intersect the path of the magnetic north pole at the point where the pole was located at the time of the fire in the Chaco site, thus dating the disaster that caused a family to flee its burning home.

Four previously unstudied campsites thought to be of pre-Anasazi age, three on sandy accumulations on the north side of Chaco Canyon and one within a shallow rock overhang on a terrace of the canyon northwest of Casa Chiquita, were excavated in the first phase of the Chaco Center's archaeological program. Archaic Stage remains were recovered from all four campsites, with an additional overlay of probable Basket Maker II materials, such as pieces of a sandal and an atlatl, triangular side-notched spear points, and red pictographs coming from the protected shelter.[11]

Next, in order to reconfirm results from Shabik'eshchee Village excavated forty-five years earlier, four Basket Maker III complexes dating to the sixth and seventh centuries were cleared or extensively tested. Each contained from two to twenty pithouses, associated storage cists, and what could now be regarded as a typical repertory of artifacts. These included globular, wide-mouthed earthenware containers that were sometimes coated with an impermanent red wash or a few crudely executed black decorations; a variety of piercing, cutting, scraping, grinding, and pounding tools; and a few ornamental objects. All the sites had been occupied into later times, often with signs of having been ransacked for construction materials by those who erected more recent structures in their vicinities.[12]

Especially interesting in this assemblage of Basket Maker III remains was the Great Kiva at Site 29SJ423 (fig. 67). This structure was found to have undergone two stages of refurbishing after construction because of fires that had destroyed its superstructure. Its final abandonment also was preceded by a fire. The floor of this chamber was thirty-three feet in diameter and was found to have been laboriously dug through a decomposed layer of sandstone down into the harder bedrock to a total depth of

Figure 66. Chaco Center archaeologists used mechanical earth-moving equipment to dig exploratory trenches, to strip away sterile overburdens, and to remove deep deposits from certain sites. When properly controlled, such practices are great time savers. *Courtesy of the National Park Service*

some three feet. The wall had been lined with stone slabs against which two benches, also faced with slabs, had been set. There was a rectangular firepit in the center of the floor; scattered around it were a number of pits of unknown use. The first Great Kiva, dated by tree-rings in poles used in its above-ground walls, was constructed between A.D. 520 and 540. Wall support was provided by posts placed around the perimeter of the pit. The second and third building phases, dated respectively by tree-rings at A.D. 540 to 550 and 557 or shortly thereafter, are believed to have had walls supported by four posts placed in a square arrangement in the floor of the structure. Wall poles rested on the top of the bench and slanted inward to lean against rafters placed on the tops of the posts. It was not determined whether in any of its stages the center of the Great Kiva had been covered by a flat roof.

In order to better identify the Chaco Pueblo I period, 6 sites of the 500 thought to be of that time were dug or tested.[13] At 2, only limited digging was done. Two others were almost completely opened, but both had seen considerable alteration or perhaps periods of nonoccupation through Pueblo II and well into Pueblo III. A fifth ruin proved to be a good exam-

Figure 67. The Basket Maker III Great Kiva at Site
29SJ423 after clearing by the Chaco Center. *Courtesy of
the National Park Service*

ple of a small Chaco Pueblo I unit, perhaps occupied by no more than a single family. It can be taken as a prototype for the period. Located on a sandy ridge extending north from the base of Fajada Butte, it included a cluster of one pithouse, a three-unit ramada or utility area, and a line of four storerooms to the rear. The excavators believed that the pithouse, two storerooms, and two ramadas made up the original settlement; later, the two additional storage chambers and another ramada were added. This might mean that the site was inhabited during a time when farming was quite productive and that the expansions were necessary in order to cache away food surpluses. The period of residence was suggested to be between about A.D. 710 and 740. The sixth Pueblo I town, at the mouth of Werito's Rincón on the south side of the canyon, was made up of three separate groupings of structures along the top of the ridge. One of them was excavated, and another was tested by trenching. The cleared unit consisted of a pithouse, several ramadas, and ten rooms, two of which were habitations and eight were for storage. It probably was a two-family establishment, with living quarters, work areas, and storage facilities reflecting seasonal activities. It may have been in use between A.D. 725 and 750. Artifacts recovered showed a slow but sure refinement of those known in the previous phase. (See fig. 68 for a map showing the growth of a typical Chaco village.)

One site perched on the crest of a winding ridge running north from Fajada Butte appeared to have been extant only during the Pueblo II horizon of the 900s.[14] The town consisted of two blocks of masonry rooms and storage cists that were separated by an intervening area that included a series of ramadas, outdoor work zones, and four kivas. Sprawled on the floor of a kiva in the eastern unit were the skeletons of two adults, an infant, and a dog. Because none appeared to have been burials, it may be that the bodies had been placed in the chamber at the time of abandonment as offerings to certain deities toward whom some religious ceremonies had been devoted. Otherwise, there were few unexpected finds in architecture or material goods.

Pueblo Alto was chosen by the Chaco Center from among the leading Pueblo III Chaco communities for extensive testing. It was selected because no such settlements outside the confines of the canyon had been thoroughly investigated and because it appeared to be a terminus for many of the roads that connected with other sites to the north of Chaco Canyon. Roads also link Pueblo Alto with Pueblo Bonito and Chetro Ketl. Furthermore, it was felt that the excavated and restored site could play an important part in the interpretative story presented to visitors by the National Park Service. Beginning in 1976, three field seasons were devoted to learning as much as possible about Pueblo Alto with a min-

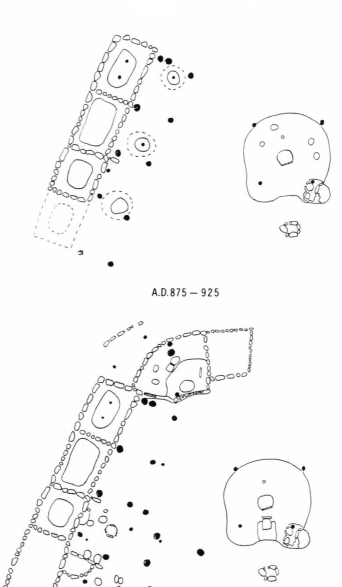

A.D. 875 — 925

A.D. 1000 — 1025

Figure 68. Characteristic growth of a small Chaco village from an initial complex containing one or more pithouses, several poorly constructed storage rooms, and a group of brush-covered ramada work areas; added to these were a number of more substantially built living and storage rooms, additional ramadas, some of them enclosed, and conversion of pithouses into kivas. *Courtesy of the National Park Service*

imum of digging. W. James Judge, assisted by Thomas Windes, directed the field work.

Since modern excavation procedures no longer consist only of digging one room after another and separating the artifacts from the debris, it was impractical to consider cleaning out the entire ruin. Also, the cost of stabilizing and maintaining an excavated ruin of the magnitude of Pueblo Alto was prohibitive. Therefore, a carefully formulated plan was devised for making a series of probes into sections of the site and back-filling most of the exposed features after they had been satisfactorily studied.

Pueblo Alto occupies a magnificent setting two-thirds of a mile back from the rim of Chaco Canyon north of Pueblo Bonito. From its lofty position, one may scan much of the Anasazi world—to the snow-clad San Juan Mountains to the north, to the Chuskas on the Navajo Reservation to the west, south to Hosta Butte and Mount Taylor, and eastward toward the Jémez Mountains. All of the uninterrupted expanses of the Chaco Plateau, and much more, are laid out in a grand full-circle vista.

William H. Jackson first visited the ruin in 1877 and named it Pueblo Alto because of its location. He recorded the tale told him by Hosta, his Jémez Indian guide, that, according to Indian tradition, a person of great importance and wealth known as "the gambler" had lived at Pueblo Alto. Some of the Navajo who helped excavate Pueblo Alto remembered that oral tradition. Had the account been passed down through generations of Anasazi and their Pueblo descendants, it could have reached the Navajo following the Pueblo Revolt of 1680, when many Pueblo families sought refuge in Navajo land including that around Chaco Canyon. During their time of coexistence, the two groups exchanged many elements of culture; legends may have been among them. The findings of the Chaco Center that Pueblo Alto in all likelihood was an important commercial establishment where goods were collected for distribution also lends some credence to the story.

Before excavation, Pueblo Alto stood out on the bleak treeless plain as a high-standing D-shaped mound of dirt and rocks from which protruded a few segments of masonry walls. A large accumulation of town trash lay to the southeast of the ruin. The first task of the excavators was to outline the ruin and its many rooms by running two-foot-deep trenches along the sides of all walls. This enabled archaeologists to make an accurate room count and study such architectural details as corner ties, wall abutments, and types of cored masonry. After all wall tops were exposed, aerial photographs of the site were taken, and a detailed map was prepared from them (fig. 69). About one hundred ground-floor rooms and eleven kivas were revealed. National Park Service stabilization crews have capped all the exposed walls.

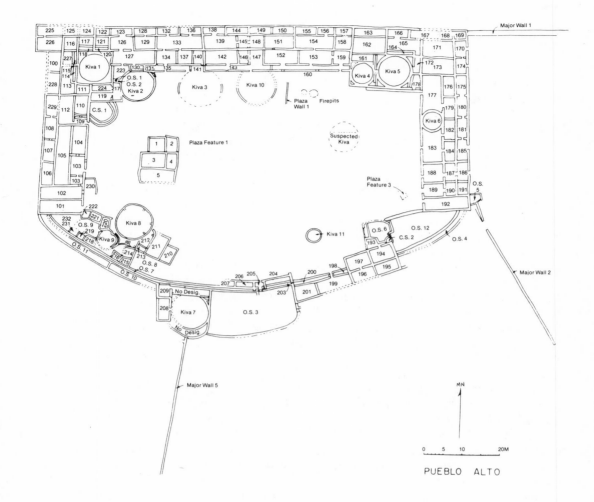

Figure 69. Map of Pueblo Alto prepared by the Chaco Center after outlining the tops of all walls in the town, extending numerous exploratory trenches, and excavating selected sections of the ruin. *Courtesy of the National Park Service*

Excavations in selected room complexes, kivas, plaza areas, and along sections of the exterior walls then commenced and were continued through the summer of 1978. The first surprise turned up by the pick and shovel was that Pueblo Alto is a single-story edifice, the only Chaco great town to be built in this manner. Prior to digging, it had been assumed, because of the height of the ruin, that some sectors of the pueblo originally had been two or more stories high. Instead, the rooms excavated proved to have very high walls that, when covered over with debris, made the ruin appear to contain multistoried units. The refuse deposit, which had been dug into in places by Frank Roberts during his analysis of Chaco Canyon ceramics in 1926, was extensively trenched for additional information about its pottery contents and for other hints of ancient ways that can be gleaned from town garbage.

Even though research on Pueblo Alto continues, it can be said that the town seems to have been planned and built over earlier pithouses and small village remains in the late tenth century as a one-story U-shaped, cored masonry block with kivas in the plaza. Additions and remodeling during the following two centuries saw the joining of a series of corridor rooms to the original building, the erection of an arc row of rooms to enclose the courtyard, and the dismantling of some of the first rooms so that kivas could be incorporated into the room block. Many of the long, high-ceilinged rooms seem to have been used solely for storage, most likely for excess foodstuffs, such as corn, beans, and dried squash and pumpkins. Other units within the pueblo probably were devoted to handicrafts, including the fashioning of ornaments from turquoise and other materials. It looks as though much of the space within Pueblo Alto was given over to specialized activities. In fact, the ratio of storerooms and workrooms to living quarters suggests that the resident population at Pueblo Alto may have been fairly small. A few dates in the early A.D. 1200s probably represent the final use of the structure during its declining days.

Three smaller ruins near Pueblo Alto were active settlements during its lifetime and possibly interacted with the larger town in various ways. Two of the communities, New Alto, 400 feet to the west, and the East Ruin, a twelve-room, one-kiva unit within Pueblo Alto, are tied to Pueblo Alto by substantial masonry connecting walls. New Alto is a typical compact McElmo-type town with one kiva and twenty-eight rooms, some of which stood two stories, having Mesa Verde characteristics. It is unexcavated, but its stabilized walls of large dimpled sandstone blocks rear high above the debris that mantles their bases. The third site, the Rabbit Ruin, is about 800 feet north of Pueblo Alto. Limited trenching of some of the walls and kivas in the prominent mound exposed two or three pueblo units built exactly in the manner of New Alto. It is believed to have been inhabited by splinter groups from the body of northern migrants who resided at New Alto.

The Pueblo Alto complex, encompassing the four sites representing both the Classic Bonito and McElmo phases, is closely associated with the Chaco road system. At least seven of the northern stretches of roads converge upon Pueblo Alto, entering the area between the main section of the town and the East Ruin through an opening, or gate, in the wall connecting the two units. The road from Chetro Ketl to the south also terminates in the same locality, and the Pueblo Bonito road passes between Pueblo Alto and New Alto to continue northward. Apparently, Pueblo Alto was the most important crossroads or terminus for the entire Chaco road system. It also occupies a vital position in the visual communication network.

With this road and signal configuration in mind and taking into consideration the great proportion of storage and work rooms in Pueblo Alto, it is not difficult to make a case for its function as a trading or redistribution center for at least the northern portion of the Chaco Plateau. It would be interesting to ascertain whether or not some of the towns just south of Chaco Canyon were as obviously critical to the economics of the southern part of the plateau.

An experiment with subsurface probing by radar was conducted at Pueblo Alto and several other Chaco ruins by the Stanford Research Institute with the cooperation of the University of Pennsylvania Museum.[15] At Pueblo Alto, a ground-penetrating radar device mounted on a cart was pulled over the plaza area of the ruin. Data from the movable radar unit were plotted, and the position of the cart was tracked simultaneously in a nearby portable laboratory. Areas where the radar signal indicated subsurface anomalies were plotted on a contour map or an aerial photograph of the site and marked on the ground. By crossing and recrossing the plaza in a number of places, small isolated areas and linear groupings were identified. Upon excavating the designated locations, walls and other buried features were encountered at some of the areas pinpointed by the radar unit.

Electronic equipment also was used to assist in verifying the existence of prehistoric garden plots just to the east of Chetro Ketl (fig. 70) which illustrate a fundamental aspect of Pueblo III life.[16] Aerial photographs of the region had pinpointed a section of the canyon floor that stood out distinctly from its surroundings; furthermore, it seemed to be crisscrossed by lines, suggesting that it had been gridded. An electronic magnetometer was run over several transects through the area to determine whether soil density changes had occurred as a result of disturbance of the alluvium by prehistoric farming activities. Data from the magnetometer were

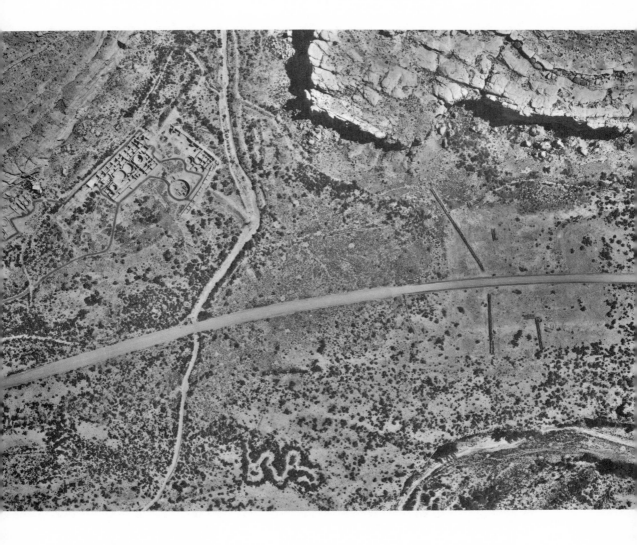

Figure 70. Aerial view of the Chetro Ketl field. It is the sparsely vegetated area to the right of the picture which is bisected by the modern road. Chetro Ketl is to the left. The photograph was taken while the Chaco Center was conducting magnetometer tests and trenching the site. *Courtesy of the National Park Service*

analyzed by computer and printed out on a contour map. Rectangular features apparent in the magnetic contours were the same size as those visible on the aerial photos and did seem to indicate former raised earthen borders around tracts where irrigation water occasionally had been impounded.

Trenches, then, were excavated along the magnetometer traverses and elsewhere within the confines of the field. Their vertical faces were carefully troweled and brushed to bring out any subtle differences in stratigraphy. By this means, a group of flat garden plots, surrounded by low earthen borders, came to light. They are estimated to have extended over about twelve acres. Analysis of the sediments covering the gridded plots indicated that the field had been irrigated by waters from the Chaco Wash, as well as by runoff from side canyons, because water-deposited soils from both sources were present on top of the gardens. Field checks located a diversion dam and a canal in the rincón to the northeast that led water on to a portion of the field. Obviously, the borders around the gardens would only have been able to trap and hold floodwaters from the Chaco Wash before the wash was as deeply entrenched as it is now. It is not obvious whether the entrenched plots were first built and then taken out of use because Chaco Wash became too deep or whether both systems were used simultaneously to supplement one another.

Another significant achievement of the Chacoans in Pueblo III first became apparent during the excavation of Site 29SJ423 (fig. 71). The ruin is predominately Basket Maker III in age, but after the original village had run its course, a Pueblo III structure was placed over the earlier remains. Immediately to the north of its already discussed Great Kiva, a curved mound of rubble suggested the presence of another such structure. However, when clearing of the area commenced, a low wall of a style of masonry not known until the eleventh century was uncovered. It obviously was not a product of Basket Maker III people. Upon completion of the excavation, the curved wall measured forty-eight feet long and is believed to have originally stood about two feet high. In the floor of the walled area a shallow hole had been dug to bedrock, and a stone bowl had been placed in it. The receptacle was covered by a large stone slab with a rectangular hole in its center (fig. 72). The hole had been neatly worked with a flange to hold a thin stone lid. When the lid was removed, the bowl was found to contain 146 small turquoise beads (fig. 73). Careful excavation around the cache recovered an additional quantity of beads and partially worked fragments of turquoise, a few unworked bits of shale, azurite, and shell, a complete shell bracelet, and a small pottery container holding a single bead of turquoise.

The style of coursed masonry in the wall definitely places its construc-

Figure 71. Pueblo III shrine–signal station at Site
29SJ423. It consists of the curved masonry wall and a
cache beneath the stack of horizontal slabs to the right
of the center of the cleared area in the photograph. The
circular pits at center and lower right are underlying
Basket Maker structures. Peñasco Blanco at upper left.
Courtesy of the National Park Service

Figure 72. The stone slab covering the cache at Site 29SJ423. The lid is in place in the rectangular opening in the slab. *Courtesy of the National Park Service*

tion in Pueblo III times. The associated cache of luxury goods implies that the feature had been a shrine or location for some kind of ritual. Another aspect of this unique site is its location, which affords clear views of the distant eastern and western horizons. The locale would have been ideal for a sun watcher's observation of the equinox and for the results, and any other messages, to be quickly transmitted for miles in all directions.[17]

While the supposed shrine-signaling station was being investigated, the excavators recalled that several other similar sites, also situated in locations with commanding views, had been recorded by the survey crews. These were reexamined and found to be in line-of-sight with one another, with Site 29SJ423, and with many of the large Pueblo III towns. These included a ruin at the westernmost tip of West Mesa, which had

Figure 73. The stone bowl which was embedded in the soil beneath the opening in the slab and which contained 146 turquoise beads. *Courtesy of the National Park Service*

been identified by the survey as a Navajo medicine hogan. Upon testing, it was determined that the structure actually is of Pueblo III age and that its characteristics and location support the hypothesis of its having been a shrine-signal station. Furthermore, it became evident that the locales for these structures had been carefully chosen, and that had the buildings been placed only short distances away, the visual contacts would have been impossible. Additional research and actual functional checking of the system have added other signaling stations to the network, tying together all of the major Chaco communities, plus the principal outlying towns and some of the lesser ones as well.

In determining the relationships of the classic towns to the visual communications system, an interesting fact came to light. In many cases, the only spot in a ruin from which another town or a signaling station can be seen is its highest point, frequently the top of a tower kiva. This may account for at least one use of these specialized chambers. One canyon floor town, Una Vida, is so located against the north cliff that it is not visible to other towns or signal places. However, the Great Kiva Kin Nahasbas, is situated a short distance away on the top of a hill from which there is visual contact with a signal station and with the tower kiva in Una Vida's west wing. It may be speculated that the enormous task of placing the Great Kiva on a steep hill, where it had to be excavated into bedrock, was due to the necessity of bringing Una Vida into the communication system.

Additional investigations may verify the assumption that the line-of-sight network linked many communities throughout the Chaco Plateau, including some along the San Juan River, and possibly extended to settlement centers as far north as the Mesa Verde country and to the vicinity of Zuñi to the south. When combined with the pattern of roads, the two systems of communication provided means for rapidly relaying news over a large territory and for facilitating the movement of peoples and goods over great distances. Together with other accomplishments of the Chacoans during their cultural apogee, they underscore possible highly organized forms of leadership and control that were felt in communal actions and economic development.

As excavation of a series of scattered sites exemplary of the various Anasazi culture stages in Chaco Canyon progressed, it was felt that a better understanding of prehistoric behavior, subsistence patterns, utilization of resources, and the like, might be grasped if one discrete geographic zone harboring a complete Chaco Anasazi continuum of sites could be located and the entire sequence excavated or thoroughly tested. Such a project would allow human events to be judged through time in a single environmental setting, rather than drawing conclusions from activities that took place in diverse environments. Of course, in studying the totality of Chaco culture, it is necessary to be aware of the differences between canyon bottom and mesa top living, and even of the cultural variations between those who dwelt on the north and south sides of the canyon. Since most of Chaco's ruins are within the canyon itself, it was deemed appropriate that a section of the canyon proper be selected.

After reviewing the recorded distribution of sites and conducting some tests, a rincón on the south side of Chaco Wash almost opposite the National Park Service Visitor Center was chosen for the experiment. The name Marcia's Rincón evolved for the area because Marcia Truell, a Chaco Center staff member, led investigations there for several field sessions. The small side canyon exhibited the proper range of sites, one of which, the Three-C Site at the old C.C.C. installation, previously had been dug by Gordon Vivian. Furthermore, the ruins were easily accessible, an important factor in setting up a long-range program, and they offered promise of being developed into a worthy interpretive feature for the monument. There are the remains of nine closely spaced settlements in the rincón, of which the Chaco Center excavated three and sampled three others.[18] Concurrent with the archaeological research, geologists and biologists analyzed in detail the physiography and ecology of the small rincón. The coordinated archaeological and environmental determinations eventually will result in an in-depth analysis of the evolution of Anasazi culture in one Chaco neighborhood.

In addition to excavating a chronological sequence of Chaco ruins, Chaco Center scientists undertook a variety of other field studies. One was to reexamine seven large masonry-walled fireboxes which Judd had encountered near Pueblo Bonito. One was circular; the others, rectangular. They averaged some four feet in greatest diameter or length and stood about two feet high. Judd had reported that all were filled with fire-reddened sand and pieces of charcoal but nothing else.[19] It was reasoned that if bits of calcined bone or bone ash could be discovered in or near them, the fireboxes might have been places for cremation of the dead, thereby accounting for the lack of burials in or around the city. It turned out that Judd had been correct. Neither burned bone nor bone ash came to light, leaving the mystery of Pueblo Bonito burials unsolved.

During the early phases of the archaeological survey of Chaco Canyon, a unique group of ten sites, characterized by remnants of oval or circular stone walls, was seen along the flat terraces above the north canyon rim between Pueblo Bonito and Wijiji. Subsequently, several others were identified along the canyon cliff tops. Most of them were within sight of a Chaco town or Great Kiva, and there were access routes between the stone circles and the communities or ceremonial centers. When the shallow sandy deposits that had drifted around several of them had been cleared away, it was seen that the walls of masonry or stone slabs had been laid upon bare exposures of bedrock. The circular walls ranged from thirty to ninety feet in greatest diameter and were estimated originally to have had a height of about two feet. Most of these sites had small, shallow basins cut into their floors. The circles invariably contained an assemblage of small, irregularly shaped ground sandstone artifacts that were faceted as though they were intended to be used as abraders or smoothing implements. Possibly the circles may have been craft centers or dance arenas to which qualified individuals came from nearby pueblos or Great Kivas to prepare ritual paraphernalia and perform ceremonies away from the eyes of the uninitiated. Similar stone circles have been found in other Anasazi population centers, such as Mesa Verde.[20]

In order to obtain a better perspective on the affiliations between the peoples who lived in or near Chaco Canyon and those who resided in surrounding localities, the Chaco Center ran a series of surveys over portions of the Chaco Plateau and made a literature search of published and unpublished reports about other archaeological work in those areas. The studies identified a sprinkling of ruins over contiguous areas that in plan, wall construction, and pottery assemblages reinforce their Bonito Phase connections. They are modest to medium-sized communities, many of which are spaced along or at the ends of the Chaco road network and are in divergent environmental zones.[21]

Some of the outliers are near extensive expanses of land suitable for farming, others are close to wooded tracts, and still others are in regions that support animal and plant life and have geological features at variance with those in Chaco Canyon. Therefore, these adjoining regions likely were important in the greater Chaco economic scheme that provided necessities and raw materials, such as timber for buildings and stones for tools and ornaments, to the populace in Chaco Canyon, as well as over the entire plateau. It even is conceivable that at times of intensified local activities, for example harvesting, planting, or road building, labor forces could have been drawn from the outlands.

Spreading horticultural endeavors over the Chaco Plateau and controlling the dispersal of goods not immediately needed would have tended to balance out the vagaries of nature typical of the region. When people in one area had a poor growing season, others in different geographic situations might have been successful enough to produce abundances. A formalized method of exchange would have made life easier for all those living in Chaco Canyon and over its entire sphere of influence. Perhaps the plan was contrived so that plateau-wide surpluses of food would have been brought together in the commodious depositories of the Chaco towns. When considering the total number of storage units in the Bonito Phase pueblos, it appears that they offered much more square footage than would have been needed for only locally produced products.

The Navajo occupation of Chaco Canyon brings the history of the Indian in this part of New Mexico up to the present. David Brugge undertook this study by correlating documented history, archaeological clues, and oral traditions to attain a fair chronology of events—but one which in parts is clouded by inconsistencies.[22] One of the problems goes back to the variations in usage of place names in the early historical accounts. For instance, one document supposedly places the Navajos in the Chaco region in the 1620s. Notwithstanding, tree-ring dates for the earliest known Chaco Navajo remains indicate their initial occupation to have occurred almost a century later.

Based upon a composite of these diverse threads of information, Brugge believes the Navajos first settled in the Chaco country in the early 1700s. However, they were in the greater Southwest several centuries earlier as part of a group of Athapascan speakers who immigrated from the north some time after Anasazi culture had passed its climax. Being nomads, the Athapascans depended upon hunting and foraging for a livelihood. Those who came in contact with the Anasazi gradually acquired some sedentary practices, including rudimentary horticulture. These were the Navajos. The others, who emerged in the historic era as the Apaches, clung to their ancestral nomadic way of life, later intensified with the adoption of the Spanish-introduced horse.

The Navajos were slow to give up some of their aggressive ways, deeply rooted in their old style of life, and found themselves periodically at war with the Pueblos, Spaniards, Mexicans, and finally the Americans. Recall that it was a United States military foray against the Navajos in 1849 that led to Lieutenant Simpson's first detailed account of the Chaco ruins. In 1864, most of the troublesome Navajos were rounded up by forces under the command of Col. Kit Carson and were removed to captivity at Fort Sumner in east central New Mexico. After remaining there for four years, where they suffered from illness, hunger, homesickness, and the misery of confinement, the Navajos were allowed to return to what is the present Navajo Nation.

By the time the Navajos took up residence in Chaco Canyon, they already had adopted many traits from the peoples about them. They herded sheep, goats, and some cattle and horses, and cultivated small plots of corn, beans, pumpkins, watermelons, chili, and possibly wheat and cotton. Usually they lived in traditional hogans, that is, conical earth-covered affairs built over a framework of forked poles. Sometimes they erected the small houses of stone, wood, and mud that they had observed being used by the Pueblos. They built rock-walled corrals to confine their livestock. Navajo settlements rarely accommodated more than one or two extended families and typically were placed in secluded locations. The rincones of Chaco Canyon and the rock-bordered terraces above the canyon were favored places, possibly because defense and protection from inclement weather were important considerations in selecting a house site. Serapes, blankets, sashes, and cloth were woven from wool and cotton, and buckskin also was used for clothing. Baskets and a small amount of pottery were made. Weaponry comprised bows, arrows, and lances. Through trade with Pueblos and Spaniards, they obtained such articles as knives, hoes, needles, cloth, beads, pottery, and tobacco.

Navajo social and religious customs probably closely paralleled those followed today. In all probability, social organization was based on kinship and placed women in a position of high status. Extended families were linked into neighboring cooperative groups and those in turn into matrilineal clans. Local leaders were men respected for their age, integrity, and wisdom who gave advice but had no formal means of control. Religious ceremonies emphasized rites of passage performed at birth, puberty, marriage, and death, and curing rites. Specialists conducted such ceremonies, but group participation was important if not necessary.

Like the Navajo as a whole, those who resided in Chaco continued to alter certain aspects of their pattern of life in response to additional innovations, greater contact with the outside world, and government-imposed controls and treaties. Most major adaptation in basic orientation had taken place before and during the exile to Fort Sumner. Guns, alcohol, Indian Agents, wheeled vehicles, job opportunities, education, and tribal organization have been responsible for many changes. A few Navajo families lived within the boundaries of Chaco Canyon National Monument until 1948, when they were excluded from the area. However, many still dwell in their scattered homes close-by. Some have found permanent or seasonal employment with the National Park Service.

One Navajo settlement, the Doll House Site, was excavated by Brugge for the Chaco Center. Located on a bench at the north edge of the Chacra Mesa opposite Wijiji, it was selected for examination because the surface remains indicated a lengthy occupation. Excavations proved this to be the case. The ten hogans, and several houses, granaries, and corrals were arranged in four chronologically distinct clusters thought to range from the mid-eighteenth century to the early 1900s. A more-or-less continuous occupation by a single kin group is implied. Time of habitation was estimated from styles of hogans and houses and types of artifacts and refuse found about the site. It is the only excavated Navajo ruin within the monument. Some parts of this former homesite have been stabilized and may be examined by visitors to Chaco Canyon.

In 1960, Gwinn Vivian completed and reported upon an archaeological reconnaissance of a portion of the Chacra Mesa south of Chaco Canyon, where he identified many early Navajo settlements and some historic Pueblo structures dating from the 1680–92 Pueblo refugee period, when many Pueblo families sought escape from the Spaniards by settling among the Navajo.[23] After the 1692 reentry of the Spaniards into the Southwest, or soon thereafter, most of the Pueblo peoples returned to their former homes, but by that time, an exchange of some cultural attributes between these two Indian groups had occurred.

In order to put together a comprehensible picture of aboriginal occupation, Chaco Center staff members have spent three times more hours in the laboratory than in the field, methodically cleaning, mending, preserving, cataloging, photographing, and, by the best means available, studying all the evidence gathered with so much expenditure of time, effort, and money. Herein lies the intellectual yeast with which life can be infused into the dry shreds of material wares. This goal demands all of a researcher's perceptive faculties, but it is absolutely necessary that he attempt to reach it, for just counting ruins or picking up potsherds is merely exercise. To his aid have come the expertise of scholars in related disciplines such as geology, chemistry, biology, astronomy, and physical anthropology, and the marvels of modern computer technology.

One such specialized laboratory analysis has been devoted to ceramics because they comprise a large proportion of the artifact collection, amounting to hundreds of thousands of potsherds and a number of whole or restorable vessels. As a result, older taxonomies and technical descriptions for some dozen types of decorated and culinary Chaco pottery have been refined, design styles have been outlined, sources of raw materials have been determined, comparisons with pottery vocabularies in other Anasazi domains have been made, and economic and social patterns involving pottery—and through it, other aspects of material culture—have been suggested. These in-depth studies have shown that during Basket Maker III and into Pueblo I times, Chaco seems to have shared a regional pottery tradition that included the Four Corners country to the north and also to have supplemented local output by obtaining a considerable quantity of clay utensils from that source. Possibly the trade alignment changed during the Pueblo II period because many intrusive wares from the Red Mesa Valley to the south and the Chuska Valley toward the southwest found their way into Chaco households. About A.D. 1050, during Pueblo III, a large amount of pottery from the Four Corners again appeared in Chaco. Despite looking elsewhere for most of the ceramic containers they needed, the Chacoans continued to produce some pottery themselves. The Chaco types usually were quite similar in form and decorative enrichment to the imported ones but were distinguishable from them in the use of local clay and tempering additives. Also, decorative pigments derived from minerals produced a different appearing end product than those from the plant juices typical of Mesa Verde pottery, although in both instances a black-on-white ware emerged. One unique type of Chaco pottery was the tall, straight-sided jar found in such great numbers in Pueblo Bonito and occasionally in other Chaco towns. The fine lined, hatchured design that appears upon some of them has elements that were deeply ingrained in local conventions, but the cylindrical form may point to influence from the south.[24]

From the first serious interest in the Chaco Canyon antiquities, the question of possible impact of Mexican or Mesoamerican concepts upon them has been voiced.[25] At first, this idea was suggested by archaeologists' greater familiarity with the southern agriculturally based high cultures and the tradition of their having evolved out of an amorphous northern culture. Later, as excavations have continued over the past century, the list of possible Mesoamerican traits steadily has grown longer and now includes such architectural features as rubble-cored masonry, square columns used in colonnades, circular structures in the form of tower kivas and tri-walled units, seating discs beneath roof support posts, and T-shaped doorways. Among ceramic objects, there are cylinder jars, effigy vessels, incense burners, stamps or seals, and certain design motifs which appear alien to the usual Anasazi conventions. Copper bells, iron pyrites used for mosaics, shell trumpets, shell beads, shell bracelets, macaws and parrots, turkey burials, bone pins, ceremonial wooden canes, altar components of wood, turquoise beads and pendants, turquoise mosaic sets, decorative techniques of cloisonné and mosaics, water control means such as dams, canals, and reservoirs, the roads and signal stations, and the alignments of architectural and other features for the purpose of observing and recording astronomical data, all of which have been noted in Chaco Canyon, are much more common in central Mexico. However, the contact with the south which may have been responsible for diffusion of these cultural expressions to Chaco probably was by way of the important pueblo of Casas Grandes in northern Chihuahua. Between A.D. 900 and 1200, it was converted by powerful Toltec merchant families, or *pochteca,* into an outpost trading and production center incorporated within a comprehensive economic webbing spreading over a large part of Mexico and Central America.[26] The parallels between Casas Grandes and Chaco Canyon include a sudden building spurt in the eleventh century with an overlay of seemingly exotic traits, a large town surrounded by smaller settlements, the installation of well-engineered water management systems, networks of roads, and signal stations. The overt manifestations of Toltec religion so prominent at Casas Grandes did not appear at Chaco, nor is there evidence for the level of organization and artistry shown in the Chihuahua center.

Possibly the Pueblo III culture of Chaco Canyon and the Toltec-implanted lifeway of the north Mexican trading entrepots were achieved independently and only came in direct contact because they both were in the merchandising business. Learning that the southern merchant-traders wished to acquire turquoise, and were willing to trade rare and valued items for it, the Chaco Anasazi could have expanded their already widespread exchange routes, which encompassed areas where turquoise was mined, to include the new marketplaces, such as Casas Grandes. Acquisition of turquoise, and perhaps other goods desired by the Mexican traders, was intensified, and stockpiles were assembled in the Chaco towns. Some of the semiprecious stone was fashioned into beads, pendants, and mosaic sets by Chaco craftsmen, but quantities of unworked turquoise also were gathered for exchange. Periodically, Chaco merchants transported their products and materials to the southern markets, traversing lands that in places were even more barren than Chaco, and bartered them for exotic articles produced or assembled there. Likewise, traders from the Casas Grandes country may have made the arduous trek north to the San Juan Basin. Realistically viewed, Chaco Canyon need not have been an actual cog in the Toltec organization of trading outposts to have been influenced by Mexican cultures, for shock waves emanating from an advanced epicenter have a way of reverberating outward to engulf otherwise removed entities.

News, ideas, and technological knowledge undoubtedly passed along the trade routes as readily as did material things, and the traveling salesmen of the times most likely played important roles in cultural diffusion. By that means, eyewitness accounts of Mesoamerican religious rituals, irrigation schemes, architectural embellishments, communication means, and other strange wonders may have reached Chaco. The descriptions may have inspired and encouraged local technicians and leaders to adopt those measures that would be beneficial to the Chacoans, such as new construction styles, ways to increase crop production, or means to improve intercourse between Chaco Canyon and its outliers. The discussions of the elaborate ceremonial rites of the Mexicans must have been listened to with fascination and awe, but Anasazi traditions being deeply ingrained, the foreign mannerisms had little impact upon the Chacoans. Moreover, the spread of religious beliefs is usually accomplished through missionary zeal or political or military dominance, none of which are recognizable in Chaco. Possibly a few alien sacred attributes temporarily colored local attitudes, but they did not have a lasting effect. Considering all the evidence, the Chaco people seem to have dealt with and benefited from contacts with the Toltec frontier in northern Mexico, but never to have been assimilated into that exploitative apparatus.

It is presumed that much of the foreign luxury goods brought to Chaco remained in the hands of the merchants, religious practitioners, and residents who could afford it; however, some items were dispersed throughout the Chaco sphere of interaction. Perhaps a stratified social structure evolved, based primarily upon occupational specialization and participation in particular economic activities. It may have elevated those in religious or secular leadership roles to high status. Below them were the merchants, the technicians, and the common laborers.[27]

Finally, attention should be called to recent investigations which have been aimed at confirming the widely held idea that the ancient Chacoans, as well as other Anasazi, made observations of the solar system in order to devise ritual and agricultural calendars. Behind this hypothesis is the knowledge that the modern Pueblos make such observations. Hence it is assumed that the practice was appreciably more elaborated in late Prehispanic times, with the sun, morning star, and moon were likely to have been regarded by the ancients as having direct bearing upon their seasonal rhythms of life. In Chaco, concerted efforts have been made to locate possible horizon observing stations, to ascertain precise alignments of features in the Chaco towns and Great Kivas, and to examine examples of rock art believed to be depictions of heavenly bodies. Many differing viewpoints of aboriginal astronomical knowledge, calendrical schemes, and levels of scientific expertise have resulted.

Observation sites consisting of artificial or natural features, or combinations of the two, that line up with the rising sun at winter or summer solstices have been found at several towns and Great Kivas, often in or near localities marked by rock art symbols representing the sun. For instance, at Pueblo Bonito two unusual third-story windows could have been used to record the winter solstice, since the view through them aligns with the point on the eastern horizon where the sun rises on that particular day. Also, painted onto the face of the cliff near Peñasco Blanco is a pictograph of a handprint, a horizontal upside-down new moon, the morning star, and the sun. Some astronomers have suggested that this possibly is a record of the advent of a supernova, or an extraordinarily bright star, in the sky of A.D. 1054. However, ethnographic evidence has been quoted to discount that interpretation and to support the belief that the site was a sun watcher's station for making observations pertinent to the solstices and the agricultural cycle. In another place, two adjacent spiral pictographs are bisected vertically by descending shafts of light at summer and winter solstices which penetrate two crevices between three rock slabs. The construct also may have been used to record the sun's movements throughout the year.

The orientation and the arrangement and number of wall niches in some of Chaco's Great Kivas have been of special concern. Sunlight has been observed to pass through certain doorways or windows in the walls of Casa Rinconada and strike particular niches at solstice times, and the alignment of selected pairs of niches and distant natural features is directed toward the equinoctial sunrise. The niches in the Great Kiva at Chetro Ketl are suspected of having been part of an ingenious calendar system, according to one researcher. If a pair of markers, one for the sun and one for the moon, were moved in a prescribed manner about the twenty-nine wall recesses, it would have been possible to operate a digital calendar to monitor the phases of the moon and the heliacal risings of Venus, to predict eclipses, and to specify dates for ceremonial and farming activities. The question has been raised as to the possible use of tower kivas, and perhaps tri-walled structures as well, as observatories from which calendar priests traced the movements of the celestial bodies. If this were the case, it is an interesting parallel with Mesoamerica, where round towers were dedicated to heavenly deities and used to make astronomical calculations. Had the Chaco towers also functioned as signal stations, as has been proposed, many messages from them must have had to do with information derived from watching the skies. Clustering of the important Chaco towns along the north side of the canyon has been interpreted by some to have been due to the fact that there is better visibility of the heavens and the horizon from that side of the canyon, and that the south-facing settlements received more direct sun and solar radiation from the cliffs during the winter months than did communities on the south side of the declivity.

A factor which some archaeoastronomers have taken into consideration when making their calculations, and others have not, is that successive renovation and stabilization of the ruins may have altered somewhat the original appearance of walls, doors, windows, and other features. Moreover, passage of the sun's rays through wall openings designated as having been important in astronomical observations in several kivas and pueblos originally may have been obstructed by roofs or contiguous walls.

The consensus is that Chacoans used astronomical phenomena as a basis for regulating the annual round of religious rites and for predicting seasonal changes that would affect the cleaning and repair of irrigation works, the preparation of fields, and the planting of crops. Evaluations of the degree of sophistication of astronomical knowledge ranges from simple sun watching in order to forecast the seasons, to a level sufficient to support an attenuated version of the Mesoamerican calendar system, to the ability to make precise observations and to employ computer-like counting devices for the purpose of predicting solstices, eclipses, and the movement of sundry celestial bodies.[28]

7 MAN AND NATURE IN CHACO CANYON

A syncopated parade of observers has amassed a formidable array of archaeological data on Chaco Canyon in the century that has passed since William H. Jackson penned the first comprehensive account. Although the goal of all has been an understanding of Anasazi civilization, the resulting interpretations of all this cultural conglomeration inevitably have differed, often discordantly. The summation to follow is based upon what appears to be a reasonably harmonious and scientifically acceptable composite of many of these views. It is our interpretation of the evidence. It can be assumed that when the Chaco Center completes the detailed analyses of the vast array of ecological and archaeological data it has gathered, somewhat different versions of natural phenomena and human events may well emerge.

THE LAND

Chaco Canyon is situated in the San Juan Basin, a major geographical configuration including most of northwestern New Mexico and a portion of southwestern Colorado. It is a circular, saucer-shaped depression about one hundred miles in diameter, whose relatively flat landscape rises to bordering mountains on the north, east, and west. On the south, where there is no well-defined edge to the basin, it is marked by a series of uplifts. The San Juan River and its tributaries carry runoff from the basin to the Colorado River to the west.

One of the tributaries to the San Juan is the Chaco Wash, an ephemeral stream sometimes dignified by the name Chaco River because of its considerable length and the violence of its floods. It is about 150 miles long and drains an area of some 4,500 square miles in the southern half of the San Juan Basin called the Chaco Plateau. This landform, whose beds rise gently to the south, is limited on the north by the San Juan River, on the east by the high country of the Continental Divide and the Canyon Largo, on the west by the Chuska Valley, and to the south by the steep-sided Dutton Plateau. The Chaco Plateau, between 5,300 and 7,500 feet in elevation, is dominated by wide, flat valleys, frequently bordered by cuestas, sloping plains whose sandstone cliffs form the north sides of the valleys. The erosive actions of wind and water have sculptured the topography into ridges, knolls, buttes, and mesas riding over 100 feet above the general plateau area. Rock exposures are mainly Upper Cretaceous sandstone and shale. Few fossils are found in the walls of Chaco Canyon, mainly casts of a giant alga, shells, and shark's teeth, attesting to the marine origin of the deposits. On the Chaco Plateau to the north of Chaco Canyon, however, there are abundant remains of petrified wood and fossils of fish, turtles, crocodiles, and dinosaurs.

The Chaco Wash bisects the plateau from east to west and, after traversing the twenty-two-mile length of Chaco Canyon in its upper course, swings sharply to the north to join the San Juan River. For most of its extent it is a typical Southwestern dry stream bed, or arroyo, which flows only after rapid melting of unusually deep snows or heavy downpours of rain. Within the last eighty years, it has become deeply entrenched throughout Chaco Canyon, forming a winding cut 20 to 60 feet deep and 75 to 300 feet wide. Flood waters up to 9 feet deep have roared down the canyon in recent years after hard summer rain storms.

One of the few gorges in the Chaco Plateau, Chaco Canyon was the seat of the Chaco Anasazi culture, although a few of the primary communities were peripheral to the canyon proper and it is now realized that an integrated "Chaco system" existed over much of the Chaco Plateau. Chaco Canyon National Monument, including a nine-mile stretch of the lower Chaco Canyon and four detached areas, encompasses an area of about thirty-three square miles, slightly over 21,500 acres. Most surrounding lands belong to the Navajo Tribe or to individual Navajo allotees. It is the seven-mile extension of Chaco Canyon between Peñasco Blanco on the west to Wijiji on the east that was the most densely occupied area of any of comparable size in the entire Anasazi world during the twelfth century. At that time, eleven of the large Chaco towns and numerous small villages thrived in that short segment of canyon bottom and on the mesas immediately to the north and south. There, the Chaco Wash has cut through the Mesa Verde group of sandstones and shales of Upper Cretaceous age to form a canyon one-half to three-quarters of a mile wide. However, excavation of the canyon is a process long since interrupted, for the wash nowhere flows on bedrock today nor does it cut laterally against the walls of the declivity. The process of canyon cutting was followed by a period of deposition resulting in the present valley fill. Elevation at Pueblo Bonito is 6,123.5 feet above sea level.

At present, the canyon floor has thick, sandy deposits mixed with clays and silts contributed by the Chaco Wash. Those soils are more impermeable than are the more purely sandy soils of the mesa tops and intercliff slopes above the canyon. Walls of the main stem of the canyon rise abruptly 50 to almost 150 feet and are bordered on both sides by series of low, steplike cliffs. The north wall of the inner canyon is steep and only slightly indented; the south wall is less abrupt and is broken by branching gulches. This asymmetrical nature of the canyon is similar to many east-west trending depressions in northern New Mexico and is the result of several factors. Most important is that the southerly rise of the sedimentary beds exposes the fairly hard Cliff House sandstone at the base of the north escarpment side, forming an almost vertical cliff, while the same formation is 50 or more feet above the canyon floor on the south side. The south cliff, therefore, is undermined with relative ease by sapping of the underlying soft Allison sandstones and carbonaceous shales, causing the fall of large, angular blocks from the harder stratum above. These blocks litter the talus slopes created by the erosion of the soft rock at the base of the canyon wall. Consequently, numerous relatively large canyons have developed. In the vicinity of Fajada Butte and opposite Pueblo del Arroyo the south canyon wall has been completely destroyed, creating broad gaps which allow easy access to the canyon from that direction. The present road entering Chaco Canyon from the south passes through the Fajada Gap. Another aspect of the difference between north and south sides of Chaco Canyon is that the south side is more shaded, a condition that leads to lower evaporation of moisture from snows and rains, which in turn has resulted in a sparse plant cover on the talus slopes. In contrast, the north wall, with its face exposed to the sun, is relatively dry. Forces of erosion also are in full swing against the sheer north cliffs but, since no talus slopes exist there, chunks and debris loosened from the wall fall clear from the rock surface and are strewn along the canyon floor next to the cliffs. Northside tributary canyons are short. Many are mere indentations in the cliffs, or the type commonly called rincons.

The uplift bordering Chaco Canyon on the south is Chacra Mesa. Away from the canyon it is a fairly flat land with steep edges whose surface is cut by minor drainages which, as noted above, have severed the mesa in a few locations and have carved unusual isolated buttes and jagged cliffs. The Chaco Plateau north of Chaco Canyon is a plain broken by wide valleys and arroyos and encompasses several extensively eroded areas, or badlands, to the north near the San Juan River.

Precipitation in Chaco Canyon has averaged 8.71 inches over the past forty years. Half of it occurs as brief but intense thunderstorms during the months of June through September. Winter snows account for about one-quarter of the total, the balance of the annual precipitation coming in the form of general rains in the fall and spring. A long-time precipitation pattern of two to five years below average separated by a single year far above the mean has been observed. Today there are few small springs and seeps in Chaco's side canyons, and on the mesa tops countless waterholes, or *tinajas,* can be seen. These are natural reservoirs cut into the sandstone exposures by running water. Although the *tinajas* collect water only during periods of runoff, they are present in sufficient numbers to have provided the prehistoric inhabitants of the Chaco with some of their water supply. Elsewhere on the moderately arid Chaco Plateau annual precipitation ranges from 6 inches on the west to 15 inches in the higher elevations to the east. Temperatures in the canyon fluctuate widely both daily and annually. Winters can be cold, summers hot but with temperatures seldom exceeding 100°F. Daily fluctuations result in generally warm days and cool to cold nights, typically a temperate climate. Winds, especially strong in late spring, are commonly southwesterly.

The Upper Sonoran vegetation of the Chaco Plateau varies according to combinations of moisture, exposure, soil, elevation, slope, and ground water. Generally speaking, the higher elevations to the east are blanketed with extensive grasslands and stretches of sagebrush in open plains. Farther up on the mesas and ridges are stands of pinyon pine and juniper. A few scattered growths of ponderosa pine and Douglas fir dot the Chacra Mesa. Lower portions of the plateau have some sagebrush, but more often the vegetation cover is a scant mixture of cacti, four-wing saltbush, rabbitbrush, and tumbleweed and other weeds. In addition to the above complex, in the wide alluvial valleys there is greasewood and the introduced tamarisk. Along the ephemeral streams cottonwoods, willows, and sedges flourish.

The vegetation of Chaco Canyon is most lush within the entrenched edges of the Chaco Wash. There, cottonwoods, willows, tamarisk, and the common reed are found. Most of the cottonwoods and willows and all of the tamarisks were introduced into the canyon over thirty years ago for erosion control. In the past, under conditions of deposition rather than erosion at which time the stream flowed between low banks, marsh grasses, rushes, and canes probably would have been included with the cottonwoods and willows. Plant life on the canyon bottom is sparse in the center along the arroyo, because the alkaline, poorly drained clay flats support only scattered black greasewood, saltbush, rabbitbush, and a little sage and tumbleweed. Additionally, alluvial fans protruding into the canyon from the side canyons have a variety of grasses. In those tributaries, especially where there are seeps or standing water after summer rains, are relatively dense stands of golden current, squaw bush, some chokecherry, and a thick undercover of grasses and herbs. The north cliff and mesa tops bear a sprinkling of grasses mixed with rabbitbrush, Mormon tea, and yucca. To the south on the Chacra Mesa, plant life is more abundant and includes grasses, Mormon tea, and patches of juniper and pinyon pine.

The matter of the distribution of ponderosa pine in and around Chaco Canyon is particularly significant in light of the enormous number of timbers used in the erection of the great Chaco towns. Calculations reveal that perhaps 75,000 to 100,000 trees, predominately pines, were cut during the eleventh century alone for construction purposes.[1] Early travelers reported, and elderly Navajo informants recalled, that a few pines formerly grew in the better watered side canyons and rincons along the

Chaco. They long since have been cut for firewood. Judd found the roots of one that had stood in the west plaza of Pueblo Bonito.[2] Furthermore, an irregular distribution of pines across the Chaco Plateau from the Continental Divide into the badlands west of Chaco Canyon may represent the remnants of a previously continuous belt of the large conifers. The two relict stands of pines closest to Chaco Canyon today are on the edge of Chacra Mesa near the head of the canyon and on Ojo Alamo Wash twenty miles to the northwest. Douglas fir, also used in some quantity by the Chacoans, still grows in some locales on Chacra Mesa and most likely was more plentiful in the past.[3]

Rodents, such as cottontail rabbits, mice, ground squirrels, pocket gophers, kangaroo rats, and a colony of prairie dogs, dominate the present-day life on the canyon floor, in Chaco Wash, and along the mesa tops. This rodent population is preyed upon by a few bobcats, badgers, coyotes, fox, birds of prey, and snakes. Mule deer have made a comeback in the canyon in recent years. The jackrabbit replaces the cottontail on the open mesas and plains. South of the Chacra Mesa one occasionally can see a herd of pronghorn antelope.[4]

183

The face of the Chaco Plateau is undergoing major changes at this writing. Beneath the desert landscape lies an untold treasure in the form of fossil fuels that were of no consequence to the Anasazi but which are of paramount importance in feeding an energy-hungry economy. Oil and gas production, already developed on a fairly large scale, will be increased. Extensive shallow coal deposits will be removed by strip mining, and uranium mining by both stripping and driving shafts into the ground will be expanded. Highways and railroads already are being built. Coal gasification plants, power generating stations, and boom towns soon will replace the occasional trading post, Navajo hogans, and grazing herds of horses and sheep as the dominant view in the Chaco country. Active or proposed energy development completely encircles Chaco Canyon National Monument. Some of these energy companies are well aware of Chaco's archaeological uniqueness and are honestly seeking ways to prevent any damage to the sites or at least to mitigate unavoidable impact upon the many ruins and fossil deposits that exist outside the monument.

Nevertheless, there are many unknowns that could have irreparable effect upon the Chaco environment and its nonrenewable archaeological resources. The water supply for the monument could quickly dry up as a result of the dozens of deep wells contemplated by the developers, which in all likelihood will drop the presently tapped water table below the reach of the well now serving the monument. Strip mining could change the drainage pattern of the upper Chaco Wash and promote even greater run-off and more erosion in Chaco Canyon than at present. And the shock waves from blasting associated with coal and uranium mining taking place within a few miles of the monument boundaries could result in structural damage to those ruins with standing walls. Even the increased visitation to the monument that will come because of the improved road network and the establishment of several fair-sized communities in the vicinity will have their impact. Anticipating foreseeable problems, the National Park Service has planned new roads, trails, and facilities so that the expected rise in visitor traffic can be accommodated while the antiquities are properly protected and preserved.

Another problem that undoubtedly will arise will be that of further illegal collecting and digging in the thousands of ruins and fossil fields that lie near the scenes of new towns and development projects. Unless the National Park Service, other federal land management agencies, and the Navajo Nation are able to work cooperatively with the developers to create measures that would protect the archaeological and paleontological resources of the Chaco Plateau, the public stands to lose entirely some of the most significant evidence for the evolution of past animal life and human culture upon the North American continent.

PALEO-INDIANS

Archaeological, geological, and biological data provide solid reasons to believe that human migrations from Asia to the New World began about 10,000 B.C., and there is growing evidence that Asiatics made even earlier forays across the Bering Sea land bridge perhaps 30,000 or more years ago.[5] Present studies indicate that Paleo-Indians, following herds of now extinct mammals, especially mammoth (elephant) and long-horned bison, made their way down the North American continent during the closing stages of the Pleistocene, or Ice Age. They drifted down an ice-free corridor in western Canada into the continental United States. Due to an increase in moisture between about 9500 and 9000 B.C., savannas and grasslands expanded, thereby allowing mammoth, bison, horse, camel, tapirs, dire wolves, ground sloths, and other species to spread widely over the west. People followed, living upon those and other animals and the many plants around the lakes and swampy areas that existed at that time.[6]

Two types of Paleo-Indian archaeological sites are known in the Southwest: campsites, where families or small bands lived briefly or periodically, and kill sites, where hunters slaughtered and processed one or more large beasts. Campsites, usually on ridges or high places, contain fire-darkened hearths; a tool assemblage characterized by projectile points, various flaked stone implements for cutting, scraping, engraving, and drilling; a rare worked piece of bone; stone chips; pieces of broken tools; and food scraps. Kill sites frequently are found at the end of ponds or stream channels, in natural cul-de-sacs, or along deep gullies, where the animals could have been surprised and dispatched while mired in muck or after being driven over cliffs. Bones and partially articulated skeletons of the slain animals are encountered, together with stone projectile points that had tipped the hunters' spears and an occasional flaked stone knife wielded in the butchering process. Most early Paleo-Indian sites contain Clovis fluted projectile points, a large channel-flaked spear point, that had been directed at mammoths. Later Paleo-Indian locations yield Folsom points, a finely chipped fluted point, and a variety of contemporary unfluted types. Bison were the principal quarry of Folsom hunters.

Judging from observation of recent nomadic hunters and the information obtained from excavated Paleo-Indian sites, one may envision the early migrants as banded together into small socioeconomic groups whose routine was geared to cyclical movements designed to take advantage of the presence at certain seasons of migratory game and the ripening of edible plants. Campsites in favorable locations were returned to periodically. Temporary shelters of poles, brush, and perhaps hide were quickly erected and then as rapidly forsaken at the time of the next move. Depending upon the season, clothing could have varied from practically nothing to simple skin robes, garments, and footgear. Fire was essential for warmth, protection, and the preparation of tools and food. The dog was a companion, an aid in hunting, and maybe a beast of burden. Nonbreakable containers suitable for carrying were fashioned from hides and basketry. Preparation of tools from stone had been developed to an art. Special forms for a variety of tasks were carefully chipped from flints and chalcedonies. Skill in tool manufacture is particularly evident in the knives and points the Paleo-Indians made for their spears, especially the fluted Folsom point and several kinds of long, thin, leaf-shaped blades. An atlatl, a short piece of wood with a hook at one end, was used to hurl spears with greater force. Grasping the handle of this instrument and engaging the butt end of the spear in the hook, the hunter in effect lengthened his arm to attain greater leverage for delivering the missile. Fundamental magical, or religious, practices probably were followed to assure success in the hunt and solace in times of crisis.

No Paleo-Indian sites on the Chaco Plateau yet have produced either Clovis points or mammoth remains. The fact that the region is ringed by locales once utilized by Clovis hunters suggests that this tableland was not particularly attractive to mammoths or their pursuers. On the other hand, a number of clues of the somewhat later Folsom hunters are known on the Chaco Plateau, though none are in Chaco Canyon itself. After about

9000 B.C., the climate became drier, causing retraction of grasslands and inevitable withdrawal of the large Pleistocene creatures. Some 500 years later when more moist conditions returned, herds of long-horned bison grazed the savannas once trampled by the mighty mammoths providing food for the Folsom people. Another relatively dry cycle after 8000 B.C. induced an eastward movement of the symbiotic bison and human forager. At this juncture, the Chaco Plateau became suitable for hunting small mammals, reptiles, and birds and for collecting edible wild vegetal crops.

THE ARCHAIC STAGE

It is not believed that the Paleo-Indian hunters evolved into the hunters and collectors subsequently resident in northwestern New Mexico. Rather, it is presumed that after they had trekked east and northward out of the area, the territory they had occupied was filled by another group of wanderers, who were dedicated to a mode of life more in tune with the conditions then prevailing on the Chaco Plateau. This ubiquitous stage of American Indian development is called the Archaic. Its content varies from area to area within the present United States, mirroring man's adjustment to differing microcosms and divergent subsistence patterns. Wherever the Archaic has been met, it speaks of a generalized lifeway dependent upon a broad spectrum of foodstuffs and an unelaborated assortment of tools prerequisite to obtaining and processing them. A variation of this food collecting pattern, once called the Desert Culture, existed over the Desert West. It has been identified in most of the arid regions of the Great Basin, parts of California, Nevada, and much of the Southwest. Even though in some zones it may have been in place as early as 8500 B.C., it does not seem to have appeared in northwestern New Mexico until about 5500 B.C.

Until the emergence of the Anasazi tradition, Archaic culture in northwestern New Mexico can be traced through a sequence of accommodations to minor climatic changes made possible by the unstructured broad-based economy of the culture. Between about 5500 and 3500 B.C., there was less effective moisture than at present, and the itinerant gatherers had to depend to a great extent upon wild plant foods. After that time, a substantial increase in moisture promoted a proliferation of animal, as well as plant, foods, An early kind of corn was introduced some time between 1700 and 800 B.C.; however, it seems to have had little immediate effect upon the dietary habits of the Archaic people.

These nomads moved from one camp to another according to available food supplies and seasonal variations in weather. Chaco Canyon was within the range of some of them. There, campsites are found in and next to shallow rock shelters, on low mesas, in sand dunes, and beside ponds. Like those of the Paleo-Indians, their places of transitory residence are marked by hearths and fire-cracked rocks, stone tools for everyday activities, and implements for killing and processing lesser game. In addition, a group of artifacts not seen in the remains of the specialized hunters is invariably present, these being grinding and crushing devices for the preparation of foods from plants. Simple flat or shallow-basin metates, together with round, single-handed manos, were employed along with choppers and hammerstones for pulverizing and grinding seeds, nuts, and tubers. Unelaborated knives and scrapers for butchering and for cutting and smoothing wood and skins were made by chipping one or more edges of stone flakes. Basketry was woven; pottery was unknown. Smaller projectile points, not as well fashioned as those of the Paleo-Indians, imply the use of spears. The atlatl was still in vogue. Clothing also resembled that of their predecessors, but there probably was more reliance upon vegetal fibers than upon hides. Although the social, economic, and religious aspects of life were synchronized into a nomadic cultural framework, there are signs of an emerging appreciation for stationary life, for the seasonal camps were occupied for longer periods of time than before.[7]

187

EMERGENCE OF THE SOUTHWESTERN TRADITION

The domestication of maize, or corn, eventually led to a revolutionary change in life for most Southwestern Indians, causing a gradual shift from nomadism to sedentism. Between 3400 and 1000 B.C., a small-eared variety of corn native to southern Mexico, together with squash, had reached the southern sectors of the Southwest, very probably via peoples who lived in the *barrancas* of the Sierra Madre Occidental of western Mexico. Additional selective breeding and cultivation resulted in types of corn suited to the varied Southwestern climatic zones, including those with shorter growing seasons and minimal rainfall. In time, the range of the plant was pushed northward to engulf the San Juan Basin. It is no coincidence, therefore, that the millenium between 1000 B.C. and A.D. 1 saw the birth of the Southwestern tradition, not only there but farther south among the Hohokam of south central Arizona and the Mogollon of southwestern New Mexico and southeastern Arizona.[8]

Dietary habits of Archaic peoples in the northern Southwest tipped in favor of reliance upon domesticated plant foods, principally corn, squash, and pumpkins in the years between 500 B.C. and A.D. 1, bringing about the coalescing of traits now termed the Anasazi Culture. Concurrent with this horticultural focus, a need arose for more permanent shelters near garden plots in order to protect and tend the crops and for storage and preservation facilities. Hence, the first substantial habitations with built-in or nearby storage units came into existence. In short, through the addition of horticulture and houses to the Desert Culture base, there followed a sedentary routine in which larger numbers of individuals lived together in permanent settlements. Settled life did not mean the complete departure from the old foraging practices. Hunting and gathering continued; but on a somewhat restricted basis, in order to obtain meat and animal by-products and to collect accustomed vegetal materials for food, medicine, and fibers.

BASKET MAKER II

The earliest Anasazi, designated Basket Maker II by archaeologists, are well known in the San Juan Basin. Thus far, they have been found at only one site in Chaco Canyon. It contained no habitations and only a limited array of artifacts. Perhaps the Anasazi dependence upon horticulture caused them to concentrate in areas adjacent to the Chaco Plateau where, during the last few centuries before Christ, moisture was greater than about Chaco. Near Durango, in southern Colorado, they chose to dwell along the edges of well-watered canyons where the bottom-lands could be cultivated and the mountains could provide an abundance of game.[9] Also in such locales, their simple habitations could be grouped beneath protective rock overhangs or erected on prepared terraces along the tops of talus slopes banking cliff bases. Individual family abodes were built in an oval shape by embedding short sections of logs horizontally in a thick mud matrix to fashion walls of head height. Next, a flat roof of poles and adobe was placed across the tops of the walls. Mud-plastered floors were slightly concave and were outfitted with various combinations of such features as firepits, warming pits into which were placed rocks that had been heated outside the structure, storage pits, and granaries that consisted of pits dug into the floor and covered by beehive-shaped superstructures of sticks and mud. Entrance probably was through a small doorway in the cribbed walls.

Household refuse and the assortment of discarded or lost tools found in and near the houses excavated verifies the consumption of two domesticated plants, corn and squash or pumpkins, and the seeds of several uncultivated plants including amaranth, wild vetch, mustard, and sunflowers. Animal bones show that deer provided the bulk of meat eaten, followed by rabbits and porcupine. Both vegetal and animal products were relied upon for clothing and some kinds of tools. A specialized artifact for separating fiber from plant leaves for the preparation of cordage was made by notching the edge of deer scapulas and ribs into comb-like implements. The metates and manos essential for plant food preparation were numerous, as were projectile points, knives, scrapers, choppers, hammerstones, and gravers. Among the collection of objects fashioned from perishable materials, some of which were especially well-preserved in the rock shelters, were many lengths of cordage made of yucca fiber and a few of human or animal hair, pieces of tanned skins, sandals of rushes and yucca, matting, twined bags, coiled basketry, and fragments of cloth woven from yucca string wrapped either with strips of rabbit fur or downy turkey feathers. Atlatls, spears, a firedrill, and a well-preserved cradle board were of wood. Animal bone was used for awls, flakers, fleshers, gaming pieces, and beads. Pottery had not yet become an Anasazi skill, but there were several examples of unfired mud containers. Ornaments, such as beads and pendants, were shaped from stone, bone, shell, and seeds. Although this inventory of the possessions of such a low-level group does not seem substantial, it did incorporate the essentials for a reasonably secure and somewhat embellished life.

Between 300 B.C. and A.D. 150 precipitation in the vicinity of Chaco Canyon has been judged to have been less than at present, a factor that would have restricted horticulture and consequently Basket Maker II settlement. The few early Basket Maker families that did exist there perhaps were not as dependent upon farming as were some of their neighbors. They may have moved from one semipermanent camp to another to take advantage of local conditions and natural resources. If simple houses comparable to those found near Durango had been built in the canyon bottom, they have been destroyed by later periods of erosion and alluviation.

BASKET MAKER III

Studies of past climatic records, as revealed by patterns of annual growth rings of trees, by geological records of erosion and valley filling, and by identification of pollen in soil deposits, demonstrate that the Chaco Plateau saw an increase in effective moisture about A.D. 150 and that precipitation continued to augment until approximately A.D. 700. The creation of conditions more suitable for sedentary life brought more people into the area, and Chaco Canyon, in Basket Maker III times, witnessed its first significant exploitation by Anasazi farmers. This essentially marked the beginning of a Chaco cultural continuum that would elaborate into the most outstanding manifestation of Anasazi culture in the Southwest.

Small settlements of Basket Maker III people grew up in Chaco Canyon, on the mesas, and on the plains to the north and south. Sites, where up to twenty pithouse dwellings were huddled together, were selected near patches of arable land so that garden crops of corn, squash, and pumpkins could be overseen and, after harvesting, could easily and quickly be carried to the villages for consumption or storage. Semisubterranean houses, with conical timber, brush, and adobe superstructures and small entrance antechambers, were multipurpose, serving as shelters, workshops, and kitchens. Also incorporated were storage facilities and features for certain kinds of religious ceremonies. Pits, frequently slab-lined, were gouged into the ground behind the habitations. In them, surplus supplies of food could be saved. Population of a village was composed of a few, probably related, families. Larger settlements had special sacred chambers, built much like the houses but on a larger scale, which seem to have been used for communal rites. Except during spells of severe weather, undoubtedly most of the everyday life was spent out-of-doors. In fact, there is reason to believe that some household chores, such as food preparation, were sometimes carried out on the flat roofs of the homes. Because some village locations did not prove satisfactory for farming, they had to be abandoned for more favorable spots. There seems to have been a fair degree of group mobility throughout the region.

Sufficient water for domestic use was obtained from natural tanks on the rims of the mesas, from seeps and springs, and from the Chaco Wash when it ran or imprisoned pools of standing water. Pottery vessels were used to transport water to the homes. Gardens were nourished by ground moisture provided by winter snows and summer rains.

Tools and weapons needed for gardening, hunting, preparing foods, gathering natural resources, and for making houses, clothing, and other essentials likely were manufactured by family members. But it is not unlikely that individuals who became especially proficient in certain crafts, as in working stone, forming pottery, or shaping wood, became part-time specialists who exchanged their output for goods or services provided by others. One wonders whether such dealings may have been confined to an intravillage arena or whether trade between villages and even with surrounding areas had emerged. Quite possibly, an informal exchange system among kinspeople of the Chaco Plateau was operative. It may have been responsible for bringing into Chaco quantities of pottery that had been produced miles to the south and north and varieties of minerals not native to Chaco which were desired for implements and ornaments. Reciprocal exchange of commodities, including horticultural products, would have helped equalize differential availability of resources as well as climatically caused short-term inequities in food productivity. Pride in workmanship and application of skills well beyond basic utilitarian requirements is shown by the decoration of pottery, baskets, and bags, the fineness of finish of some tools, and the wearing of adornments.

Garden plots were tilled with wooden digging implements, sticks with a cutting edge or tipped with blades of stone or horn, and concave scoops of wood that served as shovels. Deer, rabbits, gophers, and other animals were taken with atlatls and spears, bows and arrows, clubs, and snares. Before the period ended, the bow and arrow replaced the atlatl and spear as the common weapons. Dogs aided in hunting and also were pets and village scavengers. Baskets and bags were used to transport and store a variety of items, and pottery vessels were employed for cooking, serving, and storing food. The pots, examples of the first true Anasazi pottery, were crudely made. Local and imported wares consisted of plain, coarse, gray cooking utensils and unelaborated nonculinary white vessels enlivened with geometric black designs, many of which were direct retentions of designs woven into baskets. A few red and brown pieces probably were obtained through intercourse with peoples to the south. Stone and bone implements were necessary for butchering, preparing clothing and footgear, pulverizing food, and processing building materials. Personal jewelry was created from stone, shell, and seeds. Animal hides and plant fibers supplied raw materials for garments and sandals much like those worn in the earlier Basket Maker II period.

Despite a certain sense of security afforded by fixed towns, the raising of plants, and an expanded tool kit, life was not always easy for the Basket Maker III family. Crop failures brought on by the erratic nature of Chaco's precipitation happened rather frequently; at such times, greater reliance had to be placed upon foraging. Family food surpluses seldom lasted longer than from one growing season to the next. Winters were cold, and spring winds and unpredictable downpours were the rule. The early Anasazi lived very close to nature with survival a constant struggle. That these people sought aid from the supernatural is to be expected. The presence of a sipapu in the floor of many habitations, about which family rites were performed, implies at least some beliefs consistent with those of the historic Pueblos. If the sipapu in Pueblo mythology is recognized as the symbolic entrance to the lower world from whence the people emerged into this world and where certain deities and spirits of the dead dwell, then by inference, it suggests something about the views and practices of the ancients. Implicit in the custom of placing utilitarian objects in graves of the deceased is a concept of a hereafter where the goods, or their spirits, would be required. In addition, the presence of ceremonial chambers in some Basket Maker III towns indicates a religious complexity that may have entailed direction by specialists. Leadership, beyond that coming from heads of families, may have rested in the hands of a spiritual elite.

PUEBLO I

In the eighth century, several significant changes took place in Chacoan culture. Population increased slightly, with a greater use of the canyon floor for settlements. Even so, the mesa tops and uplands were not abandoned. Most importantly, a fundamental alteration in architectural style appeared that established a pattern for later periods: Pueblo I dwellings came up out of the ground to stand on the surface. At first, they were little more than flat-roofed, open-walled shelters built around a four-post framework, or ramada, which fronted rows of small storage rooms of mud, rock, and posts. Later, walls of the ramadas were enclosed by rows of vertical posts plastered inside and out with thick adobe to form a hut, or jacal. Pit structures grew deeper and smaller, their antechambers reduced to mere ventilators; their function as houses diminished to the point where they served primarily a religious function. This promoted the rise of the kiva, the specialized below-ground chamber devoted to family or kin group socioreligious rituals.

By A.D. 800, small multiroomed houses or compact villages had appeared. Walls of rooms were built of small posts, a few stones, and abundant adobe plaster over shallow rectangular excavations whose sides normally were lined with stone slabs. Heavier corner posts supported horizontal timbers upon which flat roofs were laid. Entrance may have been through narrow doorways or by way of the smoke hole in the roof. Arc-shaped units of a line of small storage rooms in the rear and a series of larger habitations in the front came into vogue. For every living room, and there would be from four to eight in a house, there were two or three storerooms. One or two kivas, immediately in front of the room block, completed the pueblo. As Pueblo I progressed, builders of the small houses eliminated the timbers from the walls, mixed more mud and even some loaf-shaped lumps of adobe with rocks and eventually came up with roughly constructed masonry walls in which stones predominated over mud mortar.

Advances in the ceramic art were noticeable. Some gray cooking jars continued to have plain exteriors, but the majority were elaborated by overlapping bands or pinched indentations on their necks. Black-on-white vessels showed smoother surfaces, finer line work, more intricate rectilinear decoration, and a diversity of forms. A large amount of pottery in use in Chaco during this period was imported from surrounding areas. Otherwise, the general tone of Chaco Anasazi life during Pueblo I and the paraphernalia attendant thereto were much like those of the previous horizon. Among the lesser acquisitions for the garden were protein-rich beans and some cotton that was spun and woven into textiles. Turkeys appear to have been domesticated. Larger population entities may have meant strengthened social controls and more secular and religious leadership, as well as formalization of the exchange system.

It was not unusual for those thriving Basket Maker III villages situated in advantageous locations to have been occupied into Pueblo I times. When this happened, one or more pithouses were remodeled into kivas and a small jacal or stone-walled pueblo, with its sets of living rooms and storerooms, was erected nearby. However, as population rose, limited and periodic precipitation continued to force relocation throughout the arable portions of the region. Many communities of relatively brief occupancy resulted.

EARLY PUEBLO II

Between about A.D. 850 and 920, Chaco culture can be considered archaeologically as Early Pueblo II. As in the previous stage, it is mainly a few differences in architecture and ceramics that set it apart from prior and later cultural statements.

Chaco Canyon itself continued to be favored for settlement, and clusters of small pueblos grew up near districts of farm lands. There were more people, but they were concentrated in a small number of more extensive communities. Village architecture was typified by walls of elementary coursed masonry set in mud mortar. The notion of building aggregates of living and storage cells was repeated. However, the two types of units were of almost equal size. Crescentric villages gave way to rectangular or linear communities with more or less straight rows of as many as thirty rooms. Kivas were placed near the front of the block of rooms, and their interiors were at least partially lined with masonry. Certain kiva attributes had become standard. A bench encircled the wall, a ventilator brought fresh air into the otherwise stuffy chamber, and the floor contained a slab deflector between the ventilator opening and the firepit, and possibly a sipapu. The cribbed log roof was supported by four or more posts set in the floor or resting upon the bench. A smokehole-entryway was left in the center of the roof.

Ceramic styles reveal several innovations. As in the case of previously described characteristics, most of these were not necessarily restricted to the Chaco country; up to this time, local potters had participated in a widespread Anasazi pottery tradition that shared many conventions. Frequently it is only in the use of regional materials that wares can be separated, whereas forms and decorative elements used in various sub-districts often were indistinguishable. However, the very fact that clays and tempering nonplastics varied from place to place makes it possible now for ceramic analysts to distinguish between locally produced and imported pottery. Despite its fragility, pottery seems to have been traded widely between Anasazi domains and may have been an important item in prehistoric commerce.

From the first appearance of pottery, Chaco Canyon communities appear to have obtained much of theirs from external sources. It looks as though Chaco inhabitants were not particularly interested in developing a flourishing pottery industry themselves but were content to rely to a great extent upon the efforts of others living to the south and along what is now the northern border between New Mexico and Arizona. Collections of Early Pueblo II pottery recovered in Chaco show one new type and refinements of others. The neck-banded cooking pots have narrower corrugations, sometimes with tooled bands, and a new style of cooking jar with all-over corrugations was introduced. Decorated black-on-white wares carried fine line motifs much like those of Pueblo I.

Environmental stresses, resulting from frequent localized deficiencies in precipitation, occasional periods of drought throughout the region, and, at rare intervals, an overabundance of summer rains, continued to plague Chaco farmers. Unable to respond by intensifying their horticultural output, the recourses were either to migrate to better areas or to obtain food from neighbors who had produced surpluses. Short-term food shortages possibly were handled by the latter response, but during longer periods of widespread lack of moisture, inhabitants of the entire area would suffer. Then, migration was the solution, but only as long as population density on the Chaco Plateau permitted it. When most of the arable sectors of the plateau had been occupied, there were few remaining places into which to move. During Early Pueblo II, this situation seems to have come about. As noted before, when farming did not supply sufficient food, collecting and hunting must have been intensified.

LATE PUEBLO II, EARLY BONITO PHASE, HOSTA BUTTE PHASE

Currently the term *Bonito Phase* is used to identify the climax period of Chaco Canyon culture, which actually spans two subdivisions of the conventional Pecos Classification, parts of Pueblo II and Pueblo III. In most other Anasazi provinces in the San Juan Basin, Pueblo III marks the high point in their advancement. However, Chaco Canyon Anasazi appear to have reached that stage a half-century or more before their neighbors. Furthermore, the small pueblos once thought to have preceded the rise of the classic towns but which now are seen as contemporaneous with them are identified as the Hosta Butte Phase.

The Early Bonito Phase, the century from about A.D. 920 to 1020, was a turning point in Chaco prehistory as it marked the beginning of what has become known as the Chaco Phenomenon. Whereas the Chacoans had been full-fledged San Juan Basin Anasazi up to this time, sharing a common culture with other people throughout the region, this period witnessed a transition in Chaco culture that would set it apart from the others. They continued to be Anasazi, but a very special sort.

Underlying most of the accelerating changes and innovations was a new response to the old environmental pressures. Perhaps this was forced upon the inhabitants of Chaco Canyon by the decrease in nearby favorable lands to which they could migrate during times of drought. An increasing population added even more pressure, for they could no longer depend upon surpluses obtained from others to tide them over short times of food deficiencies. Also, the Chaco Wash, which in earlier days may have allowed some flood-water irrigation of lands along its banks, may have become so entrenched that its flow was no longer available for that purpose. In any event, it seems that the first efforts at controlling surface water to bring about greater yields from Chaco gardens can be attributed to this period. The unique natural situation wherein substantial quantities of runoff water spilled over the sides of the canyon, especially on the north, and coursed down canyon-bottom arroyos finally was recognized as a valuable resource. Steps were taken to harness the periodic floods and channel them to fields. Of course, the diversion dams, canals, and ditches constructed by the Chaco farmers only functioned when there was enough precipitation to result in runoff. But when the system was operative, much greater annual yields were realized from the gardens, and surpluses large enough to get through several bad seasons could be placed in storage. Therefore, one of the resultant changes was the construction of more and larger storage facilities in the pueblos.

More of the small communities with simple masonry rooms and kivas, such as had evolved by the end of Early Pueblo II to accommodate a few families, appeared along the length of Chaco Canyon. They were spacious enough to house and offer means of storage to greater numbers of families. But more significantly, construction of at least six of the principal towns in or near Chaco Canyon—Pueblo Bonito, Chetro Ketl, Una Vida, Peñasco Blanco, Hungo Pavi, and Kin Bineola—was initiated during this time. Although none of them reached their zenith until the Classic Bonito Phase, each of these towns has sections of rather crude masonry, usually an unfaced slab type, from which tree-ring dates within the time-span of the Early Bonito Phase have been attained. This masonry is composed of irregularly shaped sandstone slabs laid horizontally in copious beds of mud mortar from the two sides of the wall so that their inner ends sometimes interlock. It differs from later modes in that it does not have a rubble core, and the surfaces, although fairly smooth, are not veneered. There are basic similarities in methods of construction, in linear or arc-shaped arrangements of rooms, and in distinction between units for household and storage purposes between the simultaneously occupied villages and the emerging towns. However, some of the latter contained more rooms and stood higher than a single story.

The best example, and the only totally excavated early stage of such a city, is at Pueblo Bonito. Its initial increment was a complex of twenty-five one-story crude masonry houses to which several additions brought the total to seventy-five ground-floor rooms placed in a wide crescentric assemblage of living rooms, each with one or two storerooms to the rear, subterranean kivas in front, and a community trash pile beyond the kivas. It probably was two stories in height in places.

The Great Kiva, which had not been much in vogue in Chaco after Basket Maker III times, was reinstalled as a prominent ceremonial adjunct and grew to immense size, indicating considerable engineering ability. During this phase, Great Kivas tended to be situated apart from the pueblos but still central to groups of them, suggesting their importance in intercommunity ritual.

Other cultural modifications were minimal. The sedentary life-style, initiated by the Basket Maker III and augmented through time by a few additions and improvements, continued to be followed. The basic Anasazi food pattern, with dependency upon corn, squash, and beans, supplemented by products acquired by hunting and foraging, had become well established. Some variations in style of footgear and clothing, basketry, pottery, projectile points, and grinding implements may be noted, but they are primarily important only to archaeologists in their attempt to separate one culture horizon from another. The significant changes, other than in architecture and irrigation which can only be inferred from the archaeological evidence, must have had to do with the social, governmental, economic, and religious segments of the society. Complexities in these activities, which grew more refined in the next stage, undoubtedly were emerging in this time of transition.

The establishment of Chaco Canyon as the population, cultural, and merchandising nucleus for the entire Chaco Plateau was taking place. And the Chaco Phenomenon, an intergrated group of communities and resource areas in and near Chaco Canyon, appears to have begun functioning as a cohesive economic system.

EARLY PUEBLO III, CLASSIC BONITO PHASE, HOSTA BUTTE PHASE, McELMO PHASE

The slow process of cultural ripening which had been under way for some 500 years reached an apogee for the Chaco Anasazi some time in the century between A.D. 1020 and 1120. It was then that such a degree of excellence had been attained in the visible arts of architecture, ceramics, jewelry making, and a host of lesser crafts that the Chacoans ranked first among their peers. From this advanced craftsmanship and the obvious burgeoning population, one must assume a concomitant enrichment of all areas of profane and sacred life. Surely the influence of the Chacoans upon other Anasazi, and perhaps upon some foreigners, was considerable.

An estimated 5,000 to 6,000 people lived in the vicinity of Chaco Canyon, occupying about 400 settlements, during the Classic Bonito Phase. These figures are double those of the previous Pueblo II times. Also, as demonstrated by the Chaco Center survey of the surrounding country, a considerable number of outlying communities exhibiting Classic Bonito Phase characteristics flourished contemporaneously with the canyon populace. Much of the Chaco Canyon population was concentrated on the floor of the canyon in relatively few large centers. A sort of urban-rural interplay may have existed between the city dwellers—the Classic Bonitians, and those who resided in the hamlets, most of whom practiced a Hosta Butte life style. Although they shared many traits, they differed markedly in preferred architectural style and technique. Perhaps the residents of the large apartment houses lived in a more completely structured society with a greater opportunity to own some luxuries.

The rural villages seldom have more than twenty-five rooms arranged in irregular blocks or rows. Plazas or courtyards are infrequent, so kivas are enclosed within the house block. In some instances, portions of these pueblos were two-storied. Roughly finished, uncored masonry walls, of the types used in the Early Bonito Phase, continued in vogue. The dead usually were buried, together with grave goods, in trash deposits and below house floors in the villages.

Meanwhile, in addition to the six towns in which construction is known to have started during the earlier period, ten more were erected during this century. They are Casa Chiquita, Kin Kletso, Kin Klizhin, Kin Ya-a, New Alto, Pueblo Alto, Pueblo del Arroyo, Pueblo Pintado, Tsin Kletzin, and Wijiji. Of these sixteen principal towns extant during the Classic Bonito Phase, nine are situated in the nine-mile stretch of the lower Chaco Canyon, one is located fifteen miles to the east of Pueblo Bonito at the head of the canyon, two are slightly to the north between

Chaco Canyon and the Escavada Wash, and four are found to the south as far distant as twenty-six miles. Twelve of the towns have their roots deep in the Chaco Canyon tradition, as do most of the villages, but four reflect one of the significant aspects of the Chaco Phenomenon, specifically the immigration of outsiders into the Chaco country. Most of these migrants seem to have emanated in the region to the north of the San Juan River, bringing with them some of their own unique ways of building pueblos and making pottery. These mannerisms and concepts of town planning distinguish the settlements from other Chaco towns, the McElmo Phase.

In essence, Late Pueblo II and Pueblo III in Chaco consist of two locally based developments, the Bonito and Hosta Butte Phases apparent in most of the villages and towns, and one intrusive group, the McElmo Phase. The latter is evident exclusively in the four towns of Casa Chiquita, Kin Kletso, New Alto, and Tsin Kletzin, and in increments in what are otherwise Chacoan structures. It would appear that relationships between the newcomers and the long-time residents were amiable and that both groups participated more or less equally in the various affairs of this period of greatest cultural elaboration in Chaco Canyon. After all, they both were Anasazi.

The Chaco towns, including those with earlier beginnings, reached their greatest size during this time. Major building projects took place in most of them after A.D. 1020 and again between A.D. 1055 and 1083. Whether they involved the addition of large units to ongoing pueblos or the razing of earlier structures and their rebuilding, these construction programs were based on predetermined plans. The erection, expansion, and refurbishing of towns continued throughout the period, but instead of proceeding in previous fashion, the cored masonry wall was introduced.

Whether this new style of masonry, involving massive walls with centers of unshaped rock and mud and veneers of shaped stones, was a local development or an introduction from Mexico has not been determined conclusively. The fact that the trait appears in Chaco Canyon about the same time as an assortment of other elements thought by many to be of Mexican derivation points up its possible southern origin. Nevertheless, among the Anasazi, cored masonry walls are unique to Chaco Canyon and the areas under Chaco influence, and became a distinct hallmark of Chaco culture. The strength of thick, cored walls of well-laid hewn stone blocks made it possible for Chaco builders to erect multistoried complexes with numerous large rooms for both living quarters and storage. Although the basic architectural style was of Anasazi tradition, the new construction technique eventually allowed buildings to reach five stories in height and to contain hundreds of rooms.

As revealed by the several excavated structures and the undug remains of others, town plans seem to have started with a compact linear or curved set of rooms to which additions of cell complexes were made, resulting in L- or E-, and D-shaped pueblos. An open courtyard, or plaza, surrounded by room blocks was the normal arrangement. Until late in their history, some communities had plazas which were open on one side. Then, an arced row of rooms or a wall completely enclosed them, by this means limiting access to the pueblo to a single restricted entrance. House units generally were terraced back from the plazas to rear tiers of rooms two to four stories high. In the case of Pueblo Bonito, the rear rooms may have stood to a height of five stories. Kivas with well-prepared masonry linings having a bench, subfloor ventilator, deflector, firepit, and four or more roof support posts set on low log and masonry foundations built upon the bench, were dug into the plazas or enclosed within the room blocks. The cribbed or flat kiva roofs, from which ladders protruded, probably were level with the plaza surface or the roof top terraces in the pueblo. Isolated Great Kivas, such as Casa Rinconada and Kin Nahasbas, were functional, but they may have been primarily for the inhabitants of the rural villages since most of the cities had one or more Great Kivas in their plazas. On the other hand, the isolated chambers could have been used to integrate residents of the towns and villages. Tower kivas, whose purpose is not entirely clear but which may have been for ritual and communication, are found in several of the Chaco towns. A lengthy local development occurred in most of the settlements, but a few, such as Pueblo del Arroyo and Wijiji, may be relatively late offshoots from larger communities.

When the remainder of the cultural inventory is reviewed, it is evident that an overwhelming number of artifacts and items of subsistence were common to the villagers and the urban populace. Still, certain things from the towns are of a particularly rich nature. These include turquoise, jet, and shell secured in inlays and mosaics or made into beads, bracelets, and pendants; pottery vessels of cylindrical, incense burner, and effigy forms; pottery stamps or seals; iron pyrites sets for mosaics; conch shell trumpets; carved and painted wood for ceremonial use; pseudo-cloisonné decoration on sandstone; ornamental copper bells; and parrots and macaws for their brilliant plumage. It may be incorrect to consider these items to have been typical of all the towns because some of them have come only from Pueblo Bonito where they may have been funerary offerings placed with important personages. Only additional excavations in other comparable towns will reveal their correct urban distribution, but it is true that none of these luxuries have been found in the rural villages.

Burial practices differed between the large and small sites. Even though there are trash accumulations near the cities, they do not contain burials as do those associated with the villages. A total of only 121 burials have been reclaimed from the excavations at Pueblo Bonito, Cheto Ketl, Pueblo del Arroyo, and Pueblo Alto. This points up a great discrepancy when taking into account population estimates and length of occupation as compared with the number of retrieved dead. When they occur, town burials are almost always in abandoned rooms or beneath floors. Extensive searches for town cemeteries have proven unsuccessful to this time.

The towns built by the McElmo Phase immigrants during the Classic Bonito Phase, and also the rooms they sometimes added on to Chaco centers, display a distinctive style of wall construction. It is the sort that they had known in their former homes, that was thinner than the Chaco cored, veneer type. It consists of large shaped sandstone blocks set in courses two stones thick. Sometimes there is a thin mud core between the opposing stones, but more commonly inner ends of these stones meet in the center of the wall. Exterior faces of the stone were smoothed and frequently dimpled with a hammer or pecking stone. These peck marks may have promoted a better bond for the mud plaster applied to the wall surfaces.

Towns of the northerners were compact, contained from thirty to seventy living and storage rooms, reached two or three stories high, and had kivas built into the rectangular blocks of rooms. Their kivas also show a northern derivation. Many are called "keyhole" because of a recess in the southern part of the otherwise circular chamber. A high, narrow bench encircles the curved part of the pit, and the floor was interrupted by a firepit and deflector. The ventilator opens at floor level into the kiva through the southern recess. A set of stone columns placed upon the bench, known as pilasters, provided support for the usual flat or cribbed roof in which an opening was left for an entryway smokehole. Great Kivas are not found in these northern towns in Chaco. However, one has a tower kiva, and the late addition by McElmo people to Pueblo del Arroyo includes a tri-walled structure, both being features more common in northern sectors.

The ceramics of the intruding colonists also differed from those of the older Chaco residents. Whereas the Chaco potters, or those to the south from whom they obtained pottery, customarily decorated their white vessels with black designs executed in mineral-based iron paint, the McElmo potters used a carbon paint obtained from plants. The distinctions between iron and carbon pigment on pottery containers or potsherds are readily discernible, as are differences in vessel shapes and design elements employed by the two schools of potters. Sites of the intruders do not yield carbon painted black-on-white pottery exclusively, but it does predominate over the associated small percentage of Chaco black-on-whites. Conversely, most of the Chaco-tradition towns have pottery complexes dominated by their iron painted pots, even though they almost invariably also have some of the carbon painted wares. Thus, each group continued to make pottery in an accustomed fashion, but adopted some products from the other. The Chacoans seem to have admired the new McElmo style pottery and to have used it in greater quantities as time passed.

If Kin Kletso is typical, the culture of the outsiders who moved into Chaco was poor by comparison in quantity and quality of goods they brought with them. For instance, luxury items, such as those recovered at Pueblo Bonito, did not occur at Kin Kletso. Moreover, the on-the-spot work in architecture by the McElmo people did not measure up to Chaco standards. Social, economic, and occupational differences between the two groups seem to have been perpetuated, and evidence is lacking for any political supremacy of one body over the other.

The Chaco Canyon water control system undoubtedly was expanded during the Classic Bonito Phase. Whether outsiders were encouraged to settle in Chaco in order to provide a labor force to enlarge the system, or whether the irrigation works had to be expanded because of the population increase is a moot point. The amount of manpower necessary to develop a unit of the system that would divert runoff water from one rincón on to bordering fields was not particularly great, which suggests that additional water diversion controls were constructed in response to growth of the local population.

But, even though more of the canyon bottom was placed under irrigation, arable land was limited and insufficient to produce the amount of food needed to feed the ballooning Chaco population. Other food sources had to be sought to supplement the canyon's produce on a continuing basis, not just periodically during times of poor yield as had formerly been the case.

Events and activities outside the canyon became as important as those within the inner canyon. It is conceivable that the loosely structured, informal distribution system that had been in operation for centuries was reorganized, and trading became formalized throughout the Chaco Plateau. Outlying communities were incorporated in the plan, and Chaco colonies were established in strategic locations in order to increase food production and obtain a number of resources unavailable or in short supply nearer Chaco. Contacts were extended to other Anasazi and their neighbors beyond the limits of the plateau for certain necessities and luxury items. The urban Chaco communities could have become the hub and power base of a far-reaching political, religious, and redistribution system united by an extensive fabric of roads and visual communication stations and operated by full-time administrators. In them, excess foods could have been accumulated for reallotment in times of need.

It is speculated that a great many people, both from the towns and villages of Chaco Canyon and from the more distant satellites, were engaged in producing foods and handcrafted goods and in hunting, gathering, and mining. Others were probably needed to transport items throughout the territory and, particularly, to stockpile in Chaco Canyon surplus foodstuffs for storage in the warehouselike units of the municipalities and to accumulate the vast quantity of timber and rock required by the local building enthusiasm. It is not improbable that labor forces were moved from place to place to assist the local inhabitants during planting and harvesting seasons, and to participate in communal projects such as constructing and maintaining water management apparatus and roads, and building the larger residential and storage facilities.

A merchant group that organized, directed, and participated in the production and distribution of basic regional commodities, and also in trade of exotics, may have come into existence and assumed considerable social status. Perhaps certain towns, Pueblo Alto for example, were scenes of periodic markets where people from near and far assembled to barter for a variety of goods and services. The most valued special goods came from a long-distance relationship with a group of Mesoamerican, Toltec-inspired, trading and production entrepots, such as Casas Grandes in northern Chihuahua, Mexico. Blue-green turquoise, highly desired by the southerners, became the principal commodity traded to the Mexicans. In return, macaws, ornamental bells of copper, shell jewelry and trumpets, and various kinds of decorative articles exhibiting artistic techniques unknown to the Anasazi, were introduced into Chaco. Probably both Chacoan and Mexican merchants traveled between redistribution centers, and an exchange of ideas between the culturally diverse groups may have led to innovations in Chaco architecture, farming procedures, communication measures, and religious activities.

No overall leadership of Chaco society is postulated. Instead, it is presumed that each community elevated, by common consent, elderly, intelligent, and respected members to positions of specialized ceremonial and political authority. Some offices, particularly those of a religious nature, may have become hereditary. The powerful merchant class probably was of slightly lower status. The majority of the Chacoans made their contributions as artists and craftsmen, skilled workers, and common laborers. Guidance for intracommunal projects and rituals was afforded by local leaders who, at times, might have formed councils to organize and direct activities that involved more than a single community.

202

The evidence at hand suggests that Pueblo Bonito had the most respected leadership and the greatest concentration of wealth of all of the Chaco communities. Certainly, it has yielded more burials of supposed high-status individuals with whom more rich funerary offerings and luxury goods had been placed than any other excavated site. But every principal center seems to have supported a basically similar set of residential, ceremonial, and commercial activities. Greater emphasis upon industrial pursuits, such as the storage of surplus foodstuffs and the production of trade goods, is evident in a few of the cities.

Chaco Canyon and its sphere of interaction was a bustling, thriving reality during the Classic Bonito Phase of Pueblo III and well deserves its reputation as the culmination of Anasazi accomplishment.

LATE PUEBLO III, LATE BONITO PHASE, McELMO PHASE

Tree-ring dates show that little new construction or remodeling of Chaco towns or villages took place after A.D. 1120. But limited building activities in some of the intrusive McElmo Phase complexes did occur after that time. Archaeomagnetic samples from a few Chaco sites, dated originally by tree-rings, and from several recently dug ruins, such as Pueblo Alto and two small units in Marcia's Rincón, are yielding construction dates in the late A.D. 1100s and very early 1200s. Still, the earlier opinion that Chaco's burst of building dwindled in the first quarter of the twelfth century is correct. The Late Bonito Phase, A.D. 1120 to 1220, witnessed the slow dissipation of the remarkable Chaco Phenomenon, then ultimately the virtual abandonment of the canyon. Thereafter, Chaco's ebullience dissipated almost as rapidly as it had blossomed.

The population decline seems to have affected all the canyon settlements, large and small, and the farflung pueblos outside its confines as well. Increasingly, larger sections of most towns were converted into handy places for the deposition of household trash. Obviously, the adverse factors were widespread and all-encompassing. The extensive Chaco province began to come apart, despite attempts to hold it together. That segments of the road system remained in use and a few of the urban centers continued with life as usual until as late as the 1200s attest to that effort. What, then, were the insurmountable conditions that led to the downfall of the well-knit organization that had elevated Chaco to its glory days?

Several previous explanations for the collapse of Chaco society no longer appear tenable. Pressure from an enemy people formerly was a popular premise. However, at present there is no concrete evidence for that. At one time, the arrival of the Navajo was considered to have triggered serious hostilities that forced the Chacoan people and other northern Anasazi to withdraw from their homelands and move elsewhere. Now it seems certain that the Navajo did not arrive until some time considerably after the abandonment of Chaco Canyon. Had an alien group been around in the twelfth century, it might well have been the ancestors of the Ute. Even so, it is unlikely that small bands of impoverished nomads would have had much impact upon the well-constructed, heavily populated Anasazi establishments. There are no indications of major skirmishes in the Chaco sites. Fires did occur, but they seem to have resulted from accidents rather than from any unfriendly actions. Defensive architectural measures, such as enclosing structures so that only a single entrance remained and plugging exterior wall openings, likely were for protection against other Anasazi rather than any foreigners.

Deforestation and agriculture have been stated to have led to accelerated erosion, arroyo cutting, and subsequent lowering of the water table, all of which seriously curtailed production of farm goods. Nevertheless, it is currently believed that the immediate vicinity of Chaco Canyon never supported a heavy growth of pines, and that the tremendous amount of wood consumed in construction had been obtained many miles distant from the canyon. Moreover, the ingenious water manipulation measures could have functioned even during cycles of erosion.

Pestilence and natural catastrophes also have been postulated as possible contributors to Chaco's cultural demise, but no clues pointing to such calamities have come to light. Drought also figured in the earlier reasoning, but the Great Drought of A.D. 1279–1299 occurred too late to have precipitated the end of Chaco Anasazi life. On the other hand, another of the cyclic periods of insufficient moisture that always plagued the Southwest may indeed have been behind many of Chaco's troubles.

Paleoecological research has shown that the entire San Juan Basin suffered a severe drought between the years A.D. 1130 and 1190. Such a lengthy, widespread lack of moisture would have brought dire consequences to the greater Chaco area. The Chaco system was capable of coping with local short-term periods of dryness, but could not sustain itself over a sixty-year span of moisture deficiency. This, then, most likely was the paramount reason for the end of the Chaco Phenomenon.

Behind the situation brought on by natural forces were devisive undercurrents among the Chaco Anasazi. Inevitably, the social fabric must have steadily eroded under the unabated pressure of food shortages. Even with intensified efforts to move surpluses from areas of plenty to areas of need, the time finally came when there were no remaining excesses and the entire society was faced with the grim specter of debilitating hunger. Nor was it just the lack of rains or snows which caused the fields to become sterile. The continuous irrigation over many centuries, without any form of soil enrichment, caused the land to choke with alkali. Also, as timber resources were depleted and the forest withdrew, so did many kinds of plant and animal life basic to the economy of the people. Labor forces that had been involved in raising and distributing food were no longer needed, the goods and products upon which the merchants depended were in short supply, and upkeep of the remaining irrigation and communication means were futile. Perhaps those who encouraged adoption of foreign ways became targets for the conservatives who found in their nonconformity to tradition a cause for the present scourge upon the land. Then social malaise and lack of confidence in those in authority, added to the insoluble problem of subsisting in such a parched area, forced the disintegration of the group.

Leaving behind the impressive masonry houses and most of their possessions, some families followed the retreating forest border eastward to the northern slopes of the Chacra Mesa and to the better watered flanks of Mount Taylor. Others continued on through the Río Puerco valley to the middle Río Grande. A considerable number headed south to the mesas and valleys near Laguna, Zuñi, and beyond, some hundred miles distant from Chaco Canyon. In those new locations, the old ways of life, free from any intrusive non-Anasazi coloration, prevailed.

At about the time Chaco Canyon was slowly being vacated, the inhabitants of the Mesa Verde region of southwestern Colorado also came under a series of severe pressures, and they, too, were forced to desert their longtime homes. Some Mesa Verde migrants moved toward the Chaco, as had their relatives in earlier times. There they found conditions no better than those from which they were retreating. Although some took up residence in the abandoned Chaco houses for a time, they soon moved on, leaving the great and small manifestations of Chaco's flowering to sink into the realm of archaeology.[10]

For several centuries after the 700-year Anasazi occupation of Chaco Canyon, there were brief periods of scattered reoccupation, perhaps by descendants of former inhabitants drawn back by tales of the region's past glory, which must have figured prominently in their oral traditions.

When the Navajo moved into the Chaco, probably in the early 1700s, they herded their stock and built their hogans in a country dotted with remains of their predecessors, whom they called Anasazi, the Ancient Ones. Although struck with wonderment at the abundance and magnitude of the Anasazi vestiges, they generally avoided them out of respect for anything associated with the dead. It remained for Spanish and American travelers and military parties to "discover" the ruins of Chaco Canyon and for three generations of archaeologists to decipher their secrets.

NOTES AND
REFERENCES

Chapter 1: Military and Survey Parties

1. David M. Brugge, *A History of the Chaco Navajos,* Reports of the Chaco Center, Division of Chaco Research, National Park Service 4 (1980), narrates in detail the history of the region, particularly in respect to the Navajo. His analysis starts with the earliest accounts of the seventeenth century and proceeds to 1948 when Chaco Canyon National Monument was fenced and the Navajo were excluded from the area. It provides more information about the early military and survey parties than is included in this chapter.

2. Josiah Gregg, *Commerce of the Prairies, The Journal of a Santa Fe Trader* (1844; reprint edition Dallas [1933]), pp. 188–89.

3. Simpson's report, "Journal of a Military Reconnaissance from Santa Fe, New Mexico to the Navajo Country, Made with the Troops under Command of Lt. Col. John M. Washington in 1849," was published in 1852 in *Senate Executive Document No. 64, 31st. Congress, 1st Session.* It was edited and annotated by Frank McNitt and reissued by the University of Oklahoma Press, Norman, in 1964 as *Navajo Expedition, Journal of a Military Reconnaissance from Santa Fe, New Mexico to the Navajo Country Made in 1849.*

4. Oscar Loew, "Report on the Ruins of New Mexico," Appendix J2 to Appendix LL of *Annual Report, Chief of the U.S. Engineers* (1875), pp. 1094–1098.

5. W. H. Jackson, "Ruins of the Chaco Canyon, Examined in 1877," *United States Geological and Geographical Survey of the Territories,* (F. V. Hayden), Tenth Annual Report (1878), pp. 431–50.

6. Lewis H. Morgan, "Houses and House-Life of the American Aborigines," United States Geographical and Geological Survey of the Rocky Mountain Region, *Contributions to American Ethnology* 4 (1881):154–71.

7. Victor Mindeleff, *A Study of Pueblo Architecture in Tusayan and Cibola,* Bureau of American Ethnology, Eighth Annual Report (1891).

8. Florence C. Lister and Robert H. Lister, *Earl Morris and Southwestern Archaeology* (Albuquerque: University of New Mexico Press, 1968), pp. 7–8.

9. F. T. Bickford, "Prehistoric Cave-Dwellings," *Century* 40 (October 1890):896–911.

Chapter 2: Collectors, Dilettantes, and Scientists

1. Frank McNitt's excellent biography, *Richard Wetherill: Anasazi* (Albuquerque: University of New Mexico Press, 1957), embraces Richard's archaeological activities, especially at Mesa Verde and Chaco Canyon, and tells of the work of the Hyde Exploring Expedition in Chaco Canyon.

2. Ibid., pp. 112–13.

3. Two of Pepper's short articles concerned themselves with ceremonial objects and ornaments: "Ceremonial Deposits Found in an Ancient Pueblo Estufa in Northern New Mexico," *Monumental Records* 1 (July 1899):1-6, and "Ceremonial Objects and Ornaments from Pueblo Bonito, New Mexico," *American Anthropologist,* n.s., 7 (1905):183-97. The third described a collection of unusual human effigy vessels: "Human Effigy Vases from Chaco Canyon, New Mexico," *Boas Anniversary Volume* (1906): 320-34; and the final one discussed the contents of a burial room: "The Exploration of a

Burial-Room in Pueblo Bonito, New Mexico," *Putnam Anniversary Volume, Anthropological Essays Presented to Frederick Ward Putnam in Honor of His Seventieth Birthday* (G. E. Stechert and Co., 1909), pp. 196–252.

4. George H. Pepper, *Pueblo Bonito,* Anthropological Papers of the American Museum of Natural History 27 (1920).

5. W. K. Moorehead, *A Narrative of Explorations in New Mexico, Arizona, etc.,* Bulletin of the Phillips Academy Department of Archaeology 3 (1906).

6. For example see, T. M. Prudden, "The Prehistoric Ruins of the San Juan Watershed in Utah, Arizona, Colorado, and New Mexico," *American Anthropologist,* n.s., 5:2 (1903):224–88.

7. Aleš Hrdlička, *Physiological and Medical Observations Among the Indians of Southwestern United States and Northern Mexico,* Bulletin of the Bureau of American Ethnology 34 (1908).

8. Professor Dodge's notes on his geological studies at Pueblo Bonito and in Chaco Canyon are contained in Pepper's account, *Pueblo Bonito* (1920), pp. 23–25.

9. Tozzer's 1901 field activities are set forth in an account by W. C. Larrabee, "Expedition to New Mexico, July 30 to September 23, 1901," filed in the Peabody Museum, Harvard. His observations about Navajo religious practices in Chaco Canyon are included in "Notes on Religious Ceremonials of the Navaho," in the *Putnam Anniversary Volume,* pp. 299–343.

10. Edgar L. Hewett, "Archaeology of New Mexico," in *Report of the Governor of New Mexico to the Secretary of the Interior* (1902), pp. 429–33.

11. S. J. Holsinger's three-volume report dated December 5, 1901, "Report on the Prehistoric Ruins of Chaco Canyon, New Mexico, Ordered by the General Land Office Letter 'P', December 18, 1900," was submitted to the General Land Office, Washington, D.C. The document is in the National Archives, Washington, D.C.

12. Cedar is the common local term for several species of juniper native to the American Southwest.

13. *Richard Wetherill: Anasazi,* by Frank McNitt, and his *The Indian Traders,* (Norman: University of Oklahoma Press, 1962) both refer to the trading post activities of the Hyde Exploring Expedition.

14. The report by Frank Grygla favoring Wetherill's homestead application was directed to the Commissioner, General Land Office, on July 5, 1905. It is in the National Archives, Washington, D.C., Record Group 79, National Park Service.

Chapter 3:   Archaeologists, Geologists, and Chronologists

1. Leading Southwestern archaeologists assembled at A. V. Kidder's field camp at Pecos, New Mexico, in 1927 thrashed out the first ordering of Anasazi cultural progression, the Pecos Classification. The event is described in an article by Kidder, "Southwestern Archaeological Conference," *Science,* 66:1716 (1927):489:91. Later, Frank H. H. Roberts, Jr. modified the stages in what has become known as the Roberts Classification. His scheme was first outlined in "A Survey of Southwestern Archaeology," *American Anthropologist* 37:1 (1935):1–35. Both systems established sequential horizons based upon diagnostic traits, such as architecture, sandals, pictographs, textiles, stone and bone implements, ornaments, and pottery, believed characteristic of each stage.

Pecos Classification	Roberts' Classification
Pueblo V	Historic Pueblo
Pueblo IV	Regressive Pueblo
Pueblo III	Great Pueblo
Pueblo II ⎫ ⎬	Developmental Pueblo
Pueblo I ⎭	
Basket Maker III	Modified Basket Maker
Basket Maker II	Basket Maker
Basket Maker I	omitted

Other classificatory methods followed. Harold S. Gladwin, founder of the Gila Pueblo research institution in southern Arizona, devised a system modeled after a tree. He felt that both the Pecos and Roberts devices, although useful as yardsticks in setting forth Anasazi cultural development on a wide scale, had shortcomings in dealing with time and space relationships, allowing sites in one area to be classified as Basket Maker III or Modified Basket Maker while at the same time the culture in an adjacent region might have progressed to the Pueblo I or Developmental Pueblo stage. In other words, all Anasazi did not turn the pages of their history at the same time. There were regional spurts and lags. Gladwin's Classification, which could be applied to the entire Southwest, not just to the Anasazi, was set forth in Winifred and Harold S. Gladwin, "A Method for Designation of Cultures and Their Variations," *Medallion Papers* XV (Globe, Arizona: Gila Pueblo, 1934). It was compared to the Pecos and Roberts classifications in Harold S. Gladwin, "The Chaco Branch, Excavations at White Mound and in the Red Mesa Valley," *Medallion Papers* XXXIII (Globe, Arizona: Gila Pueblo, 1945).

The Gladwin Classification groups cultures by the relative degree of similarities, taking into consideration temporal and spatial relationships. Roots identify the major cultural traditions of the Southwest; stems are divisions of roots that are assigned regional names; branches grow from stems and are designated by smaller geographic terms; finally, phases are named after local landmarks or ruins within the branch designation.

Depending upon preference, one could refer to a particular site or cultural manifestation in Chaco Canyon as being Pueblo III (Pecos Classification), Great Pueblo (Roberts' Classification), or Bonito Phase of the Chaco Branch of the Little Colorado Stem of the Basket Maker Root (Gladwin Classification). Or, to escape criticism of some nit-picking colleague, one could use all of them. These three cultural systematizations have survived, and according to circumstances, one or another of them is regularly employed by students of Southwestern archaeology.

The annotated edition of A. V. Kidder's *An Introduction to the Study of Southwestern Archaeology with a Preliminary Account of the Excavations at Pecos* (New Haven: Yale University Press, 1962), originally published in 1924, includes an excellent review of the status of Southwestern archaeology in the 1920s, including a section on Chaco Canyon. The introduction to the 1962 reprinting outlines more recent additions to archaeological knowledge and the recognition of stages in the Anasazi continuum. Florence C. Lister and Robert H. Lister in their book, *Earl Morris and Southwestern Archaeology* (Albuquerque: University of New Mexico Press, 1968), describe the pioneering days and flowering of the discipline of Southwestern archaeology.

2. Anonymous, "A New National Geographic Society Expedition," *National*

Geographic Society Magazine, June 1921, pp. 637–43. Neil M. Judd authored three of the *National Geographic Society Magazine* articles: "The Pueblo Bonito Expedition of the National Geographic Society," March 1922, pp. 322–31; "Pueblo Bonito, the Ancient," July 1923, pp. 99–108; and "Everyday Life in Pueblo Bonito," September 1925, pp. 227–62. A. E. Douglass wrote "The Secret of the Southwest Solved by Talkative Tree-rings," *National Geographic Society Magazine,* December 1929, pp. 736–70.

3. A. E. Douglass, *Dating Pueblo Bonito and other Ruins of the Southwest,* National Geographic Society, Contributed Technical Papers, Pueblo Bonito Series 1 (1935).

4. Kirk Bryan, *The Geology of Chaco Canyon, New Mexico, in Relation to the Life and Remains of the Prehistoric Peoples of Pueblo Bonito,* Smithsonian Miscellaneous Collections 122:7(1954).

5. Neil M. Judd, *The Material Culture of Pueblo Bonito,* Smithsonian Miscellaneous Collections 124 (1954).

6. Neil M. Judd, *Pueblo del Arroyo, Chaco Canyon, New Mexico,* Smithsonian Miscellaneous Collections 138:1(1959).

7. Neil M. Judd, *The Architecture of Pueblo Bonito,* Smithsonian Miscellaneous Collections 147:1(1964).

8. Frank H. H. Roberts, Jr., *Shabik'eshchee Village, a Late Basket Maker Site in Chaco Canyon, New Mexico,* Bulletin of the Bureau of American Ethnology 92 (1929).

9. Most of the tree-ring dates used in this text have been taken from two compilations: Bryant Bannister, *Tree-ring Dating of the Archaeological Sites in the Chaco Canyon Region, New Mexico,* Southwestern Monuments Association Publication 6:2 (Globe, Arizona, 1965); and William J. Robinson, Bruce G. Harrill, and Richard L. Warren, *Tree-ring Dates from New Mexico B, Chaco-Gobernador Area,* Laboratory of Tree-ring Research, University of Arizona (1974).

Chapter 4: Student Archaeologists

1. Unfortunately, final reports on most aspects of research at Chetro Ketl have never been written; however, some generalities about the pueblo and its excavated Great Kiva are included in Edgar L. Hewett's book, *The Chaco Canyon and Its Monuments,* (Albuquerque: University of New Mexico Press, 1936).

2. Florence M. Hawley's *The Significance of the Dated Prehistory of Chetro Ketl, New Mexico,* University of New Mexico Bulletin, Monograph Series 1:1 (Albuquerque, 1934), is one of the few complete accounts of investigations accomplished at Chetro Ketl. It describes the chronology of masonry and ceramic types and outlines the building sequence of the town.

3. R. Gwinn Vivian, Dulce N. Dodgen, and Gayle N. Hartmann, *Wooden Ritual Artifacts from Chaco Canyon, New Mexico, the Chetro Ketl Collection,* Anthropological Papers of the University of Arizona 32 (Tucson, 1978).

4. Gordon Vivian and Paul Reiter reported upon Casa Rinconada, Kin Nahasbas, and other Great Kivas in their publication, *The Great Kivas of Chaco Canyon and Their Relationships,* School of American Research Monograph 22 (1960; reprint Albuquerque: University of New Mexico Press, 1972).

5. Bertha P. Dutton, *Leyit Kin, A Small House Ruin, Chaco Canyon, New Mexico,* School of American Research Monograph 7 (Santa Fe, 1938).

6. Chaco Canyon ruins have been identified by several methods. Many of the main sites were named by Lieutenant Simpson in 1849. Additional ones were named and numbers were assigned a few sites by Jackson in 1877. Their identifications generally have been retained although spellings have varied. More recently, as additional Chaco remains have been discovered, names and numbers, some with attached prefixes, have been assigned to them. This has sometimes created considerable confusion. The University of New Mexico system of site designation was employed during the time of their operations in Chaco. It placed the prefix Bc before Chaco site numbers; the B standing for New Mexico and the lower case letter identifying a small geographic region within the state. In this format, Chaco Canyon is c. To elucidate, Bc114 is the 114th listed ruin in the Chaco Canyon area of New Mexico.

During the last few years, a comprehensive archaeological survey of Chaco Canyon has been accomplished by the National Park Service. To standardize site identification, the system followed nationwide by the Smithsonian Institution was adopted. It combines a geographical location with a sequential numbering of sites within the area, as does the University of New Mexico procedure, but its arrangement of numbers and letters is different. In this nomenclature, a Chaco Canyon archaeological feature may be designated 29SJ1220; 29 indicating the state of New Mexico, SJ San Juan County, and 1220 the 1220th site recorded in San Juan County. In an effort to further clarify matters, records of the recent Chaco survey not only refer to all remains in the Smithsonian system but also include all previously assigned names or numbers.

7. Of the six excavated small village sites near Casa Rinconada, Bc50 (Tseh So), Bc51, Bc53, Bc57, Bc58, and Bc59, collectively called the Rinconada sites, only two have been reported upon: Donald D. Brand, Florence M. Hawley, Frank C. Hibben, et al., *Tseh So, A Small House Ruin, Chaco Canyon, New Mexico,* University of New Mexico Anthropological Series 2:2 (Albuquerque, 1937), and Clyde Kluckhohn and Paul Reiter, *Preliminary Report on the 1937 Excavations, Bc50–51, Chaco Canyon, New Mexico,* University of New Mexico Anthropological Series 3:2 (Albuquerque, 1939).

Results of the excavations at the other Rinconada villages and the four talus structures, Bc52, Bc54, Bc55, and Bc56, have not been published, but student field notes and reports provide some insight into their characteristics and relationships. Refer to the Site Inventory in this volume for some information about these sites.

8. Relationships between late Pueblo II, Pueblo III, and the Bonito, Hosta Butte, and McElmo phases are shown diagramatically below:

		Hosta Butte Phase / McElmo Phase	
A.D. 1220———			———A.D. 1220
Late Pueblo III	Late Bonito Phase		
1120———			———1120
Early Pueblo III	Classic Bonito Phase		
1020———			———1020
Late Pueblo II	Early Bonito Phase		
A.D. 920———			———A.D. 920

For further discussions of the Bonito, Hosta Butte, and McElmo phases in Chaco Canyon see, Gordon Vivian and Tom W. Mathews, *Kin Kletso, a Pueblo III Community in Chaco Canyon, New Mexico,* Southwestern Monuments Association, Technical Series 6:1 (Globe, Arizona, 1965), pp. 107–11, and Harold S. Gladwin, "The Chaco Branch, Excavations at White Mound and in the Red Mesa Valley," *Medallion Papers* XXXIII (Globe, Arizona, 1945).

9. Kluckhohn's provocative critique of Southwestern taxonomic systems and his opinions about relationships between the contemporaneous village and town dwellers of Chaco Canyon are set forth in the publication edited by Clyde Kluckhohn and Paul Reiter, *Preliminary Report on the 1937 Excavations, Bc50–51, Chaco Canyon, New Mexico,* University of New Mexico Anthropological Series 3:2 (Albuquerque, 1939):151–62.

Chapter 5:   Preservation Specialists

1. Memorandum by Dale King, "Threatening Rock," in Chaco Canyon National Monument files, National Park Service (1941).

2. Reports describing two of the sites salvaged by National Park Service archaeologists have been published: Gordon Vivian, *The Three-C Site, an Early Pueblo II Ruin in Chaco Canyon, New Mexico,* University of New Mexico Publications in Anthropology 13 (Albuquerque, 1965), and Zorro A. Bradley, *Site Bc236, Chaco Canyon National Monument, New Mexico,* Division of Archeology, Office of Archeology and Historic Preservation, National Park Service (1971). Brief accounts of the others, the Headquarters sites, Lizard House, Gallo Cliff Dwelling, and Bc362, are included in the Site Inventory. Their characteristics are based upon unpublished field notes and reports compiled by the excavators.

3. Judd's discussion of the Tri-wall is in *Pueblo del Arroyo, Chaco Canyon, New Mexico,* Smithsonian Miscellaneous Collections 138:1 (1959), pp. 108–19. Gordon Vivian's description is contained in his *The Hubbard Site and other Tri-Wall Structures in New Mexico and Colorado,* National Park Service Archeological Research Series 5 (1959).

4. Gordon Vivian and Tom W. Mathews, *Kin Kletso, a Pueblo III Community in Chaco Canyon, New Mexico,* Southwestern Monuments Association, Technical Series 6:1 (Globe, Arizona, 1965).

5. Lloyd M. Pierson, "A History of Chaco Canyon National Monument," manuscript, Chaco Canyon National Monument, National Park Service (1956).

Chapter 6:   Archaeological Anthropologists and Ecologists

1. A report on the archaeological surveys in and about Chaco Canyon is in press at the Government Printing Office, Washington, D.C. In it, W. James Judge describes the sampling survey, Alden C. Hayes covers the intensive inventory survey, and David M. Brugge considers the Navajo sites recorded by the surveyors.

2. Alden C. Hayes, "A Cache of Gardening Tools: Chaco Canyon," *Papers of the Archaeological Society of New Mexico* 3 (1976):73–84.

3. Applications of remote sensing techniques to archaeological investigations, particularly as they apply to Chaco Canyon, are incorporated in the following monographs:

Thomas R. Lyons, ed., *Remote Sensing Experiments in Cultural Resource Studies: Nondestructive Methods in Archeological Exploration, Survey, and Analysis,* Reports of the Chaco Center, National Park Service and University of New Mexico 1 (1976), and Thomas R. Lyons and Robert K. Hitchcock, eds., *Aerial Remote Sensing Techniques in Archeology,* Reports of the Chaco Center, National Park Service and University of New Mexico 2 (1977).

4. Marietta Wetherill Tapes, Special Collections, Zimmerman Library, University of New Mexico (1948).

5. Neil M. Judd, *The Material Culture of Pueblo Bonito,* Smithsonian Miscellaneous Collections 124(1954), pp. 346–47, and *The Architecture of Pueblo Bonito,* Smithsonian Miscellaneous Collections 147:1(1964), pp. 141–42.

6. Dwight L. Drager, "An Analysis of a Possible Communication System in the San Juan Basin of New Mexico," manuscript, Chaco Center, Albuquerque, (1976).

7. A summary of Gordon Vivian's work appeared in Gordon Vivian and Tom W. Mathews, *Kin Kletso, a Pueblo III Community in Chaco Canyon, New Mexico,* Southwestern Monuments Association, Technical Series, 6:1 (Globe, Arizona, 1965), pp. 13– 14. See also R. Gwinn Vivian, "An Inquiry into Prehistoric Social Organization in Chaco Canyon, New Mexico," in *Reconstructing Prehistoric Pueblo Societies,* ed. W. A. Longacre (Albuquerque: University of New Mexico Press, School of American Research Advanced Seminar Series, 1970), pp. 69–74, and "Conservation and Diversion: Water-control Systems in the Anasazi Southwest," in *Irrigation's Impact on Society,* University of Arizona Press (Tucson, 1974), pp. 95–112.

8. For example see Stephen A. Hall, "Late Quaternary Sedimentation and Paleoecologic History of Chaco Canyon, New Mexico," *Geological Society of America Bulletin* 88(1977):1616–17, and Kirk Bryan, *The Geology of Chaco Canyon, New Mexico, in Relation to the Life and Remains of the Prehistoric Peoples of Pueblo Bonito,* Smithsonian Miscellaneous Collections 122:7(1954), pp. 32–37.

9. Both Neil M. Judd, *The Material Culture of Pueblo Bonito* (1954), p. 3, and Kirk Bryan, *The Geology of Chaco Canyon,* pp. 45–47, discuss how arroyo cutting and a resultant lowering of the water table would have contributed to the abandonment of Chaco Canyon.

10. Consult R. Gwinn Vivian, "Prehistoric Water Conservation in Chaco Canyon," Final Technical Report, N.S.F. Grant No. GS-3100, manuscript, Chaco Center, Albuquerque (1974), and W. James Judge, "The Emergence of a Complexity in Chaco Canyon, New Mexico," paper presented at the Seventy-sixth Annual Meeting of the American Anthropological Association, Houston, December 1, 1977, manuscript, Chaco Center, Albuquerque.

11. Tom W. Mathews and Earl H. Neller, "Atlatl Cave: Archaic-Basket Maker II Investigations in Chaco Canyon National Monument," *Proceedings of the First Conference on Scientific Research in the National Parks,* Volume II, National Park Service Transactions and Proceedings Series 5, U.S. Department of the Interior (1979), p. 873. The three excavated Archaic complexes located on Chaco's mesas and terraces, 29SJ116, 29SJ126, and 29SJ1157, yielded only lithic materials; the fourth site dug, Atlatl Cave, is situated in a dry rock shelter where stone tools and vegetal materials and artifacts of both Archaic and Basket Maker II horizons were preserved. See Site Inventory.

12. Basket Maker III sites tested or completely cleared by the Chaco Center,

29SJ299a, 29SJ423, 29SJ628, and 29SJ721, each contained a number of pithouses and associated storage cists. None was devoid of structures from later periods or of remodeling by more recent occupants. Refer to the Site Inventory.

13. Pueblo I sites 29Mc184 and 29SJ626 were only tested. Sites 29SJ627, 29SJ629, 29SJ299b, and 29SJ724 were more thoroughly excavated; however, the initial Pueblo I stages at the first two were changed markedly or were obliterated by subsequent inhabitants. Ruins 29SJ299b, near Fajada Butte, and 29SJ724, in Werito's Rincón, contained elements more typical of Pueblo I in Chaco Canyon. They are described in the Site Inventory.

14. 29SJ1360, included in the Site Inventory, is a good example of Chaco villages during Pueblo II.

15. Subsurface explorations by electronic devices at Pueblo Alto are described by Roger Vickers, Lambert Dolphin, and David Johnson in an article, "Archeological Investigations at Chaco Canyon Using a Subsurface Radar," which is part of Lyons, ed., *Remote Sensing Experiments in Cultural Resource Studies,* pp.81–101.

16. Richard W. Loose and Thomas R. Lyons, "The Chetro Ketl Field: A Planned Water Control System in Chaco Canyon," also is an article in Lyons, ed. *Remote Sensing Experiments in Cultural Resource Studies,* pp. 133–53.

17. Alden C. Hayes and Thomas C. Windes, "An Anasazi Shrine in Chaco Canyon," *Papers of the Archaeological Society of New Mexico* 2 (1975):143–56.

18. The three excavated sites in Marcia's Rincón revealed a cultural evolution from Basket Maker III into Pueblo III times. Site 29SJ628 is a Basket Maker III pithouse village showing progression toward Pueblo I characteristics. 29SJ627 and 29SJ629 both were built and inhabited during Pueblo I times, but several stages of remodeling, additions, and periods of nonoccupation, lasted through Pueblo II and during Pueblo III. Ruins 29SJ626, 29SJ630, and 29SJ633, other communities in Marcia's Rincón, were only tested by exploratory trenching. See Site Inventory.

19. Judd, *The Architecture of Pueblo Bonito,* p. 148.

20. Thomas C. Windes, *Stone Circles of Chaco Canyon, Northwestern New Mexico,* Reports of the Chaco Center, Division of Chaco Research, National Park Service 5 (1978).

21. Robert Powers, Stephen Lekson, and William Gillespie, "Preliminary Investigations into the Chacoan Outlier System: A Functional and Regional Perspective," manuscript, Chaco Center, Albuquerque (1977).

22. David M. Brugge, "Tsegai: An Archeological Ethnohistory of the Chaco Region," manuscript, Chaco Center, Albuquerque (1977), and *A History of the Chaco Navajos,* Reports of the Chaco Center, Division of Chaco Research, National Park Service 4 (1980).

23. Gwinn Vivian's archaeological reconnaissance of the Chacra Mesa is the subject of his University of New Mexico M.A. thesis, "Navajo Archaeology of the Chacra Mesa, New Mexico" (1960).

24. Refer to Robert H. Lister and Florence C. Lister, *Anasazi Pottery* (Albuquerque: Maxwell Museum of Anthropology and University of New Mexico Press, 1978), for an illustrated compendium of Anasazi ceramics including Mesa Verde and Chaco Canyon types, and to a number of detailed reports by A. Helene Warren including, "Technological Studies of the Pottery of Chaco Canyon," manuscript, Chaco Center, Albuquerque

(1976), and "Source Area Studies of Pueblo I-III Pottery at Chaco Canyon," manuscript, Chaco Center, Albuquerque (1977).

25. See particularly Edwin N. Ferdon, Jr., *A Trial Survey of Mexican-Southwestern Architectural Parallels,* School of American Research Monograph 21 (Santa Fe, 1955), and Robert H. Lister, "Mesoamerican Influences at Chaco Canyon, New Mexico," *Across the Chichimec Sea* (Carbondale: Southern Illinois University Press, 1978), pp. 233-41.

26. The comprehensive report by Charles C. DiPeso, *Casas Grandes, A Fallen Trading Center of the Gran Chichimeca,* 8 vols. (Flagstaff, Arizona: Amerind Foundation and Northland Press, 1974), describes the site and its surroundings in great detail. In Vol. 2, DiPeso makes note of similarities to and possible relationships with Chaco Canyon.

27. Interpretations of Chaco economic and social systems, based upon archaeological and ethnographic evidence, have recently been addressed by several authors including: Jeffrey H. Altschul, "The Development of the Chacoan Interaction Sphere," *Journal of Anthropological Research* 34:1 (1978):109-46; Paul Grebinger, "Prehistoric Social Organization in Chaco Canyon, New Mexico: An Alternate Reconstruction," *Kiva* (Tucson) 39 (1973):2-23; W. James Judge, "The Development of a Complex Cultural Ecosystem in the Chaco Basin, New Mexico," *Proceedings of the First Conference on Scientific Research in the National Parks,* Volume 2, National Park Service transactions and Proceedings Series 5, U.S. Department of the Interior (1979), pp. 901-5; and R. Gwinn Vivian, "An Inquiry into Prehistoric Social Organization in Chaco Canyon, New Mexico," in Longacre, ed., *Reconstructing Prehistoric Pueblo Societies,* pp. 59-83.

28. A selection of articles dealing with the results of some of the archaeoastronomical research in Chaco Canyon follows: Florence Hawley Ellis, "Pueblo Sun-Moon-Star Calendar," in *Archaeoastronomy in Pre-Columbian America* (Austin: University of Texas Press, 1975), pp. 59-87; Jonathan E. Reyman, "Astronomy, Architecture, and Adaptation at Pueblo Bonito," *Science* 193 (1976):957-62; Ray A. Williamson, Howard J. Fisher, and Donnel O'Flynn, "Anasazi Solar Observatories," *Native American Astronomy* (Austin: University of Texas Press, 1977), pp. 204-17; James R. Morgan, "Were Chaco's Great Kivas Ancient Computers of Astronomy?," *El Palacio* (Santa Fe) 83:1 (1977): 28-41; and Anna Sofaer, Volker Zinser, and Rolf M. Sinclair, "A Unique Solar Marking Construct," *Science* 206 (1979):283-91.

Chapter 7:   Man and Nature in Chaco Canyon

1. Gordon Vivian and Tom W. Mathews, *Kin Kletso, A Pueblo III Community in Chaco Canyon, New Mexico,* Southwestern Monuments Association, Technical Series 6:1, Globe, Arizona (1965), pp. 111.

2. Neil M. Judd, *The Material Culture of Pueblo Bonito,* Smithsonian Miscellaneous Collections 124 (1954), p. 3.

3. Vivian and Mathews, *Kin Kletso,* p. 7.

4. Additional details concerning the Chaco Canyon landscape and its natural resources are contained in Donald D. Brand et al. *Tseh So, A Small House Ruin, Chaco Canyon, New Mexico,* University of New Mexico Anthropological Series 2:2 (Albuquer-

que, 1937):39–65; Kirk Bryan, *The Geology of Chaco Canyon, New Mexico, in Relation to the Prehistoric People of Pueblo Bonito,* Smithsonian Miscellaneous Collections 122:7 (1954); and Vivian and Mathews, *Kin Kletso,* pp. 1–24.

5. See Jesse D. Jennings, "Origins," *Ancient Native Americans,* ed. Jesse D. Jennings (Chicago: W. H. Freeman and Co., 1978), pp. 1–41, for a comprehensive review of the geological, biological, and archaeological evidence for the beginnings of man's history in the New World.

6. Postulated climatic conditions in the Chaco Canyon area during aboriginal times are based upon correlations between archaeological research and climatic change documented by evidence of geology, palynology, and dendrochronology as are found in James Schoenwetter and Frank W. Eddy, *Alluvial and Palynological Reconstruction of Environments, Navajo Reservoir District,* Museum of New Mexico Papers in Anthropology 13 (Santa Fe, 1964); James Schoenwetter and Alfred E. Dittert, Jr., "An Ecological Interpretation of Anasazi Settlement Patterns," *Anthropological Archaeology in the Americas,* (Washington D.C.: Anthropological Society of Washington, 1968), pp. 41–66; Cynthia Irwin-Williams and C. Vance Haynes, "Climatic Change and Early Population Dynamics in the Southwestern United States," *Quaternary Research* 1:1 (1970):59–71; Stephen A. Hall, "Late Quaternary Sedimentation and Paleoecologic History of Chaco Canyon, New Mexico," *Geological Society of America Bulletin* 88 (1977):1593–1618; and Jeffrey S. Dean and William J. Robinson, "Dendroclimatic Variability in the American Southwest, A.D. 680–1970," Final Report to the National Park Service, Department of the Interior, manuscript, Chaco Center, Albuquerque (1977).

7. For further discussions of Archaic cultures in the Southwest, see two articles by Cynthia Irwin-Williams, "Archaic Culture History in the Southwestern United States," *Eastern New Mexico University Contributions in Anthropology* 1:4 (1968):48–53, and "The Oshara Tradition: Origins of Anasazi Culture," *Eastern New Mexico University Contributions in Anthropology* 5:1 (1973).

8. A discussion of the Southwestern tradition is presented by Gordon R. Willey in *An Introduction to American Archaeology,* Volume 1, *North and Middle America,* (Englewood Cliffs, N.J.: Prentice-Hall, 1966), pp. 181–87, and summarized by William D. Lipe in the chapter, "The Southwest," in Jennings, ed. *Ancient Native Americans,* pp. 341–43. Lipe's article also reviews in a general sense the Anasazi, Hohokam, and Mogollon cultural manifestations.

9. Earl H. Morris and Robert F. Burgh, *Basket Maker II Sites Near Durango, Colorado,* Carnegie Institution of Washington, Publication 604, Washington, D.C. (1954).

10. Consult Vivian and Mathews, *Kin Kletso,* pp. 111–15, for more lengthy considerations of the abandonment of the Chaco and the direction of movements away from the Chaco Plateau.

APPENDIX:
Inventory of Investigated
Chaco Canyon
Archaeological Sites

This tabulation lists all archaeological sites in, or immediately adjacent to, Chaco Canyon National Monument that have been excavated, tested, stabilized, or from which tree-ring samples have been collected. It includes all of the major Chaco Anasazi communities and most of the other ruins that have been examined by archaeologists.

The sites have been placed in culture stages and periods within the Anasazi continuum. Furthermore, the late Pueblo II and Pueblo III periods have been subdivided into the Bonito, Hosta Butte, and McElmo phases.

Many Chaco Canyon Anasazi settlements were built, occupied, and remodeled over long periods of time, spanning several culture periods. In such instances, in this scheme, sites usually are classified according to their major period of occupation, or in some cases, in respect to their initial construction.

ARCHAIC: DESERT CULTURE

Atlatl Cave

Other Designations: 29SJ1156 (National Park Service).

Location: Shallow cave on north mesa at head of first rincón west of Casa Chiquita, approximately 1.5 miles northwest of Pueblo Bonito, Chaco Canyon National Monument.

Features: A dry rock shelter containing occupational refuse and pictographs. No habitations. Area in front of and below cave used as campsite.

Excavations and Reports: Tom Mathews, Chaco Center, excavated shelter and tested campsites in 1975 and 1976. Reports on file, Chaco Center, Albuquerque. Brief note on Atlatl Cave published by Tom W. Mathews and Earl Neller in "Atlatl Cave: Archaic-Basket Maker II Investigations in Chaco Canyon National Monument," *Proceedings of the First Conference on Scientific Research in the National Parks,* Volume 2, National Park Service Transactions and Proceedings Series 5, U.S. Department of the Interior (1979) p. 873.

Dates: Carbon-14 dates from organic material collected during excavations range from 2900 to 910 B.C.

Culture Stage: Archaic and Basket Maker II.

Remarks: Only non-ceramic site to yield well-preserved artifacts of wood and fiber. Sole excavated Chaco Canyon site thought to have Basket Maker II materials.

29SJ116

Other Designations: None.

Location: North mesa, west of Cly Canyon, approximately 1 mile northwest of Pueblo Bonito, Chaco Canyon National Monument. Adjacent to rock quarry, 29SJ1118.

Features: A campsite with an assortment of lithic materials on the surface.

Excavations and Reports: Tom Mathews, Chaco Center, stripped off about two-thirds of the surface of the site in 1973. Field notes on file, Chaco Center, Albuquerque.

Dates: None.

Culture Stage: Archaic.

Remarks: Back-filled after excavation.

29SJ126

Other Designations: None.

Location: North mesa, east rim of Cly Canyon, approximately .75 mile northwest of Pueblo Bonito, Chaco National Monument.

Features: A campsite with a surface scatter of lithic materials.

Excavations and Reports: Thomas R. Lyons and Dennis Stanford, Chaco Center, extensively trenched the site in 1972. Field notes on file, Chaco Center, Albuquerque.

Dates: None.

Culture Stage: Archaic.

Remarks: The first Archaic Culture site to be excavated in Chaco Canyon. Back-filled after excavation.

29SJ1157

Other Designations: Sleeping Dune and Ant Hill Dune (Neller).

Location: Covers two sand dunes on the north mesa at head of first rincón west of Casa Chiquita, approximately 1.5 miles northwest of Pueblo Bonito, Chaco Canyon National Monument. Lies just below Atlatl Cave.

Features: A sparse scattering of chipped stone tools, cobble manos and hammerstones, fireburned sandstone flakes, and a large hearth area on ridges of deflated dunes.

Excavations and Reports: Thomas Mathews and Earl Neller, Chaco Center, trenched the site in 1975 and 1976. Preliminary reports on file, Chaco Center, Albuquerque.

Dates: None, but artifacts indicate occupation contemporary with that of Atlatl Cave.

Culture Stage: Archaic and Basket Maker II.

Remarks: Most probably a part of a long-term campsite which included neighboring Atlatl Cave.

ANASAZI: BASKET MAKER III

Half House

Other Designations: Arroyo House (Roberts), 29SJ1657 (National Park Service), Bc244, Bc373 (University of New Mexico).

Location: Exposed by arroyo cutting in the south bank of the Chaco Wash, 7 miles east of Pueblo Bonito, directly below Shabik'eshchee Village, Chaco Canyon National Monument.

Features: About half of a pithouse whose floor was 16 feet below the level of the present canyon floor. The remains indicated a house about 14 feet in diameter with firepit, sipapu, subfloor pits, and a floor ridge separating an area for culinary activities from the remainder of the unit. No postholes were apparent.

Excavations and Reports: Richard N. Adams, University of New Mexico Field Session, excavated the site in 1947. Results published in, *Half House: A Pithouse in Chaco Canyon, New Mexico.* Papers of the Michigan Academy of Science, Arts, and Letters, 35 (Ann Arbor, 1951).

Dates: Tree-ring dates from charcoal fragments are described as tenuous;- therefore, a supposed cutting date of A.D. 691 may not be reliable. But, when considering the architectural and artifactual evidence and the conditions of the fill in the house, it has been estimated that it probably was built and occupied between A.D. 691 and 740.

Culture Stage: Basket Maker III.

Remarks: First noted by Roberts and Judd in 1926. The many feet of alluvium that had accumulated over the structure since its abandonment attest to the great amount of valley fill in Chaco Canyon after Anasazi times. Site destroyed by arroyo erosion following excavation.

Shabik'eshchee Village

Other Designations: 29SJ1659 (National Park Service), Bc256 (University of New Mexico).

Location: On the north edge of the Chacra Mesa overlooking Chaco Canyon, about 9 miles east of Pueblo Bonito. Straddles the south boundary line of Chaco Canyon National Monument.

Features: Village consisted of about 20 pithouses, 1 ceremonial structure or Great Kiva, 48 storage bins, and several refuse deposits.

Excavations and Reports: Frank H. H. Roberts, Jr., Smithsonian Institution, excavated the site in 1927. Results published in, *Shabik'eshchee Village, A Late Basket Maker Site in the Chaco Canyon, New Mexico.* Bureau of American Ethnology Bulletin 92 (Washington, D.C., 1929).

Deric O'Bryan, Gila Pueblo, collected tree-ring specimens in 1940.

Alden C. Hayes and John Thrift, Chaco Center, excavated two pit structures not cleared by Roberts to obtain tree-ring samples in 1973. The two units were designated houses Y and Z. Field notes on file, Chaco Center, Albuquerque.

Dates: Initially, from specimens collected by Deric O'Bryan, House H was dated A.D. 757 and the Great Kiva 753. Reexamination of these samples resulted in a reduction in the number of dates originally established and an earlier dating of A.D. 557 and 581 for the Great Kiva. Wood specimens obtained by Hayes from a pithouse provided a date of A.D. 537.

Culture Stage: Basket Maker III.

Remarks: One of the first Basket Maker III sites in the Southwest to be carefully excavated and reported upon. The report constituted the first complete record of a major excavation in the Chaco area. Adjustment of the original dating of the site, plus additional dates, clearly place its occupation in the sixth century A.D. Shabik'eshchee Village was the type-site for this culture period in the San Juan Basin for many years. It demonstrates that the Great Kiva is an early Anasazi attribute. The site was left open and unstabilized after excavation, hence, most exposed features now badly deteriorated.

29SJ299a

Other Designations: Site 29SJ299 found to have two separate components upon excavation. This unit designated 29SJ299a.

Location: At tip of ridge north of Fajada Butte, south side of canyon, 4 miles southeast of Pueblo Bonito, Chaco Canyon National Monument.

Features: Settlement consisting of 3 Basket Maker III pithouses and a group of 10 associated storage cists. A Pueblo II kiva and a post-Basket Maker hearth intruded into the site.

Excavations and Reports: Alden C. Hayes and Richard Loose, Chaco Center, dug an estimated 90 percent of the ruin in 1973. Preliminary report on file, Chaco Center, Albuquerque.

Dates: Archaeomagnetic dates for 2 of the pithouses span the years A.D. 607 to 685.

Culture Stage: Basket Maker III.

Remarks: After abandonment, the Basket Maker III community was impacted upon by later settlements.

29SJ423

Other Designations: None.

Location: On West Mesa overlooking Chaco Canyon, .25 mile southeast of Peñasco Blanco and about 2.5 miles west of Pueblo Bonito, Chaco Canyon National Monument.

Features: Village with surface indications of at least 20 pithouses and storage cists and 1 Great Kiva. A later arch-shaped masonry shrine had been built over the earlier remains.

Excavations and Reports: Alden C. Hayes and Thomas Windes, Chaco Center, dug a small portion of the site in 1973. Notes on file, Chaco Center, Albuquerque.

Dates: Tree-ring dates for the three construction stages of the Great Kiva range from the A.D. 520s to 557.

Culture Stage: Pithouses and Great Kiva, Basket Maker III; shrine, Pueblo III.

Remarks: Another demonstration of the presence of the Great Kiva in Basket Maker III times. The shrine also appears to have functioned as a link in the Chaco visual communication system.

29SJ628

Other Designations: None.

Location: In Marcia's Rincón, south side of canyon, 3 miles southeast of Pueblo Bonito, Chaco Canyon National Monument.

Features: Six pithouses and related storage cists.

Excavations and Reports: Alden C. Hayes and Marcia Truell, Chaco Center, excavated about 80 percent of the site in 1973. Report on file, Chaco Center.

Dates: Archaeomagnetic dates indicate the majority of the pithouses were constructed between A.D. 760 and 780. The latest pit structure was dated A.D. 830.

Culture Stage: Basket Maker III and early Pueblo I.

Remarks: The series of pithouses exhibited an architectural progression typical of Basket Maker III in Chaco Canyon. Site back-filled after excavation.

29SJ721

Other Designations: None.

Location: On small knoll near mouth of Werito's Rincón, south side of canyon, 1.25 miles southeast of Pueblo Bonito, Chaco Canyon National Monument.

Features: 2 pithouses with associated storage cists and baking pits, and 1 slab-based surface room. A Pueblo III kiva was dug into the knoll long after the first occupation.

Excavations and Reports: Alden C. Hayes and Thomas Windes, Chaco Center, completely excavated the structure in 1973. Report on file, Chaco Center, Albuquerque.

Dates: Estimated in the A.D. 700s.

Culture Stage: Basket Maker III–early Pueblo I.

Remarks: Back-filled after excavation. An eleventh century Pueblo III kiva, apparently started by Pueblo III inhabitants of a nearby pueblo, appears not to have been completed.

ANASAZI: PUEBLO I

Judd's Pithouse No. 1

Other Designations: None.

Location: On south side of the canyon near Casa Rinconada, opposite Pueblo Bonito, Chaco Canyon National Monument.

Features: A shallow pithouse, 17 feet in diameter, with straight, unlined walls, and a firepit and storage bins on the floor.

Excavations and Reports: Neil Judd, National Geographic Society, partially cleared the house in 1920. He reported his findings in, "Two Chaco Canyon Pit Houses," *Smithsonian Institution, Annual Report for 1922* (Washington, D. C., 1924).

Dates: None. Cultural evidence used for general temporal placement.

Culture Stage: Pueblo I.

Remarks: The first pithouse excavated by the Pueblo Bonito Expedition. It mainly was dug by unsupervised Navajo laborers, hence details about its features are not complete.

Judd's Pithouse No. 2

Other Designations: 29SJ1678 (National Park Service), Bc194 (University of New Mexico).

Location: North bank of the Chaco Wash, about 1 mile east of Pueblo Bonito, Chaco Canyon National Monument.

Features: Partially destroyed by arroyo cutting, but remainder indicated a circular pithouse approximately 13 feet in diameter. A bench, upon which the wall poles rested and into which the four roof support posts were embedded, encircled the preserved portion of the structure. A firepit was sunk into the center of the floor. Charred remains of a portion of the superstructure were found in the fill.

Excavations and Reports: Neil Judd, National Geographic Society, salvaged the site in 1922. Report appeared in, "Two Chaco Canyon Pit Houses." *Smithsonian Institution, Annual Report for 1922* (Washington, D.C., 1924).

Dates: Two tree-ring samples produced only tentative dates. It was suggested that the site was constructed sometime after A.D. 777. Artifacts recovered from the pithouse support this temporal placement.

Culture Stage: Pueblo I.

Remarks: Completely removed by arroyo cutting.

29Mc184

Other Designations: None.

Location: Just east of Chaco Canyon–Thoreau road, 7 miles south of Monument boundary, about 11 miles southeast of Pueblo Bonito, Navajo tribal lands.

Features: A large Pueblo I community, with 4 separate house units marked by rows of upright slabs. Each house has at least 1 habitation and 3 or more storerooms fronted by a depression denoting a pithouse. Trash is concentrated beyond the pithouses.

Excavations and Reports: Alden C. Hayes and Thomas Windes, Chaco Center, ran test trenches through the trash deposits of the site in 1975. Field notes on file, Chaco Center, Albuquerque.

Dates: None, but ceramics and architecture suggest an occupation of about A.D. 750 to 800.

Culture Stage: Pueblo I.

Remarks: Test trenches back-filled after excavation.

29SJ299b

Other Designations: During excavation, Site 29SJ299 was found to have two components. This unit designated 29SJ299b.

Location: On ridge north of Fajada Butte, south side of the canyon, 4 miles southeast of Pueblo Bonito, Chaco Canyon National Monument.

Features: 4 mud-walled storerooms fronted by 3 open ramadas and a pithouse. Probably a single-family complex.

Excavations and Reports: Alden C. Hayes and Thomas Windes, Chaco Center, cleared the surface structures and about half of the pithouse in 1974. Report on file, Chaco Center, Albuquerque.

Dates: None. Architecture and artifacts indicate occupation between A.D. 710 and 740.

Culture Stage: Pueblo I.

Remarks: Back-filled after excavation.

29SJ626

Other Designations: None.

Location: On a ridge south of Marcia's Rincón, south side of canyon, about 3.25 miles southeast of Pueblo Bonito, Chaco Canyon National Monument.

Features: A small, unexcavated site with surface indications of simple slab and mud-walled rooms and possibly one or more pithouses.

Excavations and Reports: Alden C. Hayes and Thomas Windes, Chaco Center, ran a small test trench through a part of this ruin in 1975. Field notes on file, Chaco Center, Albuquerque.

Dates: None.

Culture Stage: Pueblo I.

Remarks: Test trench back-filled after excavation.

29SJ627

Other Designations: None.

Location: In Marcia's Rincón, south side of canyon, 3 miles southeast of Pueblo Bonito, Chaco Canyon National Monument.

Features: A small community that went through almost continuous remodeling and additions during its lengthy occupation. Began as a complex of pithouse dwellings, ramadas, and crude aboveground storerooms. Later changes included conversion of some storerooms to habitations, the building of additional living quarters, walling in ramadas, and converting pithouses into kivas. Trash was dumped near the village.

Excavations and Reports: Alden C. Hayes and Marcia Truell, Chaco Center, initiated excavations in 1974. Later in 1974 and in 1975, W. James Judge and Truell, Chaco Center, continued work at the site until about 80 percent of it was cleared. Four burials were found in or near the rooms. Report on file, Chaco Center, Albuquerque.

Dates: Archaeomagnetic dates verify the long occupation of Site 29SJ627, ranging from A.D. 795 to about 1200.

Culture Stage: Construction and main occupation, early Pueblo I to mid-Pueblo II; restricted use into Pueblo III.

Remarks: Demonstrates the frequent long usage and refurbishing of Chaco Canyon communities, and the utilization of simple villages into the time of the great towns. Back-filled after excavation.

29SJ629

Other Designations: None.

Location: In Marcia's Rincón, south side of canyon, 3 miles southeast of Pueblo Bonito, Chaco Canyon National Monument.

Features: A site showing a lengthy span of occupation. An initial core embracing a pithouse, ramada, and several aboveground storage rooms, built of mud and crude masonry, was enlarged by an additional pithouse, more storage rooms, some living rooms, and a kiva. Trash deposit nearby.

Excavations and Reports: W. James Judge and Thomas Windes, Chaco Center, excavated the site during the 1975 and 1976 field seasons. Report on file, Chaco Center, Albuquerque.

Dates: An extensive series of archaeomagnetic dates place the initial occupation about A.D. 875–925. Remodeling and expansion took place between A.D. 975 and 1025, followed by a period of abandonment. Reoccupation is suggested between A.D. 1100 and 1200.

Culture Stage: Late Pueblo I to Pueblo III.

Remarks: Another example of the long-time occupation of many Chaco sites, even some of the smaller villages.

29SJ724

Other Designations: None.

Location: Near mouth of Werito's Rincón, south side of canyon, 1.25 miles southeast of Pueblo Bonito, Chaco Canyon National Monument.

Features: Ruin consists of 3 complexes of surface rooms with slab and mud walls, ramadas, and pithouses built on top of a low ridge.

Excavations and Reports: W. James Judge and Thomas Windes, Chaco Center, dug one unit of the ruin and tested another in 1974. The excavated segment contained 9 surface rooms, 2 habitations fronting 7 smaller storerooms, a ramada, and a pithouse dwelling. Report on file, Chaco Center, Albuquerque.

Dates: None, but according to the village plan and method of construction, and the pottery from the site, it appears to have been in use between A.D. 725 and 750.

Culture Stage: Pueblo I.

Remarks: Following excavation, the site was back-filled.

ANASAZI: PUEBLO II

Hutch's Site

Other Designations: 29SJ838 (National Park Service), Bc126 (University of New Mexico).

Location: On canyon bottom, south side of Chaco Wash, opposite Kin Kletso, about .5 mile west of Pueblo Bonito, Chaco Canyon National Monument.

Features: Small house unit of about 11 rooms, 2 kivas, and a trash mound.

Excavations and Reports: Dug by Charles Hutchinson, J. Charles Kelley, and Albert Ely, School of American Research, in 1934. Incomplete field notes on file, Chaco Center, Albuquerque.

Dates: None.

Culture Stage: Pueblo II–Pueblo III.

Remarks: Site had been pothunted prior to the 1934 excavations.

Three-C Site

Other Designations: 29SJ625 (National Park Service), Bc243 (University of New Mexico).

Location: In the gap just west of Fajada Butte which leads south out of Chaco Canyon, about 3 miles east of Pueblo Bonito, Chaco Canyon National Monument. Site of former Civilian Conservation Corps camp.

Features: A rectangular room block of 9 houses arranged in two parallel rows. Two kivas east of the rooms and a trash deposit beyond them.

Excavations and Reports: Gordon Vivian, National Park Service, salvaged the roomblock in 1939 and returned to dig the kivas in 1949. Sixteen burials were found. His report upon the site appears in, *The Three-C Site, an Early Pueblo II Ruin in Chaco Canyon, New Mexico.* University of New Mexico Publications in Anthropology, 13 (Albuquerque, 1965).

Reexamined in 1976 by Chaco Center staff seeking samples for archaeomagnetic dating.

Dates: None, but analyses of architecture and ceramics imply construction and occupation within the years A.D. 870 to 950.

Culture Stage: Pueblo II.

Remarks: Site dug as a salvage project before being covered by the C.C.C. camp buildings. After abandonment of the camp, the facility was razed, again exposing the ruin. The pueblo has not been stabilized and is poorly preserved.

29SJ1118

Other Designations: None.

Location: North Mesa, west rim of Cly Canyon, approximately 1 mile northwest of Pueblo Bonito, Chaco Canyon National Monument. Adjacent to campsite, 29SJ116.

Features: A prehistoric rock quarry from which tabular sandstone was obtained for construction purposes.

Excavations and Reports: Tom Mathews, Chaco Center, cleared about one-half of the feature in 1973. Field notes on file, Chaco Center, Albuquerque.

Dates: None.

Culture Stage: Probably Pueblo II or Pueblo III.

Remarks: Back-filled after excavation.

29SJ1360

Other Designations: None.

Location: North foot of Fajada Butte, about 4.25 miles southeast of Pueblo Bonito, south side of canyon, Chaco Canyon National Monument.

Features: Small arc-shaped site containing 2 groups of house and storerooms, built of mud and slab walls, separated by a series of ramadas. A kiva is associated with each group of surface structures.

Excavations and Reports: Alden C. Hayes and Randall Morrison, Chaco Center, excavated about three-fourths of the ruin in 1974. Field notes on file, Chaco Center, Albuquerque.

Dates: None. Style and method of construction of the village and the complex of pottery obtained suggest occupancy between the late A.D. 900s and early 1000s.

Culture Stage: Early Pueblo II.

Remarks: Back-filled after excavation.

ANASAZI: LATE PUEBLO II–PUEBLO III, BONITO PHASE

Bromberg's Ditch

Other Designations: 29SJ1095 (National Park Service), Bc364 (University of New Mexico).

Location: Near the south bank of the Chaco Wash just east of its confluence with the Escavada Wash, below Peñasco Blanco, about 3 miles west of Pueblo Bonito, Chaco Canyon National Monument.

Features: Section of a canal associated with a water control system. Appears to have been bordered, at least on one side, by a masonry wall and a slab lining. Possibly part of an irrigation works associated with Peñasco Blanco.

Excavations and Reports: A 36-foot-long section of the canal was exposed by William Bromberg, National Park Service, as a salvage project in 1960. Report on file, Chaco Center, Albuquerque.

Dates: None.

Culture Stage: Probably Pueblo III, Bonito Phase.

Remarks: Part of the canal destroyed by arroyo cutting prior to excavations. Holsinger noted the same feature in his 1901 report and Judd observed it in 1920.

Casa Rinconada

Other Designations: 29SJ386 (National Park Service), Bc255 (University of New Mexico).

Location: .5 mile directly south of Pueblo Bonito, south side of the canyon, Chaco Canyon National Monument.

Features: The largest known isolated Great Kiva in Chaco Canyon. The central circular chamber with antechambers on the north and south has a bench which had undergone two modifications, vaults, firebox, seating pits for roof supports, an underground passage from the kiva to the north antechamber, and various lesser floor features.

Excavations and Reports: Gordon Vivian, then of the School of American Research and the University of New Mexico, excavated the great sanctuary in 1931. The site is reported by Vivian and Paul Reiter in their joint monograph, *The Great Kivas of Chaco Canyon and Their Relationships,* School of American Research Monograph 22 (Santa Fe, 1960; reprint Albuquerque: University of New Mexico Press, 1972).

Florence M. Hawley, School of American Research, is thought to have gathered a collection of tree-ring specimens from the site in 1930.

Joseph Maloney, School of American Research, demonstrated the existence of pithouses and storage cists on the slopes of the knoll upon which the Great Kiva is situated in 1936.

Dates: One tree-ring specimen is dated at A.D. 1054. Casa Rinconada's construction and occupation is felt to fall generally in the last half of the eleventh century, coincident with the major building periods at the large Pueblo III towns.

Culture Stage: Pueblo III, Bonito Phase.

Remarks: Extensive repairs to the walls and floor features were accomplished by Gordon Vivian, School of American Research, in 1933. Subsequently, National Park Service teams stabilized the chamber and its peripheral features. The presence in the upper fill of the sanctuary of pottery types introduced into the Chaco by late migrants from the Mesa Verde country suggests usage into the later stages of the Chaco Anasazi.

Chetro Ketl

Other Designations: 29SJ1928 (National Park Service), Bc246 (University of New Mexico).

Location: North side of Chaco Canyon, about .5 mile east of Pueblo Bonito, Chaco Canyon National Monument.

Features: Town contained over 500 rooms, at least 12 kivas, 2 Great Kivas, and several tower kivas. Possibly stood four stories in places. Earlier structures lie below those now standing. Extensive refuse deposit east of the community.

Excavations and Reports: Edgar L. Hewett, School of American Research, Museum of New Mexico, and University of New Mexico, excavated about one-half of the site during the periods 1920–21 and 1929–34. General statements about investigations published in Hewett's book, *The Chaco Canyon and its Monuments* (Albuquerque: University of New Mexico Press, 1936).

Florence M. Hawley, a member of Hewett's staff, conducted comprehensive studies of the trash mound, construction techniques, and ceramics, employing dates obtained from tree-rings. Results published in, *The Significance of the Dated Prehistory of Chetro Ketl, Chaco Canyon, New Mexico,* University of New Mexico Bulletin, Monograph Series, vol. 1, no. 1 (Albuquerque, 1934).

Paul Reiter, who supervised much of the field work at Chetro Ketl, presented an M.A. thesis to the University of New Mexico entitled, "The Ancient Pueblo of Chetro Ketl," in 1933. Several other M.A. theses were written on various details of Chetro Ketl archeology.

Gordon Vivian, National Park Service, and Reiter collaborated on a description of the Chetro Ketl Great Kivas in *The Great Kivas of Chaco Canyon and Their Relationships,* School of American Research Monograph 22 (Santa Fe, 1960; reprint Albuquerque: University of New Mexico Press, 1972).

Deric O'Bryan, Gila Pueblo, collected tree-ring specimens in 1940.

Gordon Vivian undertook excavations in conjunction with National Park Service stabilization projects, including the cleaning out of a room in which a collection of ritual artifacts was found, in the 1940s. Description of the wooden artifacts published by R. Gwinn Vivian, Dulce N. Dodgen, and Gayle H. Hartmann in, *Wooden Ritual Artifacts from Chaco Canyon, New Mexico, The Chetro Ketl Collection*. Anthropological Papers of the University of Arizona 32 (Tucson, 1978).

Dates: A total of 380 tree-ring dates provides Chetro Ketl with the best building sequence of all the great Chaco pueblos. Dates range from A.D. 883 to 1117, with the first major building period of the presently visible pueblo falling in the interval between A.D. 1036 and 1040. Some nonconstruction dates were derived from charcoal fragments discarded with household sweepings.

Culture Stage: Pueblo III, Bonito Phase.

Remarks: Information gained from the excavation of the Great Kiva in the east plaza provided an understanding of the construction and remodeling techniques employed in such huge sanctuaries. Rich caches of ceremonial objects from Chetro Ketl's rooms and kivas indicate elaborate Anasazi ritual pageantry. The refuse deposit, which was carefully excavated and its contents thoroughly analyzed and dated, provided many details about everyday life in the town. Contemporaneity between Chetro Ketl and the nearby talus communities implies that many of the smaller units probably were offshoots from the larger centers. Certain architectural features, such as the colonnade fronting a portion of the courtyard, are believed to demonstrate contacts with or influences from cultures to the south in Mexico. Excavated sections of Chetro Ketl have been stabilized by the National Park Service.

Headquarters Sites, Ruin A

In 1950, two sites were located and tested in the area chosen for a new National Park Service Visitor Center and Park Headquarters building. One ruin was outlined, excavated in small part, and back-filled; the other was excavated and subsequently destroyed by construction activities. They both are referred to as the Headquarters sites, but here will be separately identified as ruins A and B.

Other Designations: 29SJ515 (National Park Service), Bc211 (University of New Mexico).

Location: At the National Park Service Visitor Center, north side of canyon, 3.5 miles east of Pueblo Bonito, Chaco Canyon National Monument.

Features: A fairly extensive, deeply buried ruin with a central room block 118 feet long. At each end, there are wings of rooms extending out over 70 feet. Large rooms built of cored masonry of soft sandstone blocks. Fill of rooms contained refuse and one burial. Kiva with narrow bench, bench recess, and subfloor ventilator.

Excavations and Reports: Gordon Vivian, National park Service, tested the site in 1950 to determine its size and general characteristics. Excavations made in portions of 5 rooms and 1 kiva and back-filled. He briefly mentions the site in his joint publication with Tom Mathews, *Kin Kletso, A Pueblo III Community in Chaco Canyon, New Mexico,* Southwestern Monuments Association Technical Series, vol. 6, part 1, (Globe, Arizona, 1965).

Dates: None, but cultural contents and architecture suggest construction during second half of the eleventh century.

Culture Stage: Pueblo III, Bonito Phase.

Remarks: Buried by alluvial wash from a break in the north canyon wall. Altogether, the masonry, room size, kiva style, and ground plan suggest a small, late Chaco town somewhat like Wijiji. Contained refuse and a burial from occupants of the later Headquarters Site, Ruin B. It is intact, but completely covered by valley fill.

Hungo Pavi

Other Designations: Crooked Nose (Brand), 29SJ1918 (National Park Service), Bc247 (University of New Mexico).

Location: Slightly less than 2 miles east of Pueblo Bonito on the north side of Chaco Canyon, National Monument.

Features: Estimations indicate 73 lower-story rooms and at least 2 kivas, placing Hungo Pavi in the medium-sized town category. When occupied, it was built to a height of at least three stories.

Excavations and Reports: None. A. E. Douglass and the First Beam Expedition collected tree-ring specimens in 1922 and 1923. Subsequently, other specimens were obtained by Florence M. Hawley, School of American Research, in 1931; by Deric O'Bryan, Gila Pueblo, in 1940; and by Gordon Vivian, National Park Service, while making wall repairs in 1957.

Dates: Tree-ring dates span the period A.D. 943 to 1047. Dates as early as 943 offer the possibility that construction started at Hungo Pavi during the beginning stages of the major Chaco towns. Other dates indicate a second building spurt at around A.D. 1000 and final construction during the mid-eleventh century Chaco boom.

Culture Stage: Pueblo III, Bonito Phase.

Remarks: Hungo Pavi's standing walls have been stabilized by the National Park Service.

Hurst Julian's Niches

Other Designations: 29SJ1944 (National Park Service), Bc130, Bc133 (University of New Mexico).

Location: A series of small cavities along the base of the north cliff of the canyon between Chetro Ketl and Kin Kletso, Chaco Canyon National Monument.

Features: Most cavities are natural openings, but several had been modified by man and a few had been sealed with mud. Found cached in them were a variety of wooden artifacts, lengths of cordage, basketry, sandals, and an assortment of vegetal remains.

Excavations and Reports: Hurst Julian, Custodian of Chaco Canyon National Monument, and Dorothy Keur, School of American Research, cleaned out the niches in 1932 and 1933. A student paper by Keur, on file at the Chaco Center, Albuquerque, itemizes the specimens recovered.

Dates: None.

Culture Stage: Believed to be Pueblo III, Bonito Phase, because of their nearness to several of the great towns.

Remarks: There is no indication that this significant collection has ever been studied.

Kin Bineola

Other Designations: House of the Winds (Hewett), 29SJ1580 (National Park Service).

Location: About 10 miles southwest of Pueblo Bonito on Bineola Wash, a tributary of the Chaco Wash; a detached section of Chaco Canyon National Monument.

Features: Town containing approximately 100 ground-floor rooms and 10 kivas. Estimated to have stood four stories in places.

Excavations and Reports: None. Tree-ring samples collected intermittently between 1923 and 1963 by Douglass' First Beam Expedition, Florence M. Hawley, School of American Research, and Charles Voll, National Park Service Ruins Stabilization Unit. Minor clearing of a few rooms associated with Park Service stabilization in the 1960s.

Richard Wetherill is reported to have found many burials in a ruin near Kin Bineola in 1900.

Dates: Two well-defined clusters of tree-ring dates mark the earliest and latest dated construction periods of Kin Bineola; the first at about A.D. 943 or slightly later, the second from 1119 to 1124.

Culture Stage: Pueblo III, Bonito Phase.

Remarks: Although site is unexcavated, types of masonry and dates indicate a span of occupation comparable to other large Chaco Canyon pueblos. Extensive lands suitable for horticulture adjoin Kin Bineola, and there are remnants of water control devices in the vicinity. Standing walls have been stabilized by the National Park Service.

Kin Klizhin

Other Designations: Black House (Hewett), 29SJ1413 (National Park Service).

Location: About 6.5 miles southwest of Pueblo Bonito on a small tributary arroyo of the Chaco Wash, a detached section of Chaco Canyon National Monument.

Features: One of the smaller great towns with about 18 ground-floor rooms and 6 kivas. Some rooms surround a three-story tower kiva.

Excavations and Reports: None. Tree-ring specimens collected by Florence M. Hawley, School of American Research, in 1932.

Dates: One fragment of wood dated to A.D. 1084.

Culture Stage: Pueblo III, Bonito Phase.

Remarks: Dates and construction techniques place Kin Klizhin within range of contemporaneous Chaco Canyon classic pueblos. Nearby are remains of prehistoric irrigation works. Some standing walls have been stabilized by the National Park Service.

234

Kin Nahasbas

Other Designations: 29SJ392 (National Park Service), Bc249 (University of New Mexico).

Location: A few hundred feet west of Una Vida on the side of a sandy point protruding from the north wall of the canyon, 3 miles east of Pueblo Bonito, Chaco Canyon National Monument.

Features: An isolated Great Kiva exhibiting two periods of wall construction but only a single set of floor features. Most standard Great Kiva features are present: antechamber, bench, vaults, firebox, and seating pits to hold vertical roof support posts.

Excavations and Reports: W. W. Postlethwaite and Dorothy Luhrs, University of New Mexico, excavated the site in 1935. No final report, but Luhrs wrote a preliminary account, on file at the Chaco Center, Albuquerque.

Gordon Vivian and Paul Reiter mapped the site in 1939 in connection with their study of Chaco Great Kivas and included a description of it in their *The Great Kivas of Chaco Canyon and Their Relationships,* School of American Research Monograph 22 (Santa Fe, 1960; reprint Albuquerque: University of New Mexico Press, 1972).

Dates: No tree-ring dates from the site. Judging from dates assigned the two styles of masonry in the Great Kiva wall, representing the two periods of construction, it is proposed that the sanctuary was built between about A.D. 1030 and 1070 and renovated around 1100 or later. The pottery complex supports these dates.

Culture Stage: Pueblo III, Bonito Phase.

Remarks: Kin Nahasbas is thought to be the earliest known isolated Chaco Great Kiva which may have served more than a single community.

Kin Ya-a

Other Designations: 29SJ108 (National Park Service).

Location: About 26 miles south of Pueblo Bonito, 2 miles east of the town of Crownpoint, New Mexico; a detached section of Chaco Canyon National Monument.

Features: A medium-sized town containing about 22 one-story rooms, 2 kivas, and 1 tower kiva.

Excavations and Reports: Tree-ring specimens collected by Florence M. Hawley, School of American Research, in 1932. National Park Service stabilization crews cleared a few rooms in the 1950s.

Kin Ya-a was visited and briefly described by Jesse W. Fewkes in 1916 in *Archaeological Investigations in New Mexico, Colorado, and Utah,* Smithsonian Miscellaneous Collections, vol. 68, no. 1 (Washington, D.C., 1917).

Dates: A cluster of tree-ring dates falls about the year A.D. 1106.

Culture Stage: Pueblo III, Bonito Phase.

Remarks: A Chaco outpost, connected with the Chaco Canyon communities by a well-defined road. Surrounded by lands suited for horticulture. The high-standing walls have been strengthened and stabilized by the National Park Service.

Peñasco Blanco

Other Designations: White Rock Point (Hewett), 29SJ410 (National Park Service), Bc250 (University of New Mexico).

Location: On West Mesa bordering Chaco Canyon, about 3 miles west of Pueblo Bonito, Chaco Canyon National Monument.

Features: One of the most extensive of the Chaco towns. Unique in that all of its exterior walls are curved, forming a great elipse. Over 150 ground-floor rooms and 9 kivas may be discerned. Originally stood at least three stories high. Refuse mound to the east of the pueblo.

Excavations and Reports: None. However, a considerable amount of unrecorded digging has taken place at Peñasco Blanco, mostly in the 1890s.

Frank H. H. Roberts, Jr., National Geographic Society, cut stratigraphic trenches through the trash deposits in 1926 in connection with his studies of Chaco Canyon ceramics.

Tree-ring specimens collected by Judd, National Geographic Society, in 1922; by Douglass, First Beam Expedition, in 1923; by Florence M. Hawley, School of American Research, in 1932; and by Deric O'Bryan, Gila Pueblo, in 1946.

Some walls were partially cleared by Park Service stabilization crews in the 1960s.

Dates: Peñasco Blanco ranks third among Chaco sites in number of dated tree-ring specimens. A concentration of dates around A.D. 900 is related to the earliest building period; construction continued until at least A.D. 1088.

Culture Stage: Pueblo III, Bonito Phase.

Remarks: Peñasco Blanco has earliest dated construction stage of the large Chaco Canyon masonry towns. Site in poor condition because of extensive vandalism prior to National Park Service stabilization program.

Poco Site

Other Designations: 29SJ1010 (National Park Service).

Location: On high point of Pictured Cliff Mesa north of Chaco Canyon, about 2.75 miles northeast of Pueblo Bonito, Navajo allotment land.

Features: Apparently a nonhabitation site related to the Chaco visual and road communication networks. Test excavations delineated several low masonry-walled circular structures, one of which contained a large hearth, and a series of connecting walls. The stone circles do not appear to have been roofed. A fork from one of the roads emanating from Pueblo Alto enters the site.

Excavations and Reports: Thomas R. Lyons and Dwight Drager, Chaco Center, extensively tested the site in 1975. Report by Drager on file in the Chaco Center, Albuquerque.

Dates: An archaeomagnetic date of A.D. 1210 was obtained from a hearth in one of the circular units.

Culture Stage: Pueblo III, Bonito Phase.

Remarks: Experiments demonstrate that the Poco Site occupies a crucial position in the Chaco visual communications system. Commands views in all directions.

Pueblo Alto

Other Designations: High Town (Hewett), 29SJ389 (National Park Service).

Location: On the north mesa, .66 mile north of Pueblo Bonito, Chaco Canyon National Monument.

Features: A major Chaco town with approximately 100 one-story living and storage rooms and 11 kivas. Earlier remains beneath present structure. Large refuse mound southeast of pueblo. Pueblo Alto is the focal point of a number of roadways that extend to the north and south of the settlement. A small complex, the East Ruin, is linked to the main ruin by a masonry wall.

Excavations and Reports: Frank H. H. Roberts, Jr., National Geographic Society, trenched the refuse deposit in 1926 as part of his study of Chaco ceramics. The results were included in his 1927 doctoral dissertation at Harvard.

W. James Judge directed extensive and intensive testing of Pueblo Alto between 1976 and 1978 as a major undertaking of the Chaco Center. Most field work was supervised by Thomas Windes, Chaco Center. The top portions of all walls of the pueblo were cleared and sections of rooms and several kivas were completely cleared or thoroughly tested. The trash deposit was stratigraphically trenched. Preliminary reports and field notes on file at the Chaco Center, Albuquerque.

Dates: Tree-ring and archaeomagnetic dates place construction of various sections of Pueblo Alto between about A.D. 1000 and 1220.

Culture Stage: Pueblo III, Bonito Phase.

Remarks: Careful excavations and the utilization of a variety of detailed analytical techniques have led investigators to identify certain rooms and areas in which various specialized community activities were conducted. Pueblo Alto is unique among the large Chaco towns in being only one story in height. Its late dates place it among the last of the major communities to be inhabited. Most of the site will be back-filled following excavation, but the top portions of all walls and certain entire exterior walls are being stabilized by the National Park Service concurrent with the archaeological investigations.

Pueblo Bonito

Other Designations: Beautiful Town (Hewett), 29SJ387 (National Park Service), Bc253 (University of New Mexico).

Location: On the north side of Chaco Canyon, between the deep arroyo of the Chaco Wash and the wall of the canyon, at approximately 108°W longitude, 36°N latitude in the SW¼ sec. 12, T. 21N., R. 11W., San Juan County, New Mexico. Because of Pueblo Bonito's central location in Chaco Canyon National Monument, the position of most other sites is given in relation to it.

Features: Generally described as the largest and most important town in Chaco Canyon. Over 300 ground-floor rooms and at least 32 kivas, including 2 Great Kivas. Considering that the community stood four and possibly five stories in places, it is estimated that the room total exceeded 650. Contained over 50 rooms with intact roofs when first explored; a few remain today. Ruins of earlier settlements exist beneath the present structure. Refuse mounds to the south of the pueblo.

Excavations and Reports: George H. Pepper assisted by Richard Wetherill, Hyde Exploring Expedition, cleared 189 rooms and several kivas in the west and north sections of the town from 1897 to 1899. Field notes published by Pepper in, *Pueblo Bonito,* Anthropological Papers of the American Museum of Natural History, XXVII (New York, 1920).

Neil M. Judd, National Geographic Society, completed the excavation of the remainder of Pueblo Bonito between 1921 and 1927. The more significant reports upon archaeology and environment published as a result of the Geographic Society expeditions include:

Neil M. Judd, "Pueblo Bonito, the Ancient," *National Geographic Magazine,* July 1923.

————, "Everyday Life in Pueblo Bonito," *National Geographic Magazine,* September 1925.

A. E. Douglass, *Dating Pueblo Bonito and Other Ruins of the Southwest,* National Geographic Society, Contributed Technical Papers, Pueblo Bonito Series 1 (Washington, D.C., 1935).

Kirk Bryan, *The Geology of Chaco Canyon, New Mexico,* Smithsonian Miscellaneous Collections, vol. 122, no. 7 (Washington, D.C., 1954).

Neil M. Judd, *The Material Culture of Pueblo Bonito,* Smithsonian Miscellaneous Collections, vol. 124 (Washington, D.C., 1954).

Neil M. Judd, *The Architecture of Pueblo Bonito,* Smithsonian Miscellaneous Collections, vol. 147, no. 1 (Washington, D.C., 1964).

Gordon Vivian, National Park Service, initiated stabilization measures in Pueblo Bonito in the 1930s. Several additional rooms and another kiva have been opened as a part of the preservation procedures. Vivian and Reiter have described the two Pueblo Bonito Great Kivas in their joint monograph, *The Great Kivas of Chaco Canyon and Their Relationships,* School of American Research Monograph 22 (Santa Fe, 1960; reprint Albuquerque: University of New Mexico Press, 1972).

The prinicpal collection of tree-ring specimens was made by Judd and Douglass in 1922. Deric O'Bryan, Gila Pueblo, obtained another series in 1940.

Dates: Tree-ring dates range from A.D. 828 to 1130. Two main building periods stand out; the first in the early part of the tenth century, shortly after A.D. 919, and the second in the latter half of the eleventh century. Minor construction or reconstruction seems to have been continuous, and repairs were carried out until 1127 at the least. The total number of dated wood samples, 98, is second only to the collection obtained from Chetro Ketl.

Samples taken from logs placed as supports beneath Threatening Rock have yielded dates ranging from A.D. 1057 to 1077, showing that the Bonitians did not take measures to hold up the rock until after a large portion of Pueblo Bonito was in existence.

Culture Stage: Pueblo III, Bonito Phase.

Remarks: Pueblo Bonito is the most extensively excavated and thoroughly reported Chaco Canyon town and is the center of attention for visitors to the Monument. Several of the pueblo's rooms were used secondarily as burial places for important individuals; the undisturbed ones contained unusually rich funerary offerings, including quantities of turquoise. However, the great majority of those who died during the two centuries the pueblo was inhabited were buried in locations yet to be discovered. The depth of debris mounded over the ruins of Pueblo Bonito, and the fact that a number of rooms were found intact with floors and ceilings in place resulted in an unusual state of preservation for many artifacts of wood, basketry, cordage, shell, and other perishable materials.

Although Pueblo Bonito undoubtedly occupied a prominent place among the eleventh century Chaco towns, it is easy for the visitor to overvalue its significance because it is the featured ruin in the Park Service's interpretive story. To many people, Pueblo Bonito is Chaco Canyon. However, it must be remembered that it was but one of 16 great towns extant during Pueblo III times and that all of them contributed in varying ways to a Chaco system. Nevertheless, as a consequence of its almost complete excavation and the detailed studies of its architecture and material culture, much of our knowledge of the ancient Chacoans is based upon what has been learned at Pueblo Bonito. The National Geographic Society began programs for the repair, protection, and preservation of Pueblo Bonito in the 1920s. The National Park Service continued the work, eventually completing the enormous task of stabilizing the entire site. Today, annual maintenance is performed by local Navajo stabilization crews.

Pueblo del Arroyo

Other Designations: 29SJ1947 (National Park Service), Bc254 (University of New Mexico).

Location: One-quarter of a mile west of Pueblo Bonito, on the north bank of the Chaco Wash, Chaco Canyon National Monument.

Features: Large town containing an estimated 284 rooms and 14 kivas. Of these, only 44 rooms and 7 kivas have been cleared by controlled excavations. Main room block stood three and four stories in height. Tri-walled building and associated rooms built against the back (west) and south walls of the pueblo.

Excavations and Reports: Karl Ruppert, National Geographic Society, supervised the partial clearing of the ruin, under the general direction of Neil M. Judd, between 1923 and 1926. The site report was completed by Judd and published in, *Pueblo del Arroyo, Chaco Canyon, New Mexico.* Smithsonian Miscellaneous collections, vol. 138, no. 1 (Washington, D.C., 1959).

A. E. Douglass and Neil M. Judd, both sponsored by the National Geographic Society, collected tree-ring specimens during the Society's work at Pueblo Bonito and Pueblo del Arroyo. Deric O'Bryan, Gila Pueblo, took additional tree-ring samples in 1940.

Gordon Vivian, National Park Service, opened some features while stabilizing the site in the 1950s.

Dates: A substantial number of tree-ring dates spread from A.D. 1052 to 1103. The evidence places construction activity in the middle eleventh century, and lasting into the first decade of the twelfth century, making Pueblo del Arroyo one of the last of the major Chaco Canyon towns constructed.

Culture Stage: Pueblo III, Bonito Phase.

Remarks: A short span of utilization is postulated, perhaps falling within the last half of Pueblo Bonito's occupation. Built by a group of Chacoans, maybe an offshoot from Pueblo Bonito, some of them moved out soon after the town was completed. Bearers of a Mesa Verde–type culture moved in to take their place.

Few items of material culture recovered from excavations, and those mainly from refuse-filled rooms in the pueblo. Stones salvaged from Pueblo del Arroyo went into several of the Hyde expedition buildings. Excavated sections stabilized by the National Park Service.

Pueblo Pintado

Other Designations: Painted Town (Hewett), 29Mc166 (National Park Service).

Location: The most easterly of the large Chaco Canyon towns, it is located on the south side of the Chaco Wash approximately 17 miles east of Pueblo Bonito; detached section of Chaco Canyon National Monument.

Features: A pueblo estimated to have had 60 ground-floor rooms, 7 kivas, and possibly 1 or 2 Great Kivas. May originally have stood three or four stories high.

Excavations and Reports: None. Florence M. Hawley, School of American Research, collected wood samples for tree-ring dating in 1932, as did Deric O'Bryan, Gila Pueblo, in 1946.

Dates: The six dated wood specimens cluster at A.D. 1060-1061.

Culture Stage: Pueblo III, Bonito Phase.

Remarks: Because of its location near the frontier of the Río Grande pueblos and its situation on a high point visible from far distances, Pueblo Pintado enters into much of the early literature on Chaco Canyon. It was the first large Chaco site encountered by early travelers and military parties progressing west from the Río Grande. One account confused it with Pueblo Bonito. National Park Service archaeologists have stabilized some of the standing walls.

Roberts' Small Pueblo

Other Designations: None.

Location: At mouth of small rincón on the canyon bottom at the south bank of the Chaco Wash, below Shabik'eshchee Village. 9 miles east of Pueblo Bonito, a short distance east of the boundary of Chaco Canyon National Monument. Monument.

Features: Foundations of a planned, medium-sized pueblo of about 40 rooms that never was completed. Built in a rectangular plan around a central plaza.

Excavations and Reports: Most of the low foundations outlined by Frank H. H. Roberts, Jr., National Geographic Society, in 1926. Field notes on file Smithsonian Archives of Anthropology, Washington, D.C.

Dates: None.

Culture Stage: Pueblo III, Bonito Phase.

Remarks: Site partially destroyed by Chaco Wash. Dug at the same time Shabik'eshchee Village being tested.

Stone Circles

This group of sites, exhibiting similiar characteristics and located near one another, are lumped together.

Other Designations: 29SJ692, 29SJ866, 29SJ919, 29SJ1419, 29SJ1505, 29SJ1533, 29SJ1565, 29SJ1572, 29SJ1660, and 29SJ1976 (National Park Service).

Location: The majority of these unusual features are located on flat terraces above the north cliffs of Chaco Canyon between Pueblo Bonito and Wijiji.

Features: Isolated or groups of low oval or circular masonry walls, 30 to 90 feet in greatest dimension, placed on stretches of bedrock. Many have shallow basins cut into their rock floors. A unique assortment of crude ground stone artifacts that may have been used as abraders for working wood and hides or smoothing the bedrock within the enclosures was common to the sites.

Excavations and Reports: Thomas Windes, Chaco Center, excavated or tested these sites in 1974. His report is entitled, *Stone Circles of Chaco Canyon, Northwestern New Mexico,* Reports of the Chaco Center, Division of Chaco Research, National Park Service 5 (Albuquerque, 1978).

Dates: None. Masonry types and associated potsherds suggest construction about A.D. 1000 to 1100.

Culture Stage: Pueblo III, Bonito Phase.

Remarks: It is conjectured that the stone circles were related to the large Chaco towns and that they may have served as craft centers for the production of ritual artifacts and as places for the performance of ceremonies.

Talus Rock Shelter

Other Designations: 29SJ1936 (National Park Service), Bc98 (University of New Mexico).

Location: At the base of the cliff just behind and slightly northwest of Pueblo Bonito, Chaco Canyon National Monument.

Features: A small, natural cave in the canyon wall that had been walled up in the rear and on the side with crude stone masonry. A firepit had been dug into the floor.

Excavations and Reports: Florence M. Hawley, School of American Research, cleared the debris from the floor of the shelter and collected a few fragments of charcoal from the firepit between 1930 and 1933. No report available.

Dates: Two tree-ring dates of A.D. 1101, presumably from a single branch, were obtained from the charcoal taken from the firepit.

Culture Stage: Pueblo III (?).

Remarks: This site is similar to other small caves at the base of the cliffs rimming the north side of Chaco Canyon. Some of them, as in this case, had been walled up to form rooms which could have served as storage places or very small dwellings. The charcoal fragments may represent remains from the last fire in the hearth, placing use of the shelter contemporaneous with nearby Pueblo Bonito.

Una Vida

Other Designations: 29SJ391 (National Park Service), Bc259 (University of New Mexico).

Location: On the north side of Chaco Canyon, slightly more than 3 miles east of Pueblo Bonito, Chaco Canyon National Monument.

Features: A medium-sized town believed to have had about 100 first-floor rooms, at least 6 kivas, and possibly a Great Kiva. Northern half of the site is built on steep talus slope, making it appear to have more floors than it actually has. Three stories was probably its maximum height.

Excavations and Reports: None. However, rather extensive stabilization of the ruin in 1960 by Gordon Vivian, National Park Service, resulted in the cleaning out of a number of rooms in the northwest section of the pueblo and the collecting of a few tree-ring specimens. In 1979, these rooms were back-filled by the National Park Service after reexamination by the Chaco Center.

Florence M. Hawley, School of American Research, obtained wood samples for dating purposes in 1931 and 1932.

Sara Goddard, School of American Research, is said to have removed several burials from the vicinity in 1931.

Dates: Dated wood samples extend from A.D. 847 to 1093, with a decided clustering between A.D. 929 and 950, which represents construction during the earliest building period of the classic Chaco communities.

Culture Stage: Pueblo III, Bonito Phase.

Remarks: Una Vida was possibly one of the most long-lived of the Chaco towns. In front of the site is a large stretch of flat canyon bottom that could have been used for gardens. Closest large pueblo to the National Park Service Visitor Center.

Wijiji

Other Designations: Turquoise House (Hewett), 29SJ577 (National Park Service), Bc260 (University of New Mexico).

Location: On the north side of Chaco Canyon, 5.5 miles upstream, or east, of Pueblo Bonito, Chaco Canyon National Monument.

Features: One of the medium-sized Chaco towns. Contains an estimated 92 first-floor rooms and 2 kivas. When inhabited, may have stood a maximum of three stories.

Excavations and Reports: None. A small number of tree-ring specimens was obtained by Florence M. Hawley about 1931.

Dates: Only a single date, A.D. 1110, has been obained from Wijiji. It tells little about the site other than that the date falls in the range of dated specimens from similar, presumably contemporaneous, Chaco Pueblo III towns.

Culture Stage: Pueblo III, Bonito Phase.

Remarks: The one late date and the architectural manifestations of Wijiji lead some people to believe that it is one of the last major towns to be constructed. Standing walls have been stabilized by National Park Service personnel.

29SJ630

Other Designations: None.

Location: In Marcia's Rincón, south side of Chaco Canyon, 3 miles southeast of Pueblo Bonito, Chaco Canyon National Monument.

Features: An unexcavated small house unit marked by a rubble-strewn mound and a refuse deposit.

Excavations and Reports: W. James Judge and Robert Powers, Chaco Center, tested the trash in 1975. Field notes on file, Chaco Center, Albuquerque.

Dates: None. Estimation of culture stage based on ceramics.

Culture Stage: Pueblo III.

Remarks: Tests back-filled after excavation.

29SJ633

Other Designations: None.

Location: In Marcia's Rincón, south side of canyon, 3 miles southeast of Pueblo Bonito, Chaco Canyon National Monument.

Features: A small site with a late room block of 15 to 20 masonry-walled rooms and 3 kivas. Trash deposit near the habitation.

Excavations and Reports: Marcia Truell and LouAnn Jacobson, Chaco Center, made limited tests in 2 rooms and dug exploratory trenches in several areas of the ruin in 1978 as part of an evaluation of remote sensing techniques. Field notes on file, Chaco Center, Albuquerque.

Dates: None, but lengthy occupation implied by the assortment of pottery recovered from the tests. Main occupation probably in the late A.D. 1000s and early 1100s.

Culture Stage: Pueblo I to Pueblo III, Bonito Phase. Late use by Mesa Verde peoples.

Remarks: Back-filled after testing.

29SJ1088

Other Designations: Once referred to as the "Medicine Hogan," a misnomer implying Navajo origin, which apparently is incorrect.

Location: On a prominent part of the extreme western tip of West Mesa overlooking Padilla Wash, approximately 4 miles west of Pueblo Bonito, Chaco Canyon National Monument.

243

Features: A circle, 25 feet in diameter, of well-laid Anasazi type masonry, thought to have stood about 3 feet high and not to have been roofed. Spaced along the cliff edge for a distance of almost .25 mile are 12 carefully made stone cairns, which may or may not be related to the stone circle. The circular structure is believed to have functioned as a shrine/signal station.

Excavations and Reports: Thomas Windes and Peter McKenna, Chaco Center, excavated about 50 percent of the circular enclosure in 1975. A quantity of turquoise fragments, both worked and unworked, was recovered in and around the structure. Report on file, Chaco Center, Albuquerque.

Dates: None, but style of masonry suggests late prehistoric construction.

Culture Stage: Probably Pueblo III, Bonito Phase.

Remarks: Commands views in all directions. The ruin resembles other shrine/signal stations in the Chaco region, and experiments show that it occupies a key location in a visual communication network.

244

ANASAZI: LATE PUEBLO II–PUEBLO III, HOSTA BUTTE PHASE

Bc51

Other Designations: 29SJ395 (National Park Service).

Location: On the south side of Chaco Canyon, .5 mile south of Pueblo Bonito, Chaco Canyon National Monument. One hundred feet east of Tseh So.

Features: A small house site, or village, with at least 45 rooms and 6 kivas arranged in a single-storied elongated alignment.

Excavations and Reports: Clyde Kluckhohn, Harvard Universiiy, directed principal excavations in 1937 for a University of New Mexico field school session. Results outlined in a joint report by Kluckhohn and Paul Reiter, *Preliminary Report on the 1937 Excavations, Bc50–51, Chaco Canyon, New Mexico.* University of New Mexico Bulletin, Anthropological Series, vol. 3, no. 2 (Albuquerque, 1939).

Gordon Vivian, National Park Service, stabilized Bc51 after its excavation and opened up a few more rooms.

Dates: Two tree-ring dates, A.D. 1043 and 1077, are given in the site report, but they have not been verified by the Laboratory of Tree-ring Research at the University of Arizona. A single date of A.D. 967, however, is listed by the Tree-ring Laboratory. Bc51 is very similar to Tseh So, and the two sites are believed to have been inhabited simultaneously.

Culture Stage: Pueblo III, Hosta Butte Phase.

Remarks: See remarks under Tseh So. The Park Service has stabilized the excavated remains.

Bc53, Bc57, and Bc58

These three sites are grouped together because they are located near one another, are apparently of similar plan and content, and all are unreported.

Other Designations: 29SJ396, 29SJ397, and 29SJ398 (National Park Service).

Location: All are in the Rinconada area, .5 mile south of Pueblo Bonito, south of the canyon, Chaco Canyon National Monument. These three ruins together with Tseh So (Bc50), Bc51, and Bc59 constitute the group of 6 excavated small house villages in the rincón east of the Casa Rinconada Great Kiva.

Features: Each site is believed to contain 20 or fewer rooms arranged in alignments of contiguous units to which are attached several kivas. An earlier pit structure is said to exist beneath Bc57. An examination of the available student notes and other records on file at the Chaco Center, unfortunately, fails to add much additional information. However, Gordon Vivian was present when the ruins were excavated and undertook limited stabilization measures in them after they were dug. He has suggested that Bc53 and Bc58 were short-lived, and that Bc57 may have had a longer occupation.

Excavations and Reports: The sites were excavated in conjunction with University of New Mexico field sessions. Investigations were conducted by students at Bc53 in 1940–41, at Bc57 in 1942, and at Bc58 in 1947. Paul Reiter, University of New Mexico, was in general charge of all of the field work. There are neither published nor unpublished reports on the sites.

Dates: No absolute dates; however, evidence from architectural forms, masonry styles, and pottery types imply that these villages were inhabited during the later phases of Tseh So (Bc50), Bc51, and Bc59 in the late eleventh and early twelfth centuries.

Culture Stage: Pueblo III, Hosta Butte Phase.

Remarks: In support of a late occupation at these sites, Vivian reports late Chaco and Mesa Verde ceramics to have been present in all three ruins. The remains have not been completely stabilized and are in poor states of preservation.

Bc59

Other Designations: 29SJ399 (National Park Service).

Location: In the Rinconada area, .5 mile south of Pueblo Bonito, 300 feet east of Casa Rinconada, south side of canyon, Chaco Canyon National Monument.

Features: The excavated portion of the site contains 16 rooms and 5 kivas. A compact small house complex with kivas attached. Several periods of construction lie beneath the surface ruin.

Excavations and Reports: Paul Reiter, University of New Mexico, directed excavation in 1947. Tom Mathews supervised the group of field school students who did the digging. No published report, but fragmentary field notes on file at Chaco Center, Albuquerque.

Gordon Vivian, National Park Service, stabilized the site in 1950 for interpretive purposes, collecting a few tree-ring specimens in the process.

Dates: Four tree-ring dates, all A.D. 1110, were obtained from the upper level of a kiva, indicating that it was constructed or repaired during that year or shortly thereafter.

Culture Stage: Pueblo III, Hosta Butte Phase.

Remarks: Date falls in the period of florescence of the great Chaco towns, although the site exhibits a less advanced level of cultural attainment. Lower remains suggest occupation from Pueblo I times. Sections of the ruin have been stabilized by the National Park Service.

Bc114

Other Designations: 29SJ200 (National Park Service), Anna Shepard's Site (School of American Research).

Location: In the South Gap directly south of Pueblo del Arroyo, approximately .5 mile southwest of Pueblo Bonito, south side of canyon, Chaco Canyon National Monument.

Features: A small house ruin with rooms built around a plaza containing a single kiva.

Excavations and Reports: Anna O. Shepard, School of American Research, excavated three rooms and trenched the refuse deposit in 1929. Her brief report is on file at the Chaco Center, Albuquerque.

Dates: None. Shepard indicated the pottery from the site to be similar to that found at Chetro Ketl, implying a contemporaneity between the two ruins.

Culture Stage: Pueblo III, Hosta Butte Phase.

Remarks: Perhaps the first suggestion that some of the canyon-bottom small villages and the large towns were inhabited simultaneously, an observation based upon ceramic evidence.

Bc236

Other Designations: 29SJ589 (National Park Service).

Location: On the south bank of the Chaco Wash, about .66 mile northeast of Fajada Butte, 4.5 miles east of Pueblo Bonito, Chaco Canyon National Monument.

Features: Partially destroyed by arroyo cutting. Ten rooms and one kiva of the small pueblo remained. They were excavated as a salvage project. A portion of a Pueblo I pithouse underlay the surface ruin.

Excavations and Reports: Zorro A. Bradley, National Park Service, excavated the undamaged section of the site in 1958. His report has been published as *Site Bc236, Chaco Canyon National Monument, New Mexico,* Division of

Archeology, Office of Archeology and Historic Preservation, National Park Service (1971).

Dates: None. Analysis of pottery from the ruin and its architectural features suggest occupation of the pueblo in the latter half of the twelfth century.

Culture Stage: Pueblo III, Hosta Butte Phase.

Remarks: Bc236 continues to be subject to destruction from bank erosion of the Chaco Wash.

Bc362

Other Designations: 29SJ827 (National Park Service).

Location: On the edge of the Chaco Wash, 200 yards south of Casa Chiquita, about a mile west of Pueblo Bonito, Chaco Canyon National Monument.

Features: Small house village of 20 rooms and 2 kivas, threatened with destruction by erosion of Chaco arroyo.

Excavations and Reports: Roland Richert and Charles Voll, National Park Service, dug parts of the site as a salvage operation in 1962. A report by Charles Voll is on file at the Chaco Center, Albuquerque: "Bc362, A Small, Late 11th and Early 12th Century Farming Village in Chaco Canyon, New Mexico" (1964).

Dates: Tree-ring dates from one of the kivas range from A.D. 1061 to 1115. Two clusters, one in the late A.D. 1000s and the other in the early 1100s, imply either construction around A.D. 1088 and later repair or construction about A.D. 1109 reusing some timbers cut at earlier times.

Culture Stage: Pueblo III, Hosta Butte Phase.

Remarks: Site continues to suffer from arroyo erosion.

Kin Chinde

The proper identification of Kin Chinde is not clear in the available literature. It is said by some authorities to be the same as Unit No. 26 of the Fisher survey of 1934, but others equate it with Mound 21 of that survey. And, to further complicate matters, a site identified as Mound 20 is said to be the same as Mound 21. A consensus, whether correct or not, is that Kin Chinde is synomymous with Mound No 20.

Other Designations: Mound 20 (?), 29SJ799 (National Park Service), Bc60-1 (University of New Mexico).

Location: On the ridge to the south of Casa Rinconada, .5 mile south of Pueblo Bonito, south side of the canyon, Chaco Canyon National Monument.

Features: Believed to be a small house unit with probably no more than 5 rooms.

Excavations and Reports: None; however, Florence M. Hawley lists two tree-ring dates for the site, indicating some exploration in the unit. She also has four dates from Mound No. 20, which we assume to be the same as Kin Chinde.

Dates: Kin Chinde, A.D. 1019 and 1042; Mound 20, dates range from A.D.

247

1039 to 1045. All of these dates are tentative and have not been verified by the Laboratory of Tree-ring Research.

Culture Stage: Pueblo III according to Hawley; probably Hosta Butte Phase.

Remarks: Culture stage designation is tentative.

Leyit Kin

Other Designations: Way-down-deep House (Dutton), 29SJ750 (National Park Service), Bc26 (University of New Mexico).

Location: On the south side of Chaco Canyon, about a mile east of Pueblo Bonito, Chaco Canyon National Monument.

Features: Small house village with about 27 rooms and at least 4 kivas in a compact arrangement. Probably single-storied.

Excavations and Reports: Excavated in 1934 and 1936 by Bertha P. Dutton, School of American Research and Museum of New Mexico. Results published in, *Leyit Kin, A Small House Ruin, Chaco Canyon, New Mexico.* School of American Research Monograph 7 (Santa Fe, 1938).

Dates: Dated charcoal fragments indicate that major construction began about A.D. 1040. Earlier structures and a later reoccupation suggested by stratigraphy, masonry types, and pottery.

Culture Stage: Pueblo III, Hosta Butte Phase.

Remarks: The first two building periods of Leyit Kin are attributed to the Chacoans; the reoccupation to Mesa Verde people. Primary settlement coincides with that of the major Chaco towns. site has been partially back-filled as a preservation measure.

Lizard House

Other Designations: 29SJ1912 (National Park Service), Bc192 (University of New Mexico).

Location: Along the northwest wall of the rincón east of Chetro Ketl, about a mile east of Pueblo Bonito, north side of the canyon, Chaco Canyon National Monument.

Features: Part of a U-shaped ruin which originally had at least 20 rooms and 3 kivas. Damaged by arroyo cutting.

Excavations and Reports: William Bromberg and James C. Maxon, National Park Service, conducted salvage excavations in portions of the ruin in 1960. An unpublished report by Maxon is on file at the Chaco Center, Albuquerque: "A Report of a Salvage Archeology Excavation at Chaco Canyon National Monument, in 1960."

Dates: A single non-cutting tree-ring date of A.D. 1104 places the first phase of this site within the time span of similiar, presumably contemporaneous, Chaco villages.

Culture Stage: Pueblo III, Hosta Butte Phase.

Remarks: Ruin not stabilized, continues to suffer damage from erosion.

Talus Unit No. 1

Other Designations: 29SJ1930 (National Park Service), Bc257 (University of New Mexico).

Location: On the talus slope at the base of the cliffs behind and slightly to the northwest of Chetro Ketl, .5 mile east of Pueblo Bonito, Chaco Canyon National Monument.

Features: A small house site containing an estimated 30 rooms and 3 kivas. The compact room block formerly reached two or three stories in height.

Excavations and Reports: Paul Walter, School of American Research, commenced excavations in 1933; Margaret Woods, University of New Mexico, continued investigations in 1934–35 and 1937. Their combined efforts uncovered a major portion of the ruin. No complete excavation report has been published, but several progress reports have been included in the monthly reports of *Southwestern Monuments* (National Park Service) for August 1934, August 1935, and October 1937. Field notes are on file at the Chaco Center, Albuquerque.

Florence M. Hawley, School of American Research and University of New Mexico, obtained tree-ring specimens between 1930 and 1940. Deric O'Bryan, Gila Pueblo, collected a second group of wood specimens in 1940, and Gordon Vivian, National Park Service, obtained additional samples in 1959.

Dates: A fair collection of dates, spread from A.D. 1029 to 1069, shows no observable clustering. It seems apparent, however, that Talus Unit No. 1 was probably built, occupied, and renovated several times in the eleventh century.

Culture Stage: Pueblo III, Hosta Butte Phase.

Remarks: One of the first small houses to be judged to have existed at the same time as the classic Chaco towns. An architectural feature, described by some as resembling a platform mound, is included in a list of postulated Mexican traits in the Chaco. Most exposed walls stabilized by the National Park Service

Tseh So

Other Designations: 29SJ394 (National Park Service), Bc50 (University of New Mexico).

Location: One of the several small ruins .5 mile directly south of Pueblo Bonito and just east of Casa Rinconada, south side of the canyon, Chaco Canyon National Monument. Area locally referred to as the Rinconada area.

Features: A village consisting of 26 ground-floor rooms in a linear arrangement to which are attached 4 kivas. Evidence for a few second-story rooms. Remains of earlier habitations exist below the presently cleared ruin.

Excavations and Reports: Donald D. Brand, University of New Mexico, directed excavations in 1936 as a field session program. Results of findings published in, *Tseh So, A Small House Ruin, Chaco Canyon, New Mexico,* University of New Mexico Anthropological Series, vol. 2, no. 2, (Albuquerque, 1937).

Clyde Kluckhohn and Paul Reiter, after excavating Bc51 for the University of New Mexico, reported upon that site, noting relationship to Tseh So and discussed the position of the two sites in Chaco prehistory in, *Preliminary Report on the 1937 Excavations, Bc50–51, Chaco Canyon, New Mexico.* University of New Mexico Bulletin, Anthropological Series, vol. 3, no. 2 (Albuquerque, 1939).

Gordon Vivian, National Park Service, cleared a few other parts of the site at a later date in conjunction with stabilization activities.

Dates: A single tree-ring date of A.D. 928 does not contribute to interpretation of the site chronology.

Culture Stage: Pueblo III, Hosta Butte Phase.

Remarks: Information from Tseh So and its sister site, Bc51, was instrumental in establishing the contemporaneity of certain of the small villages on the south side of the canyon with the large towns on the north side, despite obvious difference in the cultural inventories of the two groups of sites. This fact also led to questioning of the Pecos Classification which allowed one complex of sites to be classified as Pueblo II and another as Pueblo III even though they had been inhabited, at least in part, at the same time.

Portions of Tseh So have been stabilized by Park Service personnel.

Turkey House

Other Designations: None.

Location: On the floor of Chaco Canyon at the foot of the south cliff talus, just below Shabik'eshchee Village. Nine miles east of Pueblo Bonito, just outside the boundary of Chaco Canyon National Monument.

Features: A small house of 8 or 10 rooms built in an irregular plan about a courtyard. Refuse mound nearby. Earlier structures beneath surface ruin.

Excavations and Reports: Frank H. H. Roberts, Jr., National Geographic Society, trenched the trash and dug most of the rooms in 1926. Field notes on file, Smithsonian Archives of Anthropology, Washington, D.C.

Dates: None.

Culture Stage: Probably Pueblo III, Hosta Butte Phase.

Remarks: Resembles the Hosta Butte sites in the Rinconada area, for example Bc50–51. Excavated in conjunction with the testing at Shabik'eshchee Village.

ANASAZI: PUEBLO III, McELMO PHASE

Bc52, Bc54, Bc55, and Bc56

These four small talus ruins have been tested but are unreported. They have been combined on the basis of a few bits of information about their partial clearing and the records of the survey crew, which suggest that they are generally similar and of the same age.

Other Designations: 29SJ400, 29SJ1922, 29SJ1921, and 29SJ753 (National Park Service.

Location: Bc52, at the top of the talus slope in the rincón south of the Rinconada area, about .5 mile south of Pueblo Bonito, south side of the canyon. Bc54 and Bc55, on the talus slope at the base of the north cliff of Chaco Canyon, approximately .25 mile east of Chetro Ketl and .75 mile east of Pueblo Bonito. Bc56, on the south talus slopes of Chaco Canyon, west of Leyit Kin, about 1 mile east of Pueblo Bonito. All ruins are in the Chaco Canyon National Monument.

Features: All four are small house units combining habitation and storage rooms with kivas. Bc52 is judged to have contained about 20 rooms, 2 kivas, and 1 tower kiva, and to have stood two or three stories high. Bc54 had about a dozen rooms and 3 kivas, Bc55 approximately 16 rooms and an unknown number of kivas. Bc56 apparently is a very small complex of 3 rooms and 1 kiva.

Excavations and Reports: The sites were tested by University of New Mexico field session students in 1941, directed by Paul Reiter. A few incomplete sets of student field notes are on file at the Chaco Center, Albuquerque.

Dates: None, but plans, masonry style, and surface artifacts suggest their construction late in the Chaco sequence.

Culture Stage: Pueblo III, McElmo Phase.

Remarks: Excavated sections of the ruins were left open and have suffered from the elements.

Casa Chiquita

Other Designations: Little House (Hewett), 29SJ1167 (National Park Service), Bc245 (University of New Mexico).

Location: On the north side of Chaco Canyon, west of Pueblo Bonito and 1 mile downstream from it, Chaco Canyon National Monument.

Features: A small, compact town of approximately 50 rooms and 3 kivas, the former having stood two or three stories high. Built in part over large boulders.

Excavations and Reports: None. Gordon Vivian, National Park Service, collected tree-ring specimens, during minor stabilization work in 1951.

Dates: Three tree-ring dates fall between A.D. 1058 and 1064, suggesting some construction activity in the late 1060s and a contemporaneity with its neighbor, Kin Kletso. Architectural evidence supports its occupation into the latest phase of the classic Chaco towns.

Culture Stage: Pueblo III, McElmo Phase.

Remarks: Believed to have been constructed and occupied by migrants from north of the San Juan River bearing a Mesa Verde–like culture. The Park Service has stabilized the standing walls of Casa Chiquita.

Gallo Cliff Dwelling

Other Designations: 29SJ540 (National Park Service), Bc288 (University of New Mexico).

Location: Near the mouth of Gallo Canyon, a tributary that enters Chaco Canyon from the north, approximately 4 miles east of Pueblo Bonito. On the west side of the Park Service Gallo campground, Chaco Canyon National Monument.

Features: A small 5-room 1-kiva complex built of the late-style masonry on a low talus partially beneath a shallow rock shelter. Well-preserved refuse deposit.

Excavations and Reports: Don Morris and Leland Abel, both of the National Park Service, dug the site as a salvage project in 1966 and 1967. A collection of artifacts made of perishable materials came from the dry trash deposits. A partially complete report on the excavations by Leland Abel is on file at the Chaco Center, Albuquerque.

Dates: Archaeomagnetic dates ranging from A.D. 1110 to 1370 were obtained from poor samples and are judged unreliable. Architecture and artifacts suggest late construction, probably in the twelfth century.

Culture State: Pueblo III, McElmo Phase.

Remarks: Although a minor Chaco Canyon site, the collection of artifacts made of wood and fibers that has been studied by Kate P. Kent of Denver University is of significance. Site has been stabilized by the National Park Service.

Headquarters Sites, Ruin B

Two ruins were located and tested in the area chosen for a new National Park Service Visitor Center and Headquarters building. One ruin was delineated, tested in small part, and back-filled; the other was excavated and later destroyed by construction activities. They both are referred to as the Headquarters Sites, but here will be separately identified by the letters A and B.

Other Designations: Unknown.

Location: At base of talus slope north of the National Park Service Visitor Center, 120 feet west of Headquarters Site, Ruin A, 3.5 miles east of Pueblo Bonito, Chaco Canyon National Monument.

Features: Group of not more than 4 small rooms built adjacent to large boulders which had fallen from the cliff onto the talus. Walls built of unshaped blocks without core.

Excavations and Reports: Gordon Vivian, National Park Service, trenched the site in 1950, and refers to it in the Vivian and Mathews monograph, *Kin Kletso, A Pueblo III Community in Chaco Canyon, New Mexico,* Southwestern Monuments Association, Technical Series, vol. 6, part 1 (Globe, Arizona, 1965).

Dates: None; however, potsherds and stratigraphy demonstrate that this small site was built and inhabited later than the larger Headquarters Site, Ruin A, and that it is representative of the last Anasazi occupation in Chaco Canyon.

Culture Stage: Pueblo III, McElmo Phase.

Remarks: Thought to have been constructed by a Mesa Verde group sometime after the adjacent Chaco community had been abandoned. Refuse from this site dumped into rooms of neighboring pueblo ruins after two to four feet of soil had washed into it, showing that this group either camped in part of the deserted Chaco building while constructing a habitation of their own, or used it as a trash dump, or perhaps both. The site was destroyed by construction of utility lines.

Hillside Ruin

Other Designations: 29SJ1175 (National Park Service), Bc95 (University of New Mexico).

Location: Extends approximately 300 feet east along the base of the north cliff from the terrace upon which Threatening Rock had stood, directly northeast of Pueblo Bonito overlooking the northeast foundation complex of that site, Chaco Canyon National Monument.

Features: An elongated mass of rubble with several obvious kiva depressions. Masonry said by Judd to be non-Bonitian.

Excavations and Reports: Neil M. Judd, National Geographic Society, dug 3 exploratory trenches at the west end of the mound, partially exposed the south front of the ruin, and tested 1 kiva in 1923. He briefly mentions the site in *The Architecture of Pueblo Bonito,* Smithsonian Miscellaneous Collections, vol. 147, no. 1 (Washington, D.C., 1964).

Dates: None.

Culture Stage: According to Judd's description of the architecture and the sherds he obtained from the site, it belongs to the McElmo Phase.

Remarks: Judd believed the Hillside Ruin to have been later than Pueblo Bonito, relatively short-lived, and to have been stripped of accessible building stones some time after its abandonment.

Kin Kletso

Other Designations: Yellow House (Hewett), 29SJ393 (National Park Service), Bc248 (University of New Mexico).

Location: .5 mile downstream (west) of Pueblo Bonito, north side of Chaco

Canyon, Chaco Canyon National Monument. The Chaco Wash is immediately in front of the ruin.

Features: A compact town of medium size with 55 ground-floor rooms, 4 kivas, and a tower kiva. Room block stood three stories high along its back wall. Built over and among large boulders detached from the nearby cliffs.

Excavations and Reports: Edwin N. Ferdon, Jr., School of American Research, partially cleared the site in 1934.

Gordon Vivian assisted by Tom Mathews, National Park Service, excavated the remainder of Kin Kletso in 1951. Vivian and other Park Service specialists stabilized the ruin in 1951 and 1952. Vivian and Mathews published the results of their work in, *Kin Kletso, a Pueblo III Community in Chaco Canyon, New Mexico,* Southwestern Monuments Association, Technical Series, vol. 6, part 1 (Globe, Arizona, 1965).

Florence M. Hawley, School of American Research, collected a few tree-ring samples in 1931, and the Chaco Center staff obtained samples for archaeomagnetic dating in 1976.

Dates: Tree-ring specimens from construction elements date from A.D. 1059 to a cluster at 1124. Those dates suggest that Kin Kletso underwent at least two extensive building periods, one about A.D. 1059 to 1076 and a second around A.D. 1124. Some fragments of charcoal from firepits and household refuse have yielded dates as late as A.D. 1171 and 1178, among the latest dates from the Chaco Canyon towns. They may be interpreted in two ways: one, that the pueblo was lived in at least until A.D. 1178, or two, that the firepit was used at that time but not necessarily by those who built or were permanent inhabitants of Kin Kletso. A tentative archaeomagnetic date of A.D. 1180 was obtained from Kiva D.

Culture Stage: Pueblo III, McElmo Phase.

Remarks: The only carefully excavated and reported Chaco site of what has been called the McElmo Phase. The town plan, masonry details, pottery types, and time of occupation support the view that Kin Kletso represents an intrusion into the area by Anasazi with a Mesa Verde type of culture. Some of the newcomers erected their own residences, as at Kin Kletso, others moved into ongoing Chaco towns occupied, at least in part, by the original Chaco residents. National Park Service maintenance crews keep the ruin in good repair.

New Alto

Other Designations: New Pueblo Alto, New High House (Hewett), 29SJ388 (National Park Service), Bc252 (University of New Mexico).

Location: On the north mesa, .66 mile north of Pueblo Bonito, Chaco Canyon National Monument. Four hundred feet west of Pueblo Alto.

Features: A compact, blocklike town of 28 ground-floor rooms built around a small courtyard containing 1 kiva. Walls are well preserved and stand free of fallen debris. Originally stood two stories in places.

Excavations and Reports: None.

Dates: None.

Culture Stage: Pueblo III, McElmo Phase.

Remarks: Architectural style and cultural remains place New Alto among the latest Chaco constructions. It is one of the towns attributed to migrants from the Mesa Verde area to the north. Standing walls have been stabilized by the National Park Service.

Rabbit Ruin

Other Designations: 29SJ390 (National Park Service).

Location: On the north mesa, about 1 mile north of Pueblo Bonito, Chaco Canyon National Monument. Eight hundred feet north of Pueblo Alto.

Features: High-standing, rubble-covered mound. Tracing of walls revealed 2, possibly 3, pueblo units. Wall masonry of large dimpled blocks with narrow core. Eastern unit has about 13 rooms and 3 kivas; to the west, a second complex has at least 13 small rooms and 1 kiva. Remains of a third structure were noted still farther to the west. Architecturally, very similair to New Alto.

Excavations and Reports: W. James Judge and Thomas Windes, Chaco Center, cleared portions of the site in 1976 exposing tops of most of the walls. Field notes on file, Chaco Center, Albuquerque.

Dates: A single tree-ring date from a kiva in eastern pueblo of A.D. 1088 indicates some building activity after that time.

Culture Stage: Pueblo III, McElmo Phase.

Remarks: Tops of some walls stabilized, but most test trenches back-filled.

Tri-Wall Unit

Other Designations: 29SJ1947, Pueblo del Arroyo (National Park Service), Bc254, Pueblo del Arroyo (University of New Mexico).

Location: Attached to the back (west) side of Pueblo del Arroyo, on the bank of the Chaco Wash, .25 mile west of Pueblo Bonito, Chaco Canyon National Monument.

Features: Site dominated by a circular, triple-walled unit 73 feet in diameter. Attached to it are rooms and kivas, some of which also join the walls of Pueblo del Arroyo. These are a section of a once-large community, now partially destroyed by the Chaco Wash, which extended south from the Tri-Wall and east around the south side of Pueblo del Arroyo.

Excavations and Reports: Karl Ruppert, National Geographic Society, extensively trenched the unit and cleared a few rooms in 1926. The result of that work is reported by Neil M. Judd in *Pueblo del Arroyo, Chaco Canyon, New Mexico,* Smithsonian Miscellaneous Collections, vol. 138, no. 1 (Washington, D.C., 1959).

Gordon Vivian, National Park Service, reopened the sections dug by Ruppert and excavated the remainder of the Tri-Wall in 1950 as part of the stabilization program at Pueblo del Arroyo. He has reported upon the structure in *The Hubbard Site and Other Tri-Wall Structures in New Mexico and Colorado,* National Park Service Archeological Research Series 5 (Washington, D.C., 1959).

Dates: One tree-ring specimen collected by Vivian from a room of the Tri-Wall Unit has been dated A.D. 1109.

Culture Stage: Pueblo III, McElmo Phase.

Remarks: A good example of the tri-walled structures, sometimes called towers, which extend across the Anasazi area from southwestern Colorado to the Chaco. The Tri-Wall and its associated habitations and kivas apparently were attached to Pueblo del Arroyo after its completion and are representative of the late movement of Mesa Verde peoples into the Chaco area. Most of the community and part of the Tri-Wall have been destroyed by surface and arroyo erosion, remaining sections have been stabilized by the National Park Service.

Tsin Kletzin

Other Designations: Black Wood or Charcoal Place (Hewett), 29SJ385 (National Park Service), Bc258 (University of New Mexico).

Location: 2 miles directly south of Pueblo Bonito, back from the rim of the canyon on South Mesa, Chaco Canyon National Monument.

Features: A small, compact town estimated to have had at least 45 ground-floor rooms and 4 kivas. Maximum height of three stories is postulated.

Excavations and Reports: None. A. E. Douglass collected tree-ring samples in 1926, and Florence M. Hawley obtained two specimens from the site in 1932.

Dates: Three wood specimens date A.D. 1111, 1112, and 1113. They indicate that the ruin contains rooms built during the last dated period of construction in the classic towns of the Chaco, but they, of course, do not place the ruin as a whole in time.

Culture Stage: Pueblo III, generally assigned to McElmo Phase, but exhibits some characteristics of Bonito Phase.

Remarks: Occupies a central position and visual vantage point in relation to 11 of the main Chaco settlements and many small sites.

NAVAJO

Doll House Site

Other Designations: 29SJ1613 (National Park Service).

Location: Bench on north edge of Chacra Mesa, south side of canyon opposite Wijiji, about 6.25 miles southeast of Pueblo Bonito, Chaco Canyon National Monument.

Features: A Navajo settlement exhibiting 10 hogans, 2 houses, 1 pueblito, 2 granaries, and 2 corrals, arranged in four chronologically distinct clusters. A lengthy occupation, perhaps by a single kin group, is indicated.

Excavations and Reports: David M. Brugge, Chaco Center, excavated or tested most features of the site in 1975. His report is on file at the Chaco Center, Albuquerque.

Dates: Archaeological and ethnohistoric data place the occupation of the site from the mid-eighteenth century to the early 1900s.

Culture Stage: Navajo.

Remarks: The only excavated Navajo site in Chaco Canyon National Monument. Some features stabilized by the National Park Service. Site named for a miniature replica of an Anasazi structure fashioned by a Navajo beneath a small, protective rock overhang near the settlement.

Maps of the Major Chaco Canyon Ruins

The first six sites depicted, Pueblo Bonito, Chetro Ketl, Kin Bineola, Peñasco Blanco, Hungo Pavi, and Una Vida, saw major additions to earlier increments or initial construction during the Early Bonito Phase, A.D. 920–1020.

The following six pueblos, Pueblo del Arroyo, Kin Ya-a, Pueblo Pintado, Kin Klizhin, Wijiji, and Pueblo Alto, were built primarily during the Classic Bonito Phase, A.D. 1020–1120.

The last four communities, Casa Chiquita, Kin Kletso, Tsin Kletzin, and New Alto, have been assigned to the Mesa Verde–related McElmo Phase and probably came into being coincident with the Classic Bonito Phase.

The maps are based upon aerial photographs and on ground interpolation of rubble-covered features. They have been provided through the courtesy of the Chaco Center, National Park Service, and the University of New Mexico.

Appendix

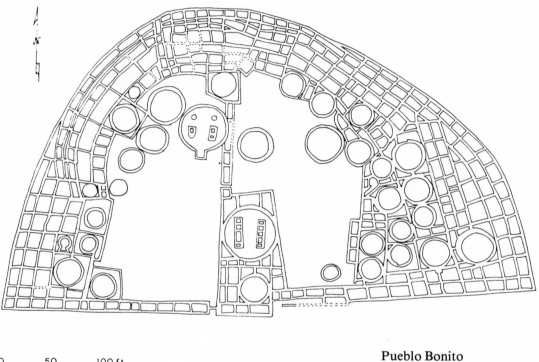

0   50   100 ft.

Pueblo Bonito

Figure 74. Map of Pueblo Bonito after extensive excavations.

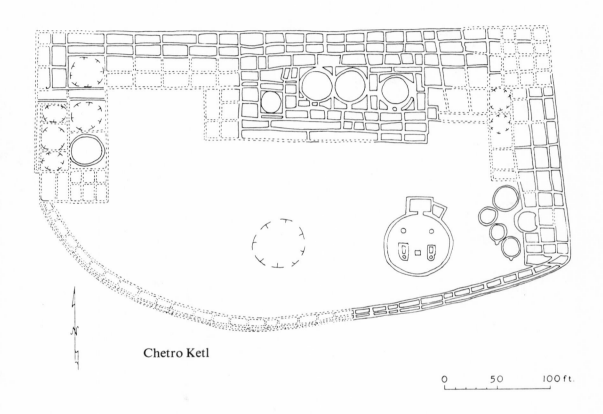

Chetro Ketl

0   50   100 ft.

Figure 75. Map of Chetro Ketl after about half the site had been excavated.

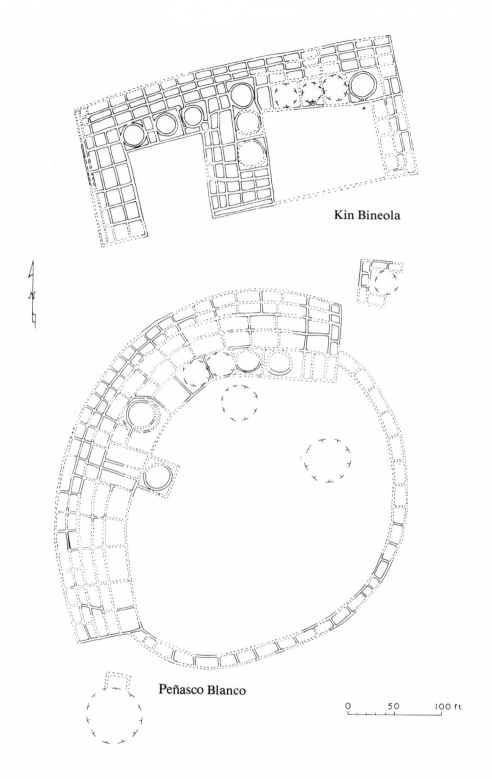

Kin Bineola

Peñasco Blanco

0   50   100 ft.

Figure 76. Maps of Kin Bineola and Peñasco Blanco.
Neither site has been excavated.

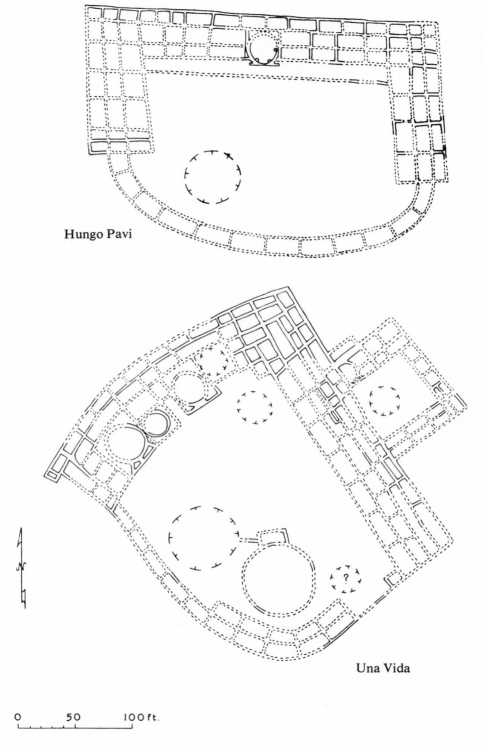

Hungo Pavi

Una Vida

0   50   100 ft.

Figure 77. Maps of Hungo Pavi and Una Vida. Both sites are largely unexcavated.

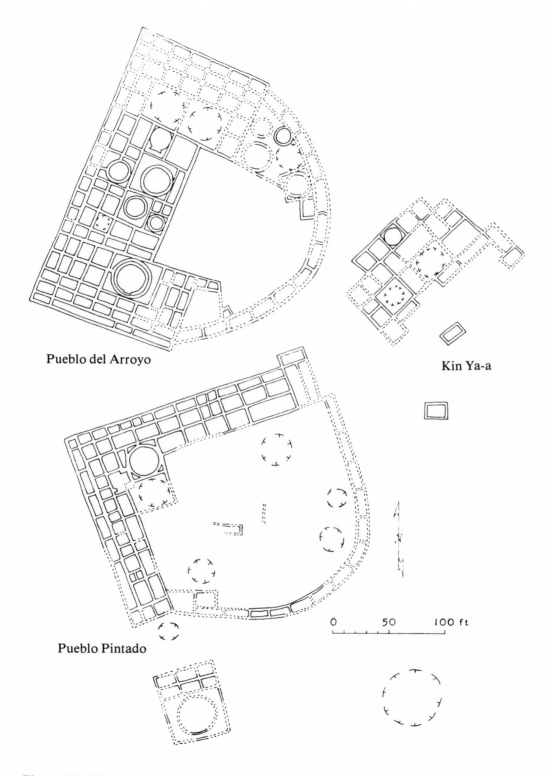

Pueblo del Arroyo

Kin Ya-a

Pueblo Pintado

0   50   100 ft

Figure 78. Maps of Pueblo del Arroyo, Kin Ya-a, and
Pueblo Pintado. Pueblo del Arroyo has been partially
cleared, the other two ruins are unexcavated.

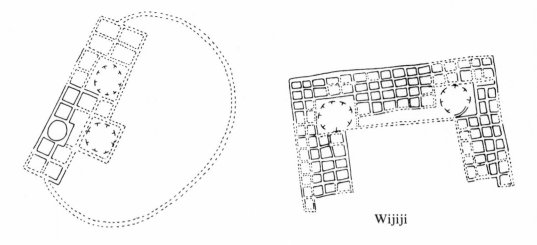

Kin Klizhin

Wijiji

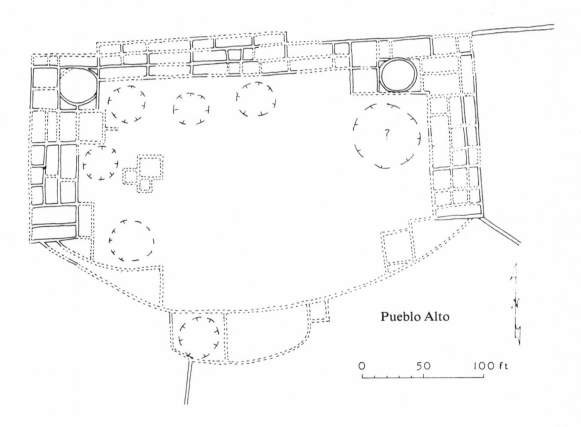

Pueblo Alto

0   50   100 ft

Figure 79. Maps of Kin Klizhin, Wijiji, and Pueblo Alto. All maps depict the sites before excavation. Pueblo Alto recently has been extensively tested by the Chaco Center. See Figure 69 for a plan of Pueblo Alto following those investigations.

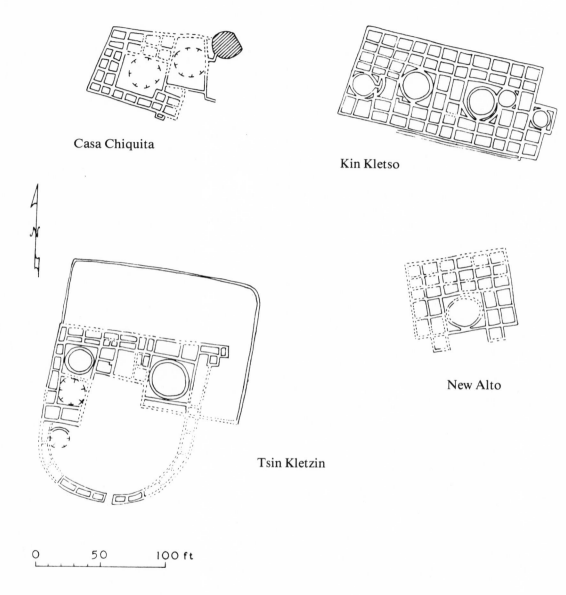

Casa Chiquita

Kin Kletso

Tsin Kletzin

New Alto

0   50   100 ft

Figure 80. Maps of Casa Chiquita, Kin Kletso, Tsin Kletzin, and New Alto. Of this group, only Kin Kletso has been cleared.

INDEX

A

Abel, Leland, 252
Adams, Richard N., 221
Aerial Remote Sensing Techniques in Archeology (Lyons and Hitchcock), 231(chap. 6, n. 3)
agriculture. *See* farming; horticulture
Agua del Ratón, 4
Agua de San Carlos, 4
Alamo Ranch, 23, 37
Albuquerque, N.M., 6, 23, 60, 61
Alluvial and Palynological Reconstruction of Environments, Navajo Reservoir District (Schoenwetter and Eddy), 216(chap. 7, n. 6)
Altschul, Jeffrey H., 215(chap. 6, n. 27)
American Museum of Natural History, 21, 23, 30, 41, 55, 61, 62, 65, 70, 73
Amsden, Monroe, 72
"An Analysis of a Possible Communication System in the San Juan Basin of New Mexico," 213(chap. 6, n. 6)
Anasazi, 50, 62, 65, 66, 67, 72, 78, 91, 93, 95, 97, 100, 105, 112, 114, 116, 117, 120, 121, 126, 129, 130, 134, 137, 138, 139, 145, 150, 153, 159, 168, 169, 173, 176, 179, 180, 183, 186, 187–205 passim, 209(chap. 3, n. 1), 214(chap 6, n. 24), 216(chap. 7, n. 8); derivation of name, 21
Anasazi Pottery (Lister and Lister), 214(chap. 6, n. 24)
"An Anasazi Shrine in Chaco Canyon" (Hayes and Windes), 214(chap. 6, n. 17)
"Anasazi Solar Observatories" (Williamson, Fisher, and O'Flynn), 215(chap. 6, n. 28)

Ancient Native Americans (Jennings), 216(chap 7, n. 8)
"The Ancient Pueblo of Chetro Ketl" (Reiter), 230
Animas River, 22
Anna Shepard's Site, 246
Ant Hill Dune, 220
Antiquities Act, 47, 58, 62, 111
Apache Indians, 171
Archaeological Institute of America, 65
"Archaeological Investigations at Chaco Canyon Using a Subsurface Radar" (Vickers, Dolphin, and Johnson), 214(chap. 6, n. 15)
Archaeological Investigations in New Mexico, Colorado, and Utah (Fewkes), 235
archaeological survey of Chaco Canyon, 137–40, 153, 169, 211(chap. 4, n. 6), 212(chap. 6, n. 1)
"Archaeology of New Mexico" (Hewett), 208(chap. 2, n. 10)
archaeomagnetic dating, 153, 203
"Archaic Culture History in the Southwestern United States" (Irwin-Williams), 216(chap. 7, n. 7)
Archaic stage, 138, 154, 186, 187, 213(chap. 6, n. 11), 216(chap. 7, n. 7)
architecture, 18, 114; alignments, 174, 176, 215(chap. 6, n. 28); arenas, 169; Basket Maker II, 188; Basket Maker III, 190; columns, 174; floors, 52, 70, 154, 188; Jackson's description of, 14; Pueblo Bonito Type I masonry, 76, 103, 113, 114; Pueblo Bonito Type II masonry, 76, 103; Pueblo Bonito Type III masonry, 76, 88, 103; Pueblo Bonito Type IV masonry, 76, 88, 103; Pueblo I,

269

271

272

273

274

275

277

beneath, 161; estimated size, 161, 162; trash, 159, 161
Pueblo Bonito, 6, 11, 13, 18, 19, 22, 23, 24, 28, 30, 36, 37, 40, 41, 47, 48, 50, 51, 52, 53, 54, 55, 56, 57, 60, 61, 62, 65, 104, 116, 119, 121, 124, 126, 130, 145, 146, 147, 157, 159, 162, 169, 173, 176, 180, 183, 195, 196, 199, 201, 203, 207(chap. 2, n. 3), 208(chap. 2, n. 4, n. 8), 213(chap. 6, n. 5), 215(chap. 6, n.28; chap. 7, n. 2), 237 (app.); abandonment, 54, 78, 84, 88; architecture, 52; burials, 24, 36, 41, 78; damage by Threatening Rock, 124, 126; domestic life, 54; earlier settlements beneath, 52, 61, 73; Hyde Expedition, 22, 23, 24, 28, 30, 41, 53, 58, 62, 73, 78; intact roof, 53; Judd's interpretations, 73, 76, 78; National Geographic Society Expedition, 67, 69, 70, 73, 90; trash mounds, 18, 24, 70, 71, 72, 76; timbers from, 52, 53; stabilization, 70, 119
Pueblo Bonito (Pepper), 208(chap. 2, n. 4, n. 8)
"Pueblo Bonito, the Ancient" (Judd), 210(chap. 3, n. 2)
"The Pueblo Bonito Expedition of the National Geographic Society" (Judd), 210(chap. 3, n. 2)
Pueblo del Arroyo, 6, 22, 47, 48, 55, 83, 88, 95, 110, 119, 124, 127, 128, 129, 181, 197, 199, 200, 239 (app.); burials, 90; National Geographic Society Expedition, 67, 73, 84, 88; trash, 90. *See also* Tri-Wall Unit
Pueblo del Arroyo, Chaco Canyon, New Mexico (Judd), 210(chap. 3, n. 6), 212(chap. 5, n. 3)
Pueblo del Ratón, 4. *See also* Painted Town; Pueblo Pintado
Pueblo Indians, 10, 21, 30, 36, 49,

53, 54, 61, 91, 111, 159, 171, 172, 176, 191
Pueblo Pintado, 4, 6, 11, 83, 146, 197, 240 (app.); Simpson cited, 10. *See also* Painted Town; Pueblo del Ratón
Pueblo Revolt, 3, 159
"Pueblo Sun-Moon-Star Calendar" (Ellis), 215(chap. 6, n. 28)
Putnam, Frederick W., 23, 41
Putnam, N.M., 56

Q

quarries, 52, 138, 140
quiver, 28

R

Rabbit Ruin, 161, 255 (app.)
radar devices, 162, 214(chap. 6, n. 15)
Rainbow Bridge, 67
ramadas, 157, 192
Ratón Springs, 4
Red Mesa Valley, 173, 209(chap. 3, n. 1)
Regressive Pueblo, 209(chap. 3, n. 1). *See also* Pueblo IV
Reiter, Paul, 95, 113, 210(chap. 4, n. 4), 211(chap. 4, n. 7), 212(chap. 4, n. 9)
religious practices: Anasazi, 54, 105, 129, 177, 191, 192, 196; Archaic, 187; Mexican, 175; Navajo, 172, 208(chap. 2, n. 9); Paleo-Indian, 185. *See also* ritual paraphernalia
remote sensing, 140, 144, 145, 147, 153, 212(chap. 6, n. 3)
Remote Sensing Experiments in Cultural Resource Studies (Lyons), 213(chap. 6, n. 3)
"A Report of a Salvage Archeology Excavation at Chaco Canyon National Monument, in 1960" (Maxon), 248

shrines, 111, 138, 214(chap. 6, n. 17). *See also* shrine/signal stations

Sierra Madre Occidental, 187

signal stations, 140, 162, 164, 174, 177. *See also* communication system; shrine/signal stations

The Significance of the Dated Prehistory of Chetro Ketl, New Mexico (Hawley), 210(chap. 4, n. 2)

Simpson, First Lt. James H., 6, 11, 13, 14, 18, 83, 88, 96, 171, 207(chap. 1, n. 3), 211(chap. 4, n. 6); cited, 10

Sinclair, Rolf A., 215(chap. 6, n. 28)

Sin-Kle-Zin, 49. *See also* Tsin Kletzin

Sipapu, 54, 91, 191, 193

Sleeping Dune, 220

Smithsonian Institution, 73, 90, 211(chap. 4, n. 6)

snares, 191

social organization, prehistoric, 213(chap. 6, n. 7), 215(chap. 6, n. 27)

Sofaer, Anna, 215(chap. 6, n. 28)

Soil Conservation Service, 126

"Source Area Studies of Pueblo I–III Pottery at Chaco Canyon" (Warren), 215(chap. 6, n. 24)

South Gap, 23, 47

"The Southwest" (Lipe), 216(chap. 7, n. 8)

"Southwestern Archaeological Conference" (Kidder), 208(chap. 3, n. 1)

Spaniards, 3, 4, 66, 171, 172, 205

spear points, 154, 185. *See also* projectile points

spears, 187, 189, 191

squash (pumpkins), 54, 161, 171, 187, 188, 190, 196

stabilization, 111, 177, 245;

National Park Service program, 119, 120; Casa Chiquita, 251; Casa Rinconada, 107, 230; Chetro Ketl, 96, 119, 230; Doll House Site, 172, 257; Gallo Cliff Dwelling, 252; Hungo Pavi, 232; Kin Bineola, 233; Kin Kletso, 129, 130, 254; Kin Klizhin, 234; Kin Ya-a, 235; Peñasco Blanco, 235; Pueblo Alto, 159, 237; Pueblo Bonito, 70, 119, 238; Pueblo del Arroyo, 127, 128, 239; Pueblo Pintado, 240; Site Bc51, 244; Site Bc59, 246; Talus Unit No. 1, 249; Tri-Wall Unit, 256; Tseh So, 250; Una Vida, 242; Wijiji, 243

stairways, 13, 53, 138, 140, 145

Stanford, Dennis, 220

Stanford Research Institute, 162

stone circles, 169, 214(chap. 6, n. 20), 241 (app.)

Stone Circles of Chaco Canyon, Northwestern New Mexico (Windes), 214(chap. 6, n. 20)

stone implements, 41, 54, 138, 169, 184, 185, 187, 189, 191, 196. *See also* knives; manos; metates; mortars; projectile points; spear points

storage units, 88, 130, 138, 153, 157, 161, 170, 188, 190, 192, 195, 196, 200, 202. *See also* bins; cists

stratigraphy, 30, 66, 72, 100, 109, 114, 164

strip mining, 183

Stubbs, Stanley, 95

A Study of Pueblo Architecture in Tusayan and Cibola (Mindeleff), 207(chap. 1, n. 7)

sun watcher, 166, 176

"A Survey of Southwestern Archaeology" (Roberts), 208(chap. 3, n. 1)

University of Arizona, 100
University of New Mexico, 95, 105, 109, 111, 112, 116, 119, 137, 211(chap. 4, n. 6)
University of Oklahoma, 154
University of Pennsylvania Museum, 162
Utah, 18, 21, 67
Ute Indians, 204

V

Vickers, Roger, 214(chap. 6, n. 15)
Vivian, Gwinn, 145, 147, 150, 172, 210(chap. 4, n. 3), 213(chap. 6, n. 7, n. 10), 214(chap. 6, n. 23), 215(chap. 6, n. 27)
Vivian, R. Gordon, 95, 104, 107, 119, 120, 127, 128, 130, 132, 145, 147, 169, 210(chap. 4, n. 4), 212(chap. 4, n. 8; chap. 5, n. 2, n. 3, n. 4), 213(chap. 6, n. 7), 215(chap. 7, n. 1, n. 3), 216(chap. 7, n. 4, n. 10)
Vizcarra, José Antonio, 4, 6
Voll, Charles, 233

W

walls: coursed masonry, 164, 193; cribbed, 188; masonry, 177; McElmo Phase style masonry, 200; pole and brush, 91; post and mud, 76, 192; rubble-cored masonry, 52, 76, 103, 174, 192, 193, 195, 198; uncored masonry, 73, 76, 103, 104, 113, 130, 196, 197. *See also* architecture; masonry
Walter, Paul, 249
Warren, A. Helene, 214(chap. 6, n. 24)
Warren, Richard L., 210(chap. 3, n. 9)
Washington, Lt. Col. John Macrae, 11

water, domestic: for ancient Chacoans, 50, 51, 83, 84, 181, 190; for modern inhabitants, 48, 50, 69, 183. *See also* irrigation; water control
water control, 138, 140, 145, 150, 153, 174, 201, 202, 204, 213(chap. 6, n. 7, n. 10), 214(chap. 6, n. 16)
Way-down-deep House, 248. *See also* Leyit Kin
weapons. *See* stone implements; wooden implements
"Were Chaco's Great Kivas Ancient Computers of Astronomy?" (Morgan), 215(chap. 6, n. 28)
Werito's Rincón, 157, 214(chap. 6, n. 13)
West Mesa, 166
Wetherill, Al, 37
Wetherill, Clate, 37
Wetherill, Marietta (Palmer), 22, 30, 37, 47, 58, 59, 60, 61, 145, 213(chap. 6, n. 4); cited, 145
Wetherill, Richard, 37, 48, 49, 57, 61, 62, 95; cited, 23; death, 60; explorations in Grand Gulch, 21, 22; explorations in Mesa Verde, 21; first visit to Chaco Canyon, 22; grave, 22, 61; homestead, 47, 55, 56, 57, 58, 59, 65, 67, 208(chap. 2, n. 14); and Hyde Exploring Expedition, 23, 24, 30, 41; pothunting, 23, 57, 58; relationship with Navajos, 58, 59; trading post, 55, 57
White Mound, 209(chap. 3, n. 1)
White Rock Point, 235. *See also* Peñasco Blanco
Wijiji, 169, 172, 180, 197, 199, 242 (app.)
Willey, Gordon R., 216(chap. 7, n. 8)
Williamson, Ray A., 215(chap. 6, n. 28)
Windes, Thomas C., 159, 214(chap. 6, n. 7)

wooden implements, 41, 111, 139, 191. *See also* hoes; lances; spears

Wooden Ritual Artifacts from Chaco Canyon, New Mexico, the Chetro Ketl Collection (Vivian, Dodgen, and Hartmann), 210(chap. 4, n. 3)

Woods, Margaret, 249

wool, 171

workrooms, 161, 162, 190

Y

Yellow House, 253 (app.). *See also* Kin Kletso

Z

Zinser, Volker, 215(chap. 6, n. 28)

Zuñi Indians, 69

Zuñi Mountains, 78

Zuñi Pueblo, 69, 168, 205